S0-BBX-925

Narrating the Rise of Big Business in the USA

"This is a story about stories, and specifically about some of the stories that Americans have told themselves about corporate economic power." In this book, Anne Mayhew focuses on the stories surrounding the creation of Standard Oil and Wal-Mart and their founders, John D. Rockefeller and Sam Walton, combining the accounts of economists with the somewhat darker pictures painted by writers of fiction to tease out the overarching narratives associated with American big business.

Mayhew argues that the diverse views about big business and its effects on welfare can be reconciled and better policies derived from a somewhat unlikely combination of ideas from the business world and from those who have dissented from the most widely accepted story told by economists. This book draws on the work of Chandler, Coase and Williamson, as well as Marx and Veblen's discussion of supply chains, to address some of the major social and economic problems of the twenty-first century.

This book will be of interest to students and researchers engaged with economic theory and public policy as well as those interested in a postmodernist take on big business in the USA.

Anne Mayhew is Professor Emerita at the University of Tennessee.

Routledge international studies in business history
Series editors: Ray Stokes and Matthias Kipping

Narrating the Rise of Big Business in the USA

How economists explain Standard Oil and Wal-Mart

Anne Mayhew

Routledge
Taylor & Francis Group

LONDON AND NEW YORK

First published 2008
by Routledge
2 Park Square, Milton Park, Abingdon, Oxon, OX14 4RN

Simultaneously published in the USA and Canada
by Routledge
270 Madison Ave, New York, NY 10016

Routledge is an imprint of the Taylor & Francis Group, an informa business

© 2008 Anne Mayhew

Typeset in Times by Wearset Ltd, Boldon, Tyne and Wear
Printed and bound in Great Britain by TJI Digital, Padstow, Cornwall

British Library Cataloguing in Publication Data
A catalogue record for this book is available from the British Library

Library of Congress Cataloging in Publication Data
Mayhew, Anne.
Narrating the rise of big business in the USA: how economists
explain Standard Oil and Wal-Mart/Anne Mayhew.
p. cm. – (Routledge international studies in business history; 14)
Includes bibliographical references and index.
1. Big business–United States–History. 2. Corporations–United
States–Case studies. 3. Standard Oil Company. 4. Wal-Mart (Firm)
I. Title.
HD2785.M38 2008
338.6'440973–dc22   2008001046

ISBN10: 0-415-77534-5 (hbk)
ISBN10: 0-203-89438-3 (ebk)

ISBN13: 978-0-415-77534-2 (hbk)
ISBN13: 978-0-203-89438-5 (ebk)

**To Patrick, Adam, and Mattie Anne
With hopes for their world**

Contents

Preface

My goals in writing this book were two. The first was to combine what can be learned from the separate and often quite different strands of literature that have dealt with the rise of large business firms in the US economy. Economists have told it one way, economic historians another, and historians of economic thought have seen a slightly different truth. Novelists, short story writers and journalists have had their own versions. What has been taught in business schools has been different still. As I have read and talked with students about the growth of business firms I have tried to cobble together the different versions into a more or less cohesive account. This book is the result.

The second goal has been to write my account so that intelligent readers who do not have specialized training in any of the academic fields from which I have drawn can understand it. This seems a worthy goal but will prove irritating to some because I have not gone into the details of a number of scholarly discussions but have summarized major points instead. I have also trespassed across disciplines and sub-disciplines and have tried to write without using the specialized language that makes for rapid intradisciplinary communication and group cohesion. I hope that in spite of all this I have managed to preserve the understanding and intent of those whose work I have read and rewritten for this purpose, and apologize if I have not.

Acknowledgments

This book has been long in the making and there are many, many teachers, students, colleagues and friends who have contributed to my understanding. My late husband, Walter C. "Terry" Neale, was both a fierce and constructive critic of everything I wrote and he made me a better scholar for it. Had he lived to read this manuscript I am sure that it would have been better than it is. My children, Kathleen and Doug, have been my very best friends, always loving and forgiving.

Several have read this manuscript in various stages of completion, among them Steve Dandaneau, Emil Friberg, Jr., Janet Knoedler, Nancy McGlasson, Mary Papke, and I thank them all, and especially Mary and Nancy for their reading as non-economists. When they said it did not make sense I went back to the keyboard and worked on it some more. To Steve, Emil, and Janet I apologize for not taking all of the advice offered. They should not be blamed. The students in English 660 and in University Honors 257 in the Spring of 2007 are the most recent in a long line of those who have challenged me to think and reread and rethink. I am most grateful.

1 Introduction

This is a story about stories, and specifically about some of the stories that Americans have told themselves about corporate economic power. Stories about the growth of corporate power and the individuals who have led that growth have been written by professional journalists; others are stories told by novelists, short story writers, and film makers; still others are the analytical accounts written by professional experts: economists, other social scientists and historians. Finally, there are the stories that are embodied in legislative history and in the public policies that deal with economic power.

These are not all the same stories, even when they purport to be about the same thing. And, the differences among the stories, differences that will be explored in detail in the pages that follow, are not simple matters of emphasis or style. There are, in fact, sharp differences between the professional views of modern economists, who now tend to see the rise of economic power as a relatively benign process driven by technological progress, and those of historians and other social scientists who take a less sanguine, or at least a less deterministic, view of the evolution of modern American capitalism. There are also sharp differences between the general view of novelists and short story writers who chronicled the lives of Americans at the end of the nineteenth and the beginning of the twentieth centuries and that of economic historians who have written about the same period. The creators of the national literature, the literature that continues to inform the view of many educated citizens, have most often described it as a time of hardship, economic unhappiness, and not infrequent destitution. Economic historians, on the other hand, generally treat this as an era of rising real incomes and increased prosperity for the majority of Americans. And, economists who are not historians tell a story of a sustained increase in affluence, marred only by the occasional recession or depression.

The same cannot be said for other academics, for in English Departments and for many historians, giant firms and their leaders tended to remain in the harsh light first cast by the muckrakers, those early twenti-eth-century journalists who created for millions of Americans a jaundiced view of the activities of the newly emerging large firms. Even among those who have taken a more analytical and less emotive stance, and espe-cially among the modern sociologists such as Fligstein (1990), Perrow (2002), and Roy (1997), who have analyzed the ways in which production came to be organized by the specific legal form of the modern corporation, the view of economic power has been much more critical than it is among economists. There has remained a strong tradition of reading business history and business function as a record of evil deeds. The result is a sharp polarization of views on most American college and university cam-puses about big business and the corporate form. Students learning about our American past must therefore choose between sharply contrasting views, the bases of which are most often left unexplored. A goal of this story of these various stories is clarification of the contrast.

In today's world we also see sharp divisions among those who write of the economic power of large corporations from the standpoint of impoverished and exploited sweatshop workers and those who stress the advantages of a "flattened" world of mass production and distribution. The contrast between the worlds described by those who protest the depredations of globalization and all-powerful corporations and those who celebrate the glories of an efficient and integrated international market in today's world are as stark as the contrast offered by Upton Sinclair in his novel of down-trodden workers in the Chicago stockyards of the early 1900s, *The Jungle*, and the statistically based accounts of the economic historians that show rising real incomes for almost all during the same period.

A major goal of this work is to understand better the causes of the great discrepancies in our narratives about corporate power. It is too easy to see such differences as a simple consequence of the economic position of the story teller. According to this rather common explanation of differences of opinion about economic matters, those who are well off, or at least expect to be well off in the near future, give happy accounts of efficiency and equity being well served by existing power. Those who are less well off are, on the other hand, likely to see exploitation and unfairness. There is some truth to this explanation, but it does not suffice to explain the differ-ences that are at the core of this account. A more complex narrative about the sources and persuasiveness of the variety of stories told is required to understand how we Americans have dealt with corporate power and how this has produced the often contradictory public policies toward large firms that have characterized the twentieth and twenty-first centuries.

In order to construct the more complex narrative that a closer approach to our multiple national stories requires, I will focus on two well-known players, John D. Rockefeller, Sr. and Sam Walton. John D. Rockefeller, Sr. founded Standard Oil of Ohio, later known simply as Standard Oil, a firm that controlled some 90 percent of world petroleum refining capacity at the beginning of the twentieth century. He also, of course, created the fortune and sired the family that has continued to be emblematic of economic power through the twenty-first century. Sam Walton, as is also well known, was the founder of Wal-Mart, now the largest firm (as measured by total revenue) in the United States and a major contributor to late-twentieth-century globalization. Simply naming these two men and their accomplishments calls to mind the division in narratives with which I propose to deal: both are simultaneously heroes of business success and villains of economic justice. As will be described in some detail in the chapters that follow, both shared many other traits as well, both in their accomplishments and in the contexts in which they worked.

Although I say my account is of two individuals, it is important to note that the success of both men came from their ability to lead and coordinate the activities of many others. As will be clear from the histories of both, neither could have succeeded alone. It is not my intent to try to unravel the separate contributions of those who served Rockefeller and Walton, nor will I venture into the scholarly discussion of the role of entrepreneurial individuals in accounting for economic and social change. The focus of this work is on how we as scholars and as interpreters of our world have told the stories of these men and their lieutenants, and not on a search for the true roles of the separate individuals. Rockefeller and Walton are emblematic of massive changes in American society. My goal is to understand how we have told ourselves about those changes.

Before turning to the stories of Rockefeller and Walton, a word about my use of the words "stories" and "narratives" may be useful. There is nothing provocative about using these words to describe the novels and shorter fiction that will be discussed as one portion of the larger American narrative about corporate power. It is also within the range of accepted usage to talk of the stories told by journalists and popular writers, but the use of this term to describe the very substantial body of expert analyses offered by professional historians, and especially by professional economists, will seem to some to be arrogant and deliberately demeaning and dismissive.[1] It is not, however, my intention to demean or to suggest that my account deserves, by reason of simple virtue, to supplant the professional stories told to date.

As an academic economic historian, my intent is, rather, to adopt a non-Whiggish and interdisciplinary approach to the history of thought about big business in America. What I will offer is not the result of research into primary sources, but rather an explicitly postmodern reading of received texts in order tell a somewhat different story. Historians of economic thought, a group whose work will be heavily used in my accounts, have in recent years carried on a fierce debate among themselves about the most appropriate way to view changing professional thought about the economy. Whiggish history is the term that this group has borrowed from other historians to describe work that treats economic science (with an emphasis on science) as a progression of scientific discoveries, which is to say a progression from error to truth. Non-Whiggish history of economic thought, on the other hand, is history that emphasizes the socioeconomic and intellectual context of new ideas, and relies more heavily upon contingency in describing new ways of thinking about an always changing economy.[2] In this book both socioeconomic change and the way we describe that change are seen as contingent, which is to say not predetermined. Things could have happened differently and we could have told ourselves different stories about how they did happen. My goal is to tell a (but not necessarily the) story of how we came to tell ourselves the stories that we have.

Adoption of a non-Whiggish perspective does not mean that I intend to abandon the protocols used by trained experts in evaluating the material that forms the substance of this account. Rather, my intent is to be as careful and professional as possible in examining all of the stories told. By professional training I am both an economist and economic historian. Although as a self-identified "Institutionalist" I have been critical of much modern economic analysis, I respect the intellectual tradition and the very considerable talent and expertise on which it is built.[3] My intent in this work is to engage with received wisdom from several groups of experts – novelists as well as economists, and political as well as economic historians. In so doing, and even as I respect the varying expertise of these groups, I will at times be guilty of the ignorance of local awareness and knowledge that always goes with trespass, but I will try to take care to avoid excessive abuse of that lack of awareness.[4] And, in the non-Whiggish spirit in which I approach my task, I will not claim that mine is a meta-story that is "true." Rather, it is simply a reexamination and retelling of an amalgam of stories, one that I hope will cast useful light upon a matter of continuing great concern: How should we Americans react to privately held economic power that affects the lives of millions of our fellow citizens and billions more around the world?

The power of large corporations and of the people who build and run them has, for more than a century now, been a matter of recurring concern to Americans. Sam Walton, founder and symbol of Wal-Mart, the giant retailing firm that has focused much of the current debate over globalization, is simply the latest of a series of admired demons, individuals who exemplify the common American dream of building a great fortune through hard work and efficiency, but who, in the eyes of many, also do so by sacrificing the interests of their fellow humans. In this work I propose to use what we know about the careers of two such men and the corporations they built to consider and reconsider some of the abiding questions about such economic powerhouses, not so much for the sake of retelling old stories but in order to ask questions about public policy.

Although the first part of this book will involve a retelling, the heart and the purpose of the work is the examination, which begins in Chapter 3, of the ways in which Americans have responded to the challenges presented by the great economic reorganization that both Rockefeller and Walton represented. Political action, action that I interpret broadly to include electoral politics, legal action, and community organization and activity, is necessarily guided by *and* creative of "expert" opinion. Because of my own training and interests, I will focus on economic expertise and examine the ways in which that expertise was formed by both public reaction and learned opinion about the behemoth that was Standard Oil, and how that expertise has, in turn, constrained discourse about Wal-Mart.

Part of my interest in undertaking this project is to understand the contingency of this evolution of thinking about issues of public policy. In a different context, some economic historians, writing in the non-Whiggish spirit already described, have made much of the fact that the keyboard that we once used on our typewriters and now use on keypads for word processing is a QWERTY keyboard. The position of the letters of the alphabet on the keyboard, including the top row for the left hand, which spells out QWERTY, was a reasonable arrangement given the technology of the typewriters of the late nineteenth century, though it may not necessarily be a technologically sensible arrangement today.[5] However, once in place, and once learned by the millions of us who do not have to think at all to know where the keys are, QWERTY has a staying power that cannot be explained "rationally." To use the language that has grown up to explain the QWERTY phenomenon, the keyboard is an example of path dependence. What is depends on a path through the past, and that path is a product of forks in the road chosen for reasons important at a specific time and place and not because of a timeless rationality. In like manner, public policy, which is always an amalgam of expert and public opinion, is also path dependent; it is, in other words, QWERTY-like in that it results from decisions that made a lot of sense in a specific time and place and then become part of the context in which we operate. In the last chapter I will argue that recognition of the QWERTY nature of public policy can be an important step to more conscious and, one hopes, more thoughtful and determined control over future paths.

Let me be clear. I do not think that such thoughtful and determined control can promise an ideal future. In the year 2008, we face real and difficult-to-answer questions about public policy toward such firms as Wal-Mart. Are workers in poor countries better off for having the opportunity to participate in a Wal-Mart supply chain than they would be if they existed quite outside the global economy? Does work in a factory that supplies Wal-Mart customers in the US with inexpensive clothing benefit both customer and worker, where workers have gained at least, but also only, a toe-hold in a "flat world" in which ambition and ability need not be constrained by geographic barriers?[6] Or, are both customer and worker simply pawns in a system created to enrich the very few while destroying both individual dignity and vital geographically based human diversity of culture? Asking questions that are less dramatically worded than are these does not, unfortunately, make answering them easier, and I will not propose a path to any easy answers. My only hope is that by examining the ways in which we Americans have responded to commercial power, we may become able to understand our current options a little more clearly.

In the pages that follow, I will use the stories of John D. Rockefeller and Sam Walton, and the fortunes they built, to do several things. After a summary in Chapter 2 of the generally agreed upon histories of the two men and their firms, Standard Oil and Wal-Mart, Chapter 3 will provide a review of popular interpretations of these histories and the larger context in which they took place. These are the interpretations found in newspapers, in political discourse, in novels and short stories, in films, and in the public imagination. My purpose in Chapters 2 and 3 is not to offer new biographies of Rockefeller or Walton or new histories of their business firms. Rather, my intent is to use the existing literature to set the stage for discussion of ways in which citizens, professional economists, and the governments that they advise have reacted to the growth of great corporate power in two different, but in many ways similar, eras.

Chapters 4 and 5 may seem to the non-economist somewhat technical, for there I trace the development of the mainstream of economic thought and public policy from Adam Smith's praise of *laissez faire* to modern acceptance of the view that large firms are the result of technological necessity and efficiencies in production that are advantageous to society as a whole. This modern consensus was not easily reached, and particularly so because economists sought to revise their treatment of competitive systems without abandoning an older conventional wisdom. In Chapter 4, the intellectual journey from Adam Smith's pin factories to John Stuart Mill's discussion of water supply in London in the middle of the nineteenth century, and on to the impact of the railroads on economic thought at the end of the century, will be used to set the stage for the debates that remade the economic theory of the firm through the twentieth century. From that remaking, and through a process that was partly political and partly scholarly, there emerged the relatively benign professional view with which most economists have viewed large firms since World War II.

Chapter 5 will present alternative views of the functioning of large firms, views that overlap in sometimes surprising ways. In this chapter the contributions of Thorstein Veblen, best known for his sarcastic treatment of the leisure class, Bela Gold, an economist who was also an industrial engineer, Alfred Chandler, who largely created the modern field of business history, and Armen Alchian and Ronald Coase, both associated with the pro-*laissez faire* Chicago School approach, will be explored.

The perspective that all of this diverse group share is one that was first articulated by Thorstein Veblen in his *The Theory of Business Enterprise* (1904), although in rudimentary form it had also been articulated by Karl Marx in *Capital*, where it was used for quite different purposes. Marx understood that the manufacturing/trading firm was the locus of a process in which $M \rightarrow C \rightarrow C' \rightarrow M'$, where M is the initial monetary outlay for C, which are the raw materials and other inputs to production, C' is the firm's output of goods, and M' is the amount realized on sales of that output. Veblen, though he did not explicitly use Marx's terminology, used the same idea to see the firm whole. In Veblen's approach the firm was not a fixed and unchanging entity facing new technologies but, rather, an evolving response to new technological and social opportunity. For Veblen, the firms that were rapidly becoming dominant in his era had emerged from a confluence of the prior existence of business enterprise as a way of organizing trade and the industrial revolution that made large-scale organization of production a feasible target for income-seeking traders. The importance of this confluence, as Veblen saw it, was that production was being embedded in organizations that had originally been designed for trade rather than production. To adequately describe such firms Veblen devised a monetary theory of production in which success came from managing the entire $M \rightarrow C \rightarrow C' \rightarrow M'$ process rather than from attention to production alone. Much more will be said about this in Chapter 5. For now it will suffice to say that in presenting the firm in this way, Veblen was able to incorporate into his book on *The Theory of Business Enterprise* a much fuller range of observations about the effects and likely consequences of the new firms of his era for American society.

Veblen was not, of course, alone in understanding that a new kind of business firm, the kind that was emerging in the age of Rockefeller, was remaking American society. As will also be described in some detail in Chapter 5, a number of his fellow economists tried to broaden the forms of analysis that economists had inherited from the English tradition created by Adam Smith. But, in spite of the availability of these broader approaches, the reforms and regulations of both the Progressive Movement and the New Deal of the 1930s tended to focus on the narrower questions of price and cost that were the focus of the theoretical developments in the English-dominated mainstream of economic thought. This narrowness of concern by economists became even more pronounced in the years following World War II, and this in spite of the ongoing evolution of the large firm as the dominant player in the functioning of the American economy. Even in the face of the massive changes associated with the growth of multinational firms that are often larger than and largely independent of traditional nation states, economists remained fairly steadfastly focused on $C \rightarrow C'$, which is to say upon production of goods, as the firm activity that really mattered, a focus for which a commodity theory of production rather than a monetary theory was most suitable. And, as will be explained in Chapter 4, economists, informed by a commodity theory, quite understandably took a benign view of the rise of corporate power.

Fortunately for this project and for our understanding of the business past, a reconciliation of the literature of damnation with that of praise for the robber barons as extraordinary entrepreneurs is available. That reconciliation, which will be described in Chapter 5, came from Alfred D. Chandler who, in 1977, published the most important work of modern business history, *The Visible Hand: The Managerial Revolution in American Business*. Rather than writing to praise or to damn, Chandler provided detailed and dispassionate accounts of how the large firms came into being. And, in doing so, Chandler, though that was not his intent, restored room in the history of American firms for the broader Veblenian notion of the firm and for a monetary theory of production, for he stressed throughput and what he initially called "economies of speed." Even with the cost advantages that derived from capital intensity and related economies of scale and scope, the big firms could not, said Chandler, "be fully realized unless a constant flow of materials through the plant or factory was maintained to assure effective capacity utilization" (Chandler 1992: 81). In other words, M has to turn with speed and consistency into C and C into C' and C' into M', and the cycle must repeat speedily if fixed capital is to be used to achieve the advantages of both scale and scope.

As it turns out, however, the kind of speed of which Chandler wrote is difficult to incorporate into the essentially static analysis on which the concepts of scale and scope rest. And, it is these static concepts of economies of scale and scope that have come to provide the core terms of analysis not only for historians of American business but even more especially for economists who concern themselves with the place of business in the American economy. Because of the troublesome lack of fit between his notion of economies of speed and the mainstream dialogue about business strategy and performance, Chandler ultimately abandoned use of the concept of "economies of speed," though he did not abandon the idea that speed and constancy of throughput were crucially important.

In the last section of Chapter 5, the modern firm in its abstract theoretical form will be considered in light of the perspective provided by Veblen's and Chandler's descriptive treatments. As it turns out, the work of theorists such as Gold, Alchian, and Coase also allow the firm to be seen whole. It is possible to restate the descriptions of both Veblen and Chandler in the abstract terms of their generalized firms and to give emphasis to the speed of throughput that Chandler emphasized and the interstitial control that Veblen stressed. However, such restatement immeasurably reduces the importance of the alternative story and does so because the power of the firm over the whole of the $M \rightarrow C \rightarrow C' \rightarrow M'$ process is compressed into the language of the commodity theory. All of firm activity is restated as a matter of $C \rightarrow C'$ and that, in effect, removes the plot line from Chandler's powerful story.

In Chapter 6 I propose a different restatement, one in which the skeletal theory of Veblen and the fully descriptive stories of Chandler are translated into the modern business theories of supply chain management. My argument will be that the Veblenian notion of interstitial control as the key to understanding the rise of big business is closely related to the notion, now common in business management literature, of value or supply chains. And, it will be argued, these concepts are key to understanding the rise of both Standard Oil and Wal-Mart and allow a more general statement of Chandler's stories as well.

Chapter 6 will make use of the various narratives provided in Chapters Two through Five to retell, in brief form, the stories of both Standard Oil and Wal-Mart using the work of both Veblen and Chandler but also that of modern management literature. If, as will be argued, we can use a monetary theory of production, which is to say supply chain analysis, with emphasis upon interstitial management, to describe more fully the process whereby both Rockefeller and Walton gained their power and fortunes, this interpretation may also serve as a template for reasonable and pragmatic approaches to current social and economic issues. The book will conclude with an exploration of this possibility in Chapter 7.

The narratives of big business, whether those created by novelists or by economists, by business historians or political activists, play a powerfully important role in shaping our reaction to current events. In the global economy of the first years of the twenty-first century, much is changing. The dominance that US manufacturing firms once enjoyed has been seriously challenged. Rather than relying on the US for goods and finance, the rest of the world increasingly looks to us to buy their goods. To deal with the shifting fortunes that have reduced US dominance in the world economy, policy makers have offered a menu of tax cuts, investment subsidies, exhortations to local officials to do a better job of educating our young, and a commitment to trade agreements to encourage greater international flow of goods. All such policies are justified as ways to increase efficiency in production of an ever larger output of goods and services.

Debate about the adequacy of these policies and the stories on which they are based is too important to leave to experts who speak knowingly, but often in ways that make it difficult for the public to follow. I have tried in all of the chapters of this book to present all of our national stories about big business, including the stories of the experts, in a way that can be understood by intelligent and diligent readers even though they have no training in economics or business history. Though this is a story about stories of the past, it is not a story that has ended. Where we take the American narrative about big business is up to us all. I hope that this story about stories told will provide some useful perspective as additional chapters in our national narrative are added.

2 The agreed upon stories

What did John D. Rockefeller, Sr. and Sam Walton have in common? One answer is obvious. Both made a lot of money and were among the wealthiest men of their time. But, there was much more to it than that. Both Rockefeller and Walton made their fortunes by reorganizing important parts of the American economy. Both presided over sharply falling prices for the products for which they organized the production and distribution. The quantity of goods that their organizations distributed – petroleum products in the case of Rockefeller and a wide variety of consumer goods for Walton – increased manyfold during their lifetimes. Both were seen as unfair competitors who drove honest men and women out of business. Both were, and still are, simultaneously held in contempt and praised as heroes. And, both men became symbols of their times. Brief accounts of their rise as successful business heroes and as villains may be given as follows.

John D. Rockefeller, Sr. and Standard Oil[1]

John D. Rockefeller built his fortune in the oil business, an industry that began in 1859 with the drilling, in northwest Pennsylvania, of the first successful oil well. A combination of pressing need for more and better illuminants that led to widespread use of kerosene lamps and easy access into both drilling and refining, using existing technologies, created a booming and chaotic industry. Between 1862 and 1873, the output of crude oil is estimated to have increased from three million to ten million barrels per year (Williamson and Daum 1959: 118). If this growth rate seemed impressive at the time, a comparison to the current domestic US production of over eight million barrels *a day* (8.69 in 2004), and much more than that worldwide, makes it clear that this was indeed an infant industry when Rockefeller first became involved.

In 1862, three years after the first oil well, Rockefeller was on his way, along with a partner, Maurice B. Clark, to local success in Cleveland, Ohio, as a produce merchant. He had come to this position by way of working, while still a teenager, as a bookkeeper for a commission and shipping firm in Cleveland. By saving some of his own salary and with a loan (at an above market rate of interest!) from his itinerant father, whom biographer Chernow describes as a flim-flam man, John D. was able to scrape together the $2,000 that represented his share of the initial investment that founded the Clark and Rockefeller firm in 1858.[2] His success in the new firm and his reputation led to the invitation to help finance a local refinery. In 1863, Excelsior Works began operation as a partnership between Rockefeller, Clark, and Samuel Andrews, "a self-taught chemist" who had, while working in a lard-oil refinery, figured out how to use sulfuric acid to produce kerosene from crude oil (Chernow 1998: 77). Rockefeller and Clark provided the business knowledge; Andrews brought the technical knowledge. In 1866, a second refinery was built in Cleveland, and an office to handle exports was established in New York. The decade of establishment and initial expansion was capped off in early 1870 when a new firm, capitalized at $1 million, was incorporated as Standard Oil of Ohio (Williamson and Daum 1959: 301–2).

Although there are differences of opinion about the degree of nefariousness involved (differences that will be explored more fully in the next chapter), all agree on what Rockefeller and his associates both had and had not done to achieve this initial success. What they had *not* done was to become directly involved in oil production and they had *not* brought to the refining industry itself any new and superior techniques or processes. What they *had* done was to achieve control of transportation. To understand the importance of this achievement, a brief history of the technology of drilling, refining, and transport of oil is required.

As the new industry developed, both drilling and refining techniques that had been adopted from other uses were gradually modified by users but without any dramatic breakthroughs. The first successful well, that of Colonel Edwin Drake in western Pennsylvania, had been based on a method used for salt wells, a method improved throughout the 1860s and early 70s "as practical oilmen responded to the particular problems encountered in the fields" (Williamson and Daum 1959: 136).[3] Nevertheless, drilling remained, at least by twentieth-century standards, a relatively simple and inexpensive process. Williamson and Daum estimate that prior to 1862, "...wells seldom exceeded 200 feet in depth [and] drilling costs ranged between $1,200 and $1,500," whereas by the early 1870s, depths were much greater, with averages of over 800 feet and ranging up to 1,600 feet (Williamson and Daum 1959: 156–8). In spite of the increasing costs associated with deeper drilling and improved technology, and in spite of falling prices for crude in the early 1870s that might have dampened enthusiasm, the boom mentality persisted. Drilling and crude production were carried on by thousands of eager wildcatters and it was not until the 1890s that Rockefeller and others sought to control the production of crude.

In refining, the 1860s and early 70s also saw substantial though not dramatic improvements in techniques, but there, too, Rockefeller and his associates played a relatively minor role. The techniques for converting crude oil into kerosene were largely carried over from those used for coal oil production in the decades prior to the Civil War and involved a simple process which introduced no substantial barriers to entry because of initial capital costs. Here is how Williamson and Daum describe it:

> In its crudest, earliest form this method of refining involved little more than a 5-barrel, cast-iron still, in effect merely a closed kettle, in which the crude oil was cooked over an open fire. The rising vapors were piped from an opening near the top to a worm where they were condensed back into liquids. The typical worm condenser comprised about 100 feet of coiled-copper pipe submerged in water to obtain cooling. If the distiller embarked on refining, then understood to embrace the art of chemical treating, he added a tin- or zinc-lined agitating tank, and a wooden dasher, similar to that used in a churn, which sufficed to stir the mixture. If he did not undertake treating, he needed only a settling tank into which the condensed vapors could be collected. He might add a little hut, often of stone, to protect his apparatus from the elements, and perhaps fence it in with some rough boards.
>
> (Williamson and Daum 1959: 212)

A good mental picture emerges from Williamson and Daum's conclusion that "these petroleum distilleries were as portable and operated at about the same level as the numerous moonshiners' stills in western Pennsylvania and elsewhere" (1959: 212).

The refineries with which Rockefeller began in 1863 were certainly not portable stills, but the technology that they embodied was not greatly different from that used in the crude stills described by Williamson and Daum as costing a few hundred dollars. Refineries did, however, grow larger both as a consequence of production of more by-products (kerosene remained the major product) and of increases in still sizes, with stills of 500–600 barrels regarded as generally the most efficient size, and with multi-still plant size "typically" running at 1,000 barrels in new plants.[4]

Although his refineries were among the largest, Rockefeller did not gain his preeminent position through straightforward economies of scale of operation. (Much more will be said about this later.) Rather, what he did do was to make the use of existing techniques of refining as efficient as possible, and, much more importantly, he stationed himself and his firm at the crucial intersection of transport, first of transport of crude oil to the refineries and then of transport of refined products to final markets.[5] There is no doubt whatsoever that John D. Rockefeller set out to create a cartel of oil refiners and that he succeeded in doing so by recognizing and taking advantage of a crucial bottleneck in the sequence whereby oil was extracted from the ground, refined, and transported to consumers.[6]

From the very beginning, transport was a serious problem for the new petroleum industry. For kerosene to be competitive with coal-oil as an illuminant, estimates were that petroleum had to be available at the refinery at a cost of no more than $12.00 a barrel (Williamson and Daum 1959: 105). As transportation and handling charges amounted to two-thirds or more of the cost, the importance of transport is clear. But the problem was not simply one of direct cost. It was also a matter of scheduling, which was made difficult by the fact that the producing region was not initially served by rail so that barrels had to be shipped "twenty to forty miles to railhead or wharf," over roads and streams subject to the vagaries of weather (Williamson and Daum 1959: 106). Add to this the loss through seepage and fire associated with shipping barrels of crude oil on flat and unprotected railcars, and it is clear that transport was a crucial issue. Early solutions to these problems were found through shipments by river to Pittsburgh, facilitated by use of small dams to maintain sufficient water flow, but much more importantly by construction of local rail lines into the producing region (Williamson and Daum 1959: 164–170). Soon the major trunk lines in alliance with their affiliated local feeders were doing battle for dominance, a dominance that would determine not only earnings for the railroads themselves but also locational advantages for refining and distribution.[7]

It was into this fray between the major railroads, their local feeder lines, and the major cities and regions that Rockefeller stepped with authority. And, it was with this step that Standard Oil began its dramatic ascent. Remember that it was in early 1870 that Standard came into existence with a capital value set at $1 million. Williamson and Daum quote Ida Tarbell on local perceptions of the empire that was coming into existence:

[Local competitors] ... began to suspect something. John Rockefeller might get his oil cheaper now and then, they said, but he could not do it so often. He might make close contracts for which they had neither the patience or the stomach. He might have an unusual mechanical genius in his partner. But these things could not explain all. They believed they bought, on the whole, almost as cheaply as he, and they knew they made as good oil and with as great, or nearly as great, economy. He could sell at no better price than they. What was his advantage?

(Williamson and Daum 1959: 303 quoting from Tarbell 1904: 45–6)

Williamson and Daum answer Tarbell's question, as have all others who have written about Standard Oil, by pointing to negotiated concessions from the railroads. Apparently the first of these was obtained in 1867 from the Lake Shore Railroad which had recently built into Cleveland. Henry M. Flagler, another successful merchant who had recently joined Rockefeller's team, obtained a rebate per barrel shipped for the firm, as, however, did other Cleveland refiners. But then in 1868, Rockefeller and associates joined with two other refiners to acquire an interest in Allegheny Transportation Company, a gathering line in the Oil Regions, which itself had a deal with the Atlantic and Great Western Railway. Williamson and Daum conclude their description of these and other agreements that followed with these words:

> How much these arrangements contributed to the growth of Standard's refining capacity (estimated at about 1,500 barrels of crude daily in 1870) is impossible to measure. But whatever their influence, the effects tended to be cumulative. Every increase in refining capacity further strengthened the firm's bargaining position in maintaining or increasing its special concessions from transportation companies.
>
> (Williamson and Daum 1959: 305)

And, more special concessions were forthcoming, for in 1870 Flagler was able to obtain from the Lake Shore line highly favorable rates on oil shipped from the producing region to Cleveland and on refined products from Cleveland to New York. Other refiners were told, when they complained, that they could have the same deal if they could guarantee the same volume of traffic.

Economic events of the early 1870s made it possible for Rockefeller and the new Standard Oil to move quickly to consolidate their advantages. In a turbulent economic context of financial panic and business insolvency, the petroleum industry was in particularly dramatic turmoil. The prominent role that Cleveland played in refining was threatened by further rate wars between the railroads, who could have, had they wished, switched advantage to refiners elsewhere. There was substantial excess refining capacity, which was estimated by Williamson and Daum to be roughly twice the amount of crude oil actually received by refineries (Williamson and Daum 1959: 344). Whether through underhanded action by Rockefeller acting in cahoots with the railroads or, as Rockefeller himself had it, as part of a consolidation plan that involved fair recompense for firms that Standard either purchased outright or brought under effective control, order was achieved. By the end of 1872, Rockefeller had control of virtually all of the refining capacity in Cleveland. He had put that city in a position of preeminence in the ongoing regional rivalry for dominance in refining and had moved further into control of refining on the eastern seaboard. Although the precise steps and the economic morality and justice of those steps may be in dispute, as we shall see in the next chapter, there is no doubt that cooperation (collusion is the way others would put it) with the railroads was crucial. Chandler describes the strategy this way: "The control of transportation provided a weapon to keep out new competitors and a threat to prevent those who joined Standard from dropping out of the cartel" (Chandler 1977: 321).

With control of roughly one-fourth of the total daily refining capacity in the nation by 1872 and 1873, Rockefeller and associates consolidated and improved holdings in Cleveland by expanding the range of refined products sold by Standard, expanding exports, and, in general, centralizing and improving management of what was by then a substantial multiplant enterprise. According to Williamson and Daum, by the end of 1873,

> Standard was supplying about one-third of the industry's total output of refinery products from Cleveland, which added to the product of New York plants probably raised the proportion to a figure between 30 and 40 percent. Considering the fact that Standard's share of the market in January, 1871, was about 10 percent, this was a remarkable advance. But Rockefeller and his associates were fully aware that their position in the industry was by no means secure: the fact that Standard's refineries were operating at about two-thirds capacity only emphasized the over expanded condition of the refining industry generally.
>
> (Williamson and Daum 1959: 366–8)

The Rockefeller combine reacted to this danger by moving aggressively to consolidate their control, using their power over railroads and then pipelines to work deals and entice allegiance or force mergers. Although Rockefeller's direct control was only over refineries, this gave him effective control over the producers of crude, who became increasingly resentful of Standard. At first, it was sufficient to have leverage over the railroads, which were willing to cooperate because of the volume that such cooperation guaranteed. But, in 1878, when plans surfaced for building a trunk pipeline that would carry crude a substantial distance from the producing region to a railroad that was not under effective Standard control (the Reading Railroad), Standard's control over the producers was seriously challenged (Chandler 1977: 322–3; Williamson and Daum 1959: 440–52).

The new technology for transporting oil not only threatened Standard Oil by reducing the effectiveness of railroad rates as a way of controlling producers of crude; it also offered advantages of management and challenged the existing locational advantage that Rockefeller had created in Cleveland. Rockefeller and his associates

> realized [that pipelines] transported crude oil far more cheaply than railroads did. The lines also provided excellent storage. Their existence made possible the scheduling of a much greater and steadier refinery throughput than was possible using rail shipments. Moreover, because the pipeline could carry crude oil to processing facilities but not refined products to market, the completion of long-distance lines called for relocation of refinery capacity at centers close to the market, particularly at the ports where ships loaded the refined products for the great European markets.
>
> (Chandler 1977: 323)

Standard Oil responded to the pipeline challenge by building its own and then, in 1883, by entering a market-sharing arrangement with the Tidewater Line, the construction of which had set off the initial rush to build the pipelines.

The move to build and control pipelines also set off organizational changes in Standard Oil. In 1882, shareholders in the companies that formed alliances with Standard Oil, often through transfer of company stock to trustees who were officers of Standard Oil, were given, in exchange for their stock in those companies, trust certificates in a new company, Standard Oil Trust. This clever use of existing legal practice avoided questions of what would happen in case of death of a trustee, served to consolidate managerial control, which allowed for closure of a number of refineries, and also allowed for continued operation of Standard behind a veil of, if not total, then relatively effective secrecy.

Meanwhile, Standard, with "carefully scheduled throughput" (Chandler's phrase to which I will return later), lowered costs of refining inputs, including but not limited to costs of crude, and in combination with efficiencies of operation, managed to cut the cost of refined goods substantially. They also extended their reach into marketing of final output. Though not planned initially, this move was in reaction "to the need to assure a steady flow of the high volume output from the new centralized refining facilities to the consumer" (Chandler 1977: 324).

By the early 1890s, Chandler notes, Standard had a "national sales organization managed through regionally defined subsidiaries," owned a British distributor, owned a fleet of tankers, and had a joint venture with two German distributors. Standard had also begun to produce its own crude oil (Chandler 1977: 325).

Throughout this period, the prices of the refined products fell, and fell more rapidly than the overall price level (Williamson and Daum 1959: 728). This was in large measure due to a fall in the price of inputs, including crude oil but of other refining inputs as well. It was also due to efficiencies in operation, some of which may have been associated with scale of operation, a point to which we will return later. And, certainly, Standard was able to operate with lower margins because of its assured throughput as it controlled, as of the early 1880s, approximately 90 percent of the refining capacity of the country.

As everyone knows, Standard did not maintain its end-of-century hegemony. The creation of other integrated companies both in the US and abroad and, much more importantly, the discovery of new oil fields in 1901, dramatically illustrated by the gusher Spindeltop which was located in East Texas, more than a thousand miles to the southwest of the original producing region, signaled a new era for the industry. This was followed by legal changes when, in 1911, the dissolution of Standard Oil was ordered by the Supreme Court, a move that further reduced the degree of dominance of the firm. The irony, as Chernow notes, was that dissolution of Standard Oil was "the luckiest stroke of [Rockefeller's] career," for it "converted [him] from a mere millionaire ... into something just short of history's first billionaire" (Chernow 1998: 556). The saga of Rockefeller's continued wealth as holder of shares in the allegedly independent firms that were spun off by the decision is not the subject of this work. For present purposes, it is sufficient to note that Rockefeller's was an unprecedented economic empire at the end of the nineteenth century, one from which the wealth, income flows, and power that had been amassed continue to be important even in the twenty-first century.

Sam Walton and Wal-Mart[8]

Unlike Rockefeller, Sam Walton did not get in at the beginning of a new industry or even close to it. Retailing of a wide variety of consumer goods in a large store supplied by many different producers goes back a long way, with the first department store usually acknowledged to have been Le Bon Marché in Paris, where, beginning in the 1850s, a variety of goods were stocked and sold at fixed prices. In the US, department stores and then, as perhaps more directly lineal ancestors of Wal-Mart, the mail-order catalog distributors began to serve as middlemen between producers and consumers on a massive scale in the decades just after the Civil War. Nor was Sam Walton the first to initiate "big box" retailing in modern America. What, then, did Walton do?

What Walton did that was very like what Rockefeller achieved was to develop and put in place a plan for systemic change in an industry that was undergoing substantial revision. How much of the plan evolved as it was implemented and how much was there in the beginning it is difficult to say. Nor is it any easier to distinguish the contributions of Walton from those whom he hired as he built Wal-Mart than it is to sort out the separate contributions of Rockefeller and his associates. What is clear, however, is that in both cases much more was involved than simple building of *a* firm. Rather, new technologies and new opportunities were exploited to create a system of control of the movement and transfer of goods from producer to final consumer. In both cases, the dramatic accomplishment was in the creation of a *system* where none had existed before.

Sam Walton's story begins simply enough. After earning a college degree with a major in economics at the University of Missouri, he worked at a J. C. Penney store in Des Moines as a trainee and then, following service in the army from 1942 until 1945, started his climb as a semi-independent retailer with a Ben Franklin franchise in Newport, Arkansas.[9] Like Rockefeller, he established connections with a bank in the early stages, in his case by marrying the daughter of a banker in Claremore, Oklahoma, and thus ensured himself the funding that he needed to get started. In 1951, having lost the lease on the building in which the original store was located, he opened another Ben Franklin franchise in another small town, Bentonville, Arkansas. This site was not his first choice. He wanted to buy a department store in St. Louis, but his wife Helen insisted that they live in small towns, specifically in a town with fewer than 10,000 inhabitants (Slater 2003: 26 and Walton 1992: 21). The move to Bentonville, which was to grow well beyond the limit of 10,000 because of Walton's success, occurred in 1951, and by 1962 Walton had sixteen franchise stores, all in the tri-state area of Arkansas, Missouri, and Kansas. This made him one of the larger independent variety store operators in the country, but beyond the adoption of self-service and acquisition of a plane and pilot's license so that he could visit all of the stores regularly, he had done nothing to this point to indicate the innovations to come.

Walton had, however, come to appreciate small towns as underserved and to recognize that "[t]he real future … was in discounting – buying directly from manufacturers and displaying the merchandise in bulk – rather than in five-and-dimes supplied by traditional wholesalers" (Slater 2003: 26). Most of small-town America, when Walton began his ascent, was still served by highly traditional stores that offered few of the price reductions or the variety of goods that were becoming features of new stores opening in larger population centers.

The gap between what was available in small towns and in cities and larger towns was widened when, in 1962, Kresge opened the first Kmart, Woolworth started Woolco, and Hudson opened the first Target. All were large stores with emphasis on discounting and were located in suburban areas. Walton, too, wanted to operate his Ben Franklin franchises as discount stores, but the parent company was concerned about profit margins and said no (Slater 2003: 28). It was at this point that Walton created the first Wal-Mart, and from there the chain grew rapidly, becoming a publicly owned company in 1970. In that year there were thirty-two Wal-Marts, with total sales of $31 million. By 1980 there were 276, with total sales of $1.2 billion (Walton 1992: 120).

At first, Wal-Marts, which were then devoted solely to general merchandise, were placed in small towns and in geographic proximity to already established Wal-Marts. This strategy of gradually spreading from secured locations had much to do with distribution of goods and showed an early appreciation for the importance of logistics. In his autobiography, Walton describes the strategy as one of "spreading out, then filling in." Here is what he wrote:

> while the big guys were leapfrogging from large city to large city, they became so spread out and so involved in real estate and zoning laws and city politics that they left huge pockets of business out there for us. Our growth strategy was born out of necessity, but at least we recognized it as a strategy pretty early on. We figured we had to build our stores so that our distribution centers, or warehouses, could take care of them, but also so those stores could be controlled. We wanted them within reach of our district managers, and of ourselves here in Bentonville, so we could get out there and look after them. *Each store had to be within a day's drive of a distribution center.* So we would go as far as we could from a warehouse and put in a store. Then we would fill in the map of that territory, state by state, county seat by county seat, until we had saturated that market.
>
> (Walton 1992: 110, italics added)

And then they would build a new distribution center and move into another area.

As Wal-Mart spread from Arkansas and adjacent states, stores were placed on the edges of larger towns (a pattern already established by the other big box chains). Wholesale "clubs" were added in 1982 and later in that decade supercenters offering both general merchandise and groceries. The result of the hub-and-spoke strategy has led, in the words of geographers Matthew Zook and Mark Graham, to "remarkable geographic coverage." Using GIS (Geographic Information Systems) techniques and language, they estimate that, as of 2005,

> fully 60 percent of the entire U.S. population lives within 5 miles of a Wal-Mart location and 96 percent are within 20 miles. With the exception of extremely remote and sparsely populated locations, almost all citizens of the United States are also within the Wal-Mart nation's catchment of consumption.
>
> (Zook and Graham 2006: 20)

Growth was so rapid that by 2001 Wal-Mart had become the largest company in America as measured by total revenues, and in 2003, with sales of $256.3 billion, it would have ranked twentieth among the income of nation states as measured by gross domestic product (Hugill 2006: 3). In the meantime, some direct competitors (Kmart for example) had largely fallen by the wayside or established smaller niches (Target, for example, with its image of a more upscale discounting), and Wal-Mart was expanding (though not without some difficulty) into retailing in a number of countries other than the US.

Almost all accounts of this remarkable rise to preeminence in retailing mention as causes Walton's insistence on close and careful management, on cost containment, on clever marketing of specific products, on initial location in small towns, on "EDLP" (every day low pricing), and on a culture of folksiness and friendliness offered up by "associates" (employees) who are told they are part of a team. (Wal-Mart's treatment of its "associates" is, of course, a subject of considerable contention, and much more will be said about it in the next chapter.) Walton also noted that the pattern of expansion helped the chain minimize outlays on advertising as they relied heavily upon word of mouth. While these were undoubtedly important elements in the rise of Wal-Mart, it seems clear from all of the accounts that an early emphasis on inventory management and rapid distribution was the key component of Wal-Mart's success.

In the beginning, Walton relied on clever marketing to move goods quickly from his stores to purchasers, but it is also clear that he understood, even in the 1960s when computers were still very new to the civilian world, that a revolution was in the making. Although Walton apparently relished the image of himself as a good old country boy who was ignorant of and resistant to new technology, the facts do not support such a view.

In 1966 Walton attended an IBM school for retailers that was held in Poughkeepsie, New York. There Walton sought out Abe Marks, the president of the National Mass Retailers' Institute, and subsequently visited him to learn more. Here is Marks' account of their interaction:

> Our system [at Hartfield-Zody's, a women's apparel chain that filed for bankruptcy in 1974] was rudimentary by today's standards, but it was very advanced for the 1960s. Very few companies controlled their merchandise the way we did. Sam spent a lot of time reviewing these operations and he brought some of his people up to review them.... What we helped him with in the early days was really logistics. It's like in the Army. You can move troops all over the world, but unless you have the capacity to supply them with ammunition and food, there's no sense putting them out there. Sam understood that. He knew that he was already in what the trade calls an 'absentee ownership' situation. That just means you're putting your stores out where you, as management, aren't. If he wanted to grow he had to learn to control it. So to service these stores you've got to have timely information: How much merchandise is in the store? What is it? What's selling and what's not? What is to be ordered, marked down, replaced? To get more technical, that helps you control what we call turn, or inventory turnover – the ratio of sales to inventory.... [Walton] realized – even at the rudimentary level he was on in 1966, operating those few stores that he had – that he couldn't expand beyond that horizon unless he had the ability to capture this information on paper so that he could control his operations.... He became, really, the best utilizer of information to control absentee ownerships that there's ever been.... You've got to realize this too. By being at that conference, he was absolutely in the right place at the right time. There were no such things in those days as minicomputers and microcomputers. He was really ten years away from the computer world coming. But he was preparing himself. And this is a very important point: without the computer, Sam Walton could not have done what he's done.
>
> (Walton 1992: 85–6)

Management of inventory turnover in the stores was not the only problem that Walton attacked early on. At the same conference where he met Marks, he learned of a computerized warehouse in Green Bay, Wisconsin, visited that, and put an expert in charge of the first of what would be many distribution centers where goods were brought in and moved out in a controlled and speedy manner.[10]

Here is Walton's own account of how the distribution centers came to work once fully integrated into the system that he was building:

> When ... [it] all comes together at one of our distribution centers, it's really a sight to behold. You really have to see one of these places in action to appreciate them. Start with a building of around 1.1 million square feet, which is about as much floor space as twenty-three football fields, sitting out somewhere on 150 acres. Fit it high to the roof with every kind of merchandise you can imagine.... Everything in it is bar-coded, and a computer tracks the location and movement of every case of merchandise, while it's stored and when it's shipped out. Some six hundred to eight hundred associates staff the place, which runs around the clock, twenty-four hours a day. On one side of the building is a shipping dock with loading doors for around thirty trucks at a time – usually full. On the other side is the receiving dock, which may have as many as 135 doors for unloading merchandise.
>
> These goods move in and out of the warehouse on some $8\frac{1}{2}$ miles of laser-guided conveyer belts, which means that the lasers read the bar codes on the cases and then direct them to whatever truck is filling the order placed by one of the stores it's servicing that night. On a heavy day, these belts might handle up to 200,000 cases of goods. When the thing is running full speed, it's just a blur of boxes and crates flying down those belts, red lasers flashing everywhere, directing this box to that truck, or that box to this truck.
>
> (Walton 1992: 211)

It was not, of course, sufficient merely to build distribution centers with conveyer belts. Walton and his associates also realized that a coding system was essential, and here, too, they moved quickly to seize the advantage. To understand this, a brief history of modern coding and inventory management is required. Before the late 1960s and the introduction of computers into the retailing process, inventory management was highly labor intensive, and the process of reorder slow. An early improvement in department stores involved use of a Bureau of Standards-backed system of optical character recognition. Clerks typed in a numbered code for each item as it was sold, which at least allowed the tracking of goods as they moved off the shelves. However, the system was awkward and slowed checkout (Ortega 1998: 129). The bar code system that has become a familiar part of American shopping today was already being used in grocery stores and involved use of a uniform product code, which allowed simple scanning.

In general retailing, the OCR (optical character recognition) system had been the initial choice of most because the uniform product code (UPC) did not have the capacity to handle the large number of different goods carried by most department stores. Walton and his associates nevertheless made the decision to go ahead and began using UPC, even in the early 1980s, in part because so many of the goods they carried were also sold by grocery stores and so were already part of the UPC system, and in part because they thought that capacity would grow. In this they were absolutely correct. A Voluntary Interindustry Commerce Standards (VICS) initiative led by a number of retailers began to pressure suppliers to tag products before they were delivered and to adopt the UPC. According to Petrovic and Hamilton,

> The UPC requirement was [but] the first VICS recommendation. There soon followed electronic data interchange (EDI) standards and codes for shipping containers and intermediate products. By 2000, over 90 percent of the entire nonfood consumer goods industry in the US (in terms of volume), as well as a large number of global companies, were members of VICS and promulgated its standards.
>
> (Petrovic and Hamilton 2006: 118)

As all of this happened, those companies that had not moved quickly to adopt the UPC were forced to catch up and faced higher costs as a result. Whether through foresight or with a degree of luck as well, all portions of the Wal-Mart system were coming together to give them a decided advantage over competitors. Consider that another reason why Wal-Mart moved so quickly to adopt the UPC was that 80 percent of the goods that Wal-Mart stocked went through their own distribution system where tickets were already put on. Bar codes could be readily attached to these (Ortega 1998: 129–30).

The experience of Kmart provides a telling contrast. Only 30 percent of their stock went through their own distribution network, and there the decision had been made to stick with the OCR system and even then in a fairly half-hearted manner, for Kresge had maintained a largely decentralized system and resisted turning over inventory tracking and management to centralized control. This was in part due to resistance from store managers who thought that centralization would undermine the value of their own expertise and authority (Ortega 1998: Chapter 7). In the Wal-Mart organization, such resistance would not have been tolerated. The consequence of the difference between the two giant discounters is reflected in the fact that in 1983 Kmart spent five cents on distribution for every dollar of goods sold, while Wal-Mart spent only two cents per dollar (Ortega 1998: 130).

As Wal-Mart built their computer systems and implemented their use throughout their operations, they also outgrew the ability of the telephone system to service their needs adequately. In 1983 they began using their own specially constructed satellite. In Walton's words,

> The satellite turned out to be absolutely necessary because, once we had those scanners in the stores, we had all this data pouring into Bentonville over phone lines. Those lines have a limited capacity, so as we added more and more stores, we had a real logjam of stuff coming in from the field. As you know, I like my numbers as quickly as I can get them. The quicker we get that information, the quicker we can act on it. The [satellite] system has been a great tool for us, and our technical people have done a terrific job of figuring out how to use it to our best advantage.
>
> (Walton 1992: 213)

As Wal-Mart built their capacity to track inventory and to distribute it quickly from receipt by the company to consumers, opportunities for even greater control of the supply chain were recognized and seized.[11] Here again, new technology provided the opportunity. In 1956, just six years before the first Wal-Mart opened, the first ship carrying goods in the kind of large containers that have become ubiquitous sailed from Newark, New Jersey, to Houston, Texas. What followed was dramatic:

> An enormous containership can be loaded with a minute fraction of the labor and time required to handle a small conventional ship half a century ago. A few crew members can manage an oceangoing vessel longer than three football fields. A trucker can deposit a trailer at a customer's loading dock, hook up another trailer, and drive on immediately, rather than watching his expensive rig stand idle while the contents are removed. All of those changes are consequences of the container revolution. Transportation has become so efficient that for many purposes, freight costs do not much affect economic decisions.
>
> (Levinson 2006: 1)

More precisely, Levinson estimates that prior to the time when containers were used internationally, ocean freight costs amounted to 12 percent of the value of US exports and 10 percent of the value of imports. To that had to be added the costs of domestic shipping, and as had long been recognized by some students of international trade, such costs were often more significant than the more often discussed tariffs. Particularly important were the port costs; the total of shipping and handling meant that selling internationally often did not make economic sense. The adoption of containers, with all of the related changes involved for ships, trucks, and ports, reduced the cost dramatically and changed the volume and nature of international trade.[12]

The cost of moving goods across oceans had not been the major financial barrier for some time. Rather, what was costly was loading and unloading goods at ports and, as Walton recognized, from trucks to warehouses and back to trucks. Containers, and the ships and trucks designed to haul them, as well as the computer systems that developed to track them and direct the machines responsible for loading and offloading, drastically reduced those costs. These changes also affected the time required to move goods. Here is how Levinson describes it:

> Transport efficiencies, though, hardly begin to capture the economic impact of containerization. The container not only lowered freight bills, it saved time. Quicker handling and less time in storage translated to faster transit from manufacturer to customer, reducing the cost of financing inventories sitting unproductively on railway sidings or in pierside warehouses awaiting a ship. The container, combined with the computer, made it practical for companies like Toyota and Honda to develop just-in-time manufacturing, in which a supplier makes the goods its customer wants only as the customer needs them and then ships them, in containers, to arrive at a specified time. Such precision, unimaginable before the container, has led to massive reductions in manufacturers' inventories and correspondingly huge cost savings. Retailers have applied these same lessons, using careful logistics management to squeeze out billions of dollars of costs.
>
> (Levinson 2006: 11)

Levinson estimates that non-farm inventories in the US had a value of approximately $1 trillion *less* in 2004 than they would have had if the ratio of inventories to sales had been the same as it was in the 1980s (Levinson 2006: 267).

Interestingly enough, the advent of container shipping had locational effects not unlike those associated with the railroad rebates and charges during the build-up of Standard Oil. Levinson points out that container shipping abolished the advantage that a New York City location once held for manufacturing because of its proximity to ocean shipping but also, and in general, reduced the importance of distance.

Distance matters, but not hugely so. A doubling of the distance cargo is shipped ... raises the shipping cost only 18 percent. Places far from the end market can still be part of an international supply chain, so long as they have well-run ports and a lot of volume.... Shippers in places with busy ports and good land-transport infrastructure not only enjoy lower freight rates, but they also benefit from the shortest shipping times.

(Levinson 2006: 268–9)

In other words, locational advantage can be constructed.

Wal-Mart took advantage of this fact of the modern world first by their hub-and-spoke distributional system but also by their management of the shipment of goods. Although the story of Walton's rise to wealth is often told as a story of overcoming what are assumed to be intuitively obvious disadvantages of starting in a remote corner of Arkansas, the context in which he was working meant that locational advantage went to the aggressive and early managers of supply chains. Wal-Mart owned their own fleet of trucks, which were tightly managed.[13] They built their distribution centers to move goods quickly and cheaply from truck to truck. And, they required their suppliers to pack in units designed for distribution to the stores to which they were going so that containers could be quickly and easily broken into shipment units within the distribution centers.

And, that requirement is, of course, only one component of the most notorious, and certainly most powerful, element of the entire Wal-Mart system: the control over their suppliers. Crucial to this control is something called "Retail-Link," which was implemented in 1991. This system allows suppliers to use the internet to get daily updates on the quantity of their products selling at each Wal-Mart, to download purchase orders, and to check other aspects of their dealings with the firm (Slater 2003: 151; Soderquist 2005: 246; Bonacich and Wilson 2006: 234–5; Lichtenstein 2006: 133). The relationships with suppliers are a source of pride for Walton and his associates, and in writing about them they often focus on the happy side of mutual cooperation for mutual gain. For example, Don Soderquist, a top lieutenant who joined Wal-Mart in 1980, writes glowingly of how a canoe trip taken by Walton and a senior executive at Procter & Gamble led to a change from the traditional adversarial relationship between buyer and seller into a relationship based on mutual recognition that both wanted "to sell more of our merchandise to our customers" (Soderquist 2005: 166–7).

From this and other meetings, Retail-Link was developed so that

our [Wal-Mart's] technology people work directly with their technology people, our logistics people work directly with their logistics people, and our accounts-payable department works directly with their accounts-receivable department. We streamlined both ordering and invoicing processes by transmitting orders and invoices electronically, directly into each other's computers, and letting the computers do the translating.

(Soderquist 2005: 171)

For those firms large enough to care, data is updated eight times a day, allowing rapid response by the supplier. Walton and Soderquist also acknowledge a point made more often and more forcefully by critics of the Wal-Mart system, namely that Wal-Mart is a ferocious negotiator for low prices from their suppliers. On this point, much more will be said in the next chapter.

Wal-Mart's ability to demand lower costs, tagged products, and, more recently, radio-frequency identification tagged products, and to place orders for specified size of shipments to minimize re-sorting costs in Wal-Mart distribution centers are all a result, in some large measure, of their monopsonistic power, power similar to that enjoyed by Standard Oil in their dealings with the suppliers of crude.[14] Bonacich and Wilson estimate that Wal-Mart accounts for only about 7 percent of US retail sales but in six states they account for close to 20 percent of retail sales, with varying degrees of dominance for specific commodities (Bonacich and Wilson 2006: 235). For many individual suppliers, it seems fairly obvious that a route through the Wal-Mart system can be of critical importance.

Will Wal-Mart eventually lose their dominant place in the American retail market? Will they be able to extend their dominance abroad? Will they suffer the relative loss of preeminence that befell Standard Oil? As this is being written, there are threats to Wal-Mart's position. Their efforts to move into somewhat more up-scale fashion have not been successful and they have retreated (Barbaro 2007b). And, some business writers see the British firm Tesco as a potential rival in American markets, while internationally Wal-Mart has found planned expansion into many countries a difficult task (Smith 2007). At the same time, Wal-Mart executives continue to expand efforts to reach and serve in new ways, most notably with an expansion into the banking arena via introduction of a prepaid debit card (Barbaro and Dash 2007). They have also begun to advertise more on TV in order to shore up demand in the holiday season of 2007 and have initiated programs designed to make the firm more environmentally friendly. Whether or not they will succeed in any of these programs is by no means clear.[15] What is clear, even from this close perspective of time, is that Wal-Mart has become a major economic power in the world and that, like Standard Oil, the fortunes made and the power accumulated will continue to play an important role in the twenty-first century.

A preliminary comparison

In Chapter 3, the circumstances that made what Rockefeller and Walton achieved so pivotal in the American economy will be explored, and the larger narratives of which they are part will be examined. Before turning to those larger narratives, however, it is worth noting some of the ways in which the careers of the two men were alike. Neither man created new industrial or commercial processes, but both were quick to see and take advantage of important new technologies as they became available. Neither could have accomplished what they did on their own; they were in a sense superb generals who selected and managed colleagues and employees in pursuit of their own visions.[16] Both reacted swiftly as new opportunities and dangers arose and both were, in the modern parlance, risk takers. And yet, both were extremely thrifty, both in personal and in business expenditures, and both paid close attention to detail. Finally, both men were extremely lucky, for they sought their goals in contexts that had as much to do with their success as their own undoubted virtues. These contexts, which are the subject of the next chapter, led to the fortunes and the denunciations that are also part of the larger American story.

3 Popular accounts and wider contexts

Around the bare bone stories of the rise of John D. Rockefeller's Standard Oil of Ohio and Sam Walton's Wal-Mart as recounted in Chapter Two, there are other, larger narratives that have become part of the American legacy. These narratives blur distinctions between the actions of the leaders of Standard Oil and Wal-Mart and their firms and changes in the larger social, political, and economic context in which they operated. They are, for the most part, narratives of judgment and blame that have served political and economic debate as well as historical scholarship. Because the larger, more inclusive narratives are part of evolving American public understanding of economic and corporate power, these narratives have also shaped the scholarship of the economists and other social scientists who have articulated the issues that such power presents in a democratic society. These larger narratives and the role they have played in shaping social and political history, economic history, and American literature are the subject of this chapter.

Public understanding has come from many sources. In the case of the Standard Oil, the journalists and other writers who came to be known collectively as muckrakers gave a nation their views of the depredations of the firms of Rockefeller and other "robber barons" of his era. They found allies among the farmers who had already begun to organize themselves to protest their changing circumstances and among those who deplored the revelations in word and photograph of the often miserable living conditions found in the rapidly growing cities. At the Federal level, investigations by the Industrial Commission established at the end of the 1890s and the earlier efforts of many state legislators to regulate the railroads all contributed to the public perception of what Standard Oil was and what it was doing. And, of lasting importance were the many, some of them hugely popular, novels and short stories that depicted the changing economic conditions of farmers, laborers, as well as business owners, novels and stories that continue to be read in high school and college classrooms even today.[1]

In the case of Wal-Mart, novels and short stories, at least as read in colleges and universities, have played a less important role than they did in creating the context of the end of the nineteenth century. This is not surprising, for non-print forms of information are much more important today. There are books such as Barbara Ehrenreich's *Nickel and Dimed*, and other works of non-fiction, as well as countless news stories that both denounce and praise the giant firm. However, television features, as well as full-length movies, both documentary and fictional, as well as web sites such as Wal-Mart Watch helped articulate widespread concern about growing income inequality and social injustice.[2] There is also, as of 2007, an off-Broadway Musical – *Walmartopia* – which bills itself as "a musical on a mission." In other words, the forms have changed but the amount of public chatter about Wal-Mart is in volume and tone not unlike that which documented Standard's rise in the public arena.

Concern and, indeed, anger about income disparity is the common theme of popular reaction to both Standard Oil and Wal-Mart. Ironically, though both John D. Rockefeller and Sam Walton lived their lives with relative frugality, both were also associated with times of high living by their rich and super-rich brethren. The highly visible wealth of Rockefeller's era, particularly as it contrasted with the poverty of the tenements, which photography and journalism made visible to the American public, was a vivid backdrop to all discussions of his firm. A second, though less obvious, common theme has had to do with the use, or misuse, of new forms of transportation and communication. The impact of the railroads, still a relatively new form of transportation in the 1870s, and particularly the use made of the railroad system by Rockefeller, was as much and more a part of his story as was his organization of the technical aspects of oil refining. In parallel, globalization and outsourcing, aided and abetted by computerized management of the chains of transactions required to stock the shelves of Wal-Marts, as well as new forms of transport, have been to Walton's legacy what the railroads were to Rockefeller. Both the concern with income distribution and the use of new technologies that formed the public's larger stories of Standard and Wal-Mart are inescapably part of the challenge to economists as they have sought to explain the growth of economic power in what is supposed to be a competitive economy. Because of this it is important to understand these larger stories alongside the narrower narratives laid out in Chapter 2.

Rockefeller's context

John D. Rockefeller and his associates built Standard Oil during four decades that have been characterized as the "gilded age," as the era of "robber barons," and, in more mundane fashion, as a time of rapid economic growth that also entailed considerable misery in cities and on farms. It was a time of growth, of urbanization, and of industrialization. Between 1870 and 1900, population in the United States almost doubled, growing from just under forty million to almost seventy-six million people, an increase of 90 percent, fueled in part by a birth rate that remained high by modern standards in spite of a sharp decline over the whole of the nineteenth century but also by massive immigration. The population of urban areas grew more rapidly than the population as a whole, roughly tripling during the period. And, even though approximately 60 percent of the population lived in rural areas in 1900, where rural areas are defined to include towns of 2,500 or fewer, and the total number of people living on farms actually increased, the percentage of population that was directly involved in agriculture declined, as both native-born and immigrant populations poured into the cities, many to work in the new factories.[3] In 1870, no city in the US had a million people; by 1900, there were three such places, and the population that lived in cities of 500,000 or more had quadrupled, from 1.6 million to over eight million. And, the growth of output more than kept pace with the growth of population.[4] For those living through the decades that brought the US to the role of twentieth century economic superpower, however, attention was less on aggregates than on the actions of those firms and individuals effecting the change.

From early on in its history, Standard Oil was the subject of public scrutiny as state legislative bodies and the US Congress, responding to loud complaints from constituents and eventually from reformers, investigated the company. Not surprisingly, given the story told in Chapter 2, the heart of the complaints almost always had to do with Standard and the railroads. In her classic muckraking account, Tarbell borrowed the phrase the "unholy alliance" that was used by angry oil producers in the Oil Regions to denounce the South Improvement Company, one of the early but abortive efforts that Standard made to reach agreement on production levels and shipment with producers and to offer lower freight rates to those who were cooperative.[5] To understand the resonance that the phrase had and the depth of fury that the railroads caused across much of the country, a temporary sidetrack is required.

Understanding the railroads and, most importantly, the railroad system that was completed in the last decades of the nineteenth century is crucial to understanding *all* of the narratives of the period. Economic historians have had their own technical and somewhat inconclusive debate about the net contribution that this rail network made to aggregate economic growth, but there can be little doubt that railroads transformed the organization of virtually every sector and aspect of American life and, in doing so, riled many.[6]

By all accounts, and there are indeed many, the railroads changed American consumption patterns, altered the location of production, caused drastic reorganization in the distribution network, changed the way in which business was organized, as well as its accounting and management practices, and, ultimately, changed American law. They did all of this by virtue of providing, for the first time in human history, a low-cost, speedy, and reliable way of transporting people and goods, including goods that were very heavy relative to their market value.[7] Alfred Chandler has observed that the source of success of the railroads over competing forms of transport is obvious: "[f]or the first time in history, freight and passengers could be carried overland at a speed faster than that of a horse," and this was true even over mountains and on a direct line between towns, routes not easily or always available for waterways (Chandler 1977: 83). The multiple and far-reaching changes were also a result of two crucial facts about railroads: they were expensive to build and much of the cost was fixed, which is to say that it did not vary greatly with the amount of traffic on the road. You could build and move canal or river boats on a small scale, using portage if necessary, and you could go into the business of hauling people or goods overland with one wagon and a simple trail, but you could not run a railroad without a system of tracks, engines, and rolling stock.

Even though a system of canals and river transport had been built in the early decades of the nineteenth century, transport of both people and goods remained time-consuming and uncertain until the railroads were built. There was simply no reasonable way to organize production of bulky goods for widespread distribution through the countryside or to small towns or for farmers to ship produce to distant markets. As eager as American farmers and merchants may have been to improve their economic lot by selling what they produced, the difficulties and costs of transportation served to organize American life on a local scale. In some areas, farmers took produce to centralized markets in winter months, but for the most part they produced for their own consumption and for limited local markets (Berry 1943 and Lebergott 1984: Chapter 17). Families that moved out onto the frontier made do with what they could produce along with a few store-bought goods purchased on occasional trips to distant stores or purchased from peddlers. Except along the coasts and on some of the rivers, towns were largely isolated from each other and, by twentieth-century standards, were remarkably self-contained and self-sustaining.

Approximately 43,000 miles of rail lines were built prior to 1870, and then another 41,000 miles were added in that decade alone. Net new miles continued to be added into the twentieth century, though some miles of track were also abandoned as new systems of interconnected lines were organized. Total mileage peaked in 1916. Prior to the Civil War, most of the rail mileage had been east of the Mississippi, and lines were not well integrated. After the War, there was a rapid extension of rail lines to the west, and a well-integrated system was eventually created, though not without great difficulty.[8] The impact of the extension and integration of the rail lines was widespread and dramatic, and for simple and straightforward reasons:

> millions of farmers, thousands of small manufacturers, and dozens of giant trusts [seized] the opportunity to expand their sales (and profits) by moving into new markets. Some of these new markets were a hundred miles from their base. Others were located thousands of miles away in Europe and Asia.
>
> (Lebergott 1984: 268)

Without recounting the long debate among economic historians over exact measures of the contribution of the railroads to economic growth, and even in the absence of any precise comparison of the early costs of moving goods by rail as opposed to wagon, it is reasonable to say that the railroads fundamentally altered the context of economic life of most inhabitants of the nation.

Not only did the railroads change fundamentally the way in which goods were distributed, but they also changed consumption patterns:

> During the pre-railroad age in America western storekeepers made semi-annual visits to the cities of the East, bought supplies for the coming season, and personally supervised the shipment of their goods to their stores in the interior. For example, a merchant from one of the small settlements in Michigan, purchasing his stock in Albany in 1825, arranged first for its shipment via the Erie Canal to Buffalo. At Buffalo he supervised its transfer to a lake boat on which he took passage to Detroit. At Detroit he arranged for transshipment to his own or hired wagons which finally carried his new stock to his place of business.
>
> (Taylor and Neu 1956: 49)

For those settlements further removed from water transport, the likelihood of receiving goods from the East was much smaller, and until the railroads came, traveling peddlers and, in many cases, home production had to suffice. Taylor estimates that two-thirds of clothing in the US was produced at home in the first decades of the nineteenth century, but this mode of production gradually disappeared along with other home manufactures as inexpensive and reliable transportation spread (Taylor 1951: 211). In the case of another basic product, soap – the product of "one of the nastiest of a woman's duties" – home production using vats of boiled animal fat gave way to factory production, as, for example, in the Cincinnati plant of Procter & Gamble (Morris 2005: 162). In a move that echoes all the way to the twenty-first-century story of Wal-Mart, P&G became a major supplier in the 1880s of a variety of kinds of soap that were used in homes throughout a large area of the US even though soap making continued to be a home process in more remote regions of the country into the twentieth century.

The availability of "store-bought" soap, cloth, clothing, and, increasingly, food was of enormous benefit to the women who had previously had to produce all such things at home and, in turn, to all consumers of both sexes and all ages:

> History had never seen an explosion of new products like that in the America of the 1880s and 1890s. Branded foods followed the lead of the meatpackers, starting in the 1880s. Store shelves offered Cream of Wheat, Aunt Jemima's Pancakes, Postum, Kellogg's Shredded Wheat, Juicy Fruit gum, Pabst Blue Ribbon Beer, Durkee's salad dressings, Uneeda Biscuits, Coca-Cola, and Quaker Oats, Pillsbury and Gold Medal wiped out local flour millers.... The Great Atlantic and Pacific Tea Company, A&P, was the first national grocery chain, and Frank Woolworth's "nickel-stores" were sweeping through the country.
>
> (Morris 2005: 177)

At the end of the nineteenth century, these products were still far more likely to be found in towns and cities than on the farms, but as the century ended, more and more of the new goods of the era also went to farms. Montgomery Ward was specifically designed to serve rural areas, and Sears and other mail-order firms followed in the same path. As Morris notes, it was not the intention but it was certainly the effect of investment in railroads that small-town depots and post offices became part of a massive system of distribution of consumer goods. Ironically,

> [w]hen railroad men and their investment banks adopted their "if you build it, they will come" strategy, they were not thinking of a consumer revolution. Gould, Vanderbilt, and Scott went to war over grain, iron, and oil freights, not corsets and ribbons.
>
> (Morris 2005: 176)

However, corsets and ribbons flowed across America as surely as did grain and oil, and the impact was most pronounced for farmers and their families. The farmers were in many ways well served by the railroads, but, as will become evident, they were also mightily unhappy with them. First, however, consider the benefits that came to farm families across the country.

After the railroads were built, farm families not only sold a large share of their output and purchased what they had once produced at home but also added niceties. They purchased, that is, signs of success, of which perhaps the most important for families in the late nineteenth century was the piano. Amazingly enough, you could buy one from the Montgomery Ward catalog. In 1860, just under 22,000 pianos were produced in the US, in 1870 just over 24,000, but by 1890, 232,000 were rolled out. These were largely upright pianos designed for the parlors of American homes, many of which were farmhouses (www.cantos.org, accessed June 2007).

The fact that there were parlors in which to put the pianos is, of course, another telling piece of evidence that many farm families were doing quite well and in a manner that is probably understated in the numbers of the national income accounts. In the 1830s, a new way of building houses was developed in Chicago, one that involved use of factory-produced nails and precut two-by-four studs. In contrast to earlier housing that required considerable expertise and labor time, the resulting "balloon houses" could be put together by two workers who had only basic carpentry skills.[9] Across the prairies and plains, frame houses replaced dugouts and sod, and the railroads brought new finery to these new homes. A passage from Willa Cather's novel *O Pioneers!* captures well how it was on a prospering farm:

> The table was set for company in the dining-room, where highly varnished wood and colored glass and useless pieces of china were conspicuous enough to satisfy the standards of the new prosperity. Alexandra had put herself into the hands of the Hanover furniture dealer, and he had conscientiously done his best to make her dining-room look like his display window. She said frankly that she knew nothing about such things, and she was willing to be governed by the general conviction that the more useless and utterly unusable objects were, the greater their virtue as ornament. That seemed reasonable enough. Since she liked plain things herself, it was all the more necessary to have jars and punch-bowls and candlesticks in the company rooms for people who did appreciate them. Her guests liked to see about them these reassuring emblems of prosperity.
>
> (Cather 1933: 56)

Cather's account of the successful Alexandra Bergson and her friends and kin, like many other accounts, both fictional and documentary, also tells the tale of failure and of hard years. However, it is impossible to come away from Cather's *O Pioneers!*, and *My Antonia*, without a sense that the years between early settlement and the end of the century were years of growing prosperity.

But, there was another story, a much sadder one, that was also told in novels and the popular press. To take one dramatic example, in *The Octopus*, Frank Norris tells a tragic tale of prospering ranchers and farmers in California whose hard work and success was undermined by the very railroads that allowed the possibility of their success in the first place. Based on an actual gun battle between a sheriff's posse sent to evict farmers from leased land owned by the Southern Pacific Railroad, Norris's novel is a story of the unhappy consequences of land policy in one particular locale, but it was also an effective muckraking attack upon the railroads that farmers across the country had come to hate for reasons that overlapped with those that led the crude oil producers of the Oil Region to decry the "unholy alliance" of Standard and the railroads.

To understand how the context in which public reaction to Standard Oil and other large firms of the era was formed, it is important to recognize the extent to which the same farm families that would seem to have been prime beneficiaries of the rail network led in articulating the reasons why those same railroads were the cause of much evil. Complaints against the railroads were at the heart of the farm protests and reform efforts that were prominent in political debate and electioneering during the decades following the Civil War. The farmers, through their various organizations and in exercise of their very considerable political power, were able to stamp their own interpretation of their woes upon the nation's understanding and memory. And, in concert with the Pennsylvania oil producers, railroad and industrial workers, and many others, they found the actions of railroads to be fundamentally and destructively unfair.

Why, given the obvious benefits that the railroads brought to farmers and their families, did farmers lead the way in seeking to control them? The rhetoric employed by Alliance members, the Grange, and the Populists makes it clear that they were not seeking friendly amendments to the behavior of otherwise benign organizations when they sought a variety of forms of public control over the railroads. They regarded the railroads as their enemies, and the question is why this was so. A second question will follow from answers to the first: why did the railroads adopt the practices that were deemed so harmful to the interests of the farmers and, in turn, to crude oil producers and merchants who joined the farmers in their decades-long battle to control what Norris, in apt reflection of the views of many, called the octopus?

The first question is a complicated one. The railroads made it possible for settlers to move out beyond navigable waterways to produce for distant markets and live relatively comfortable lives. If we did not have the accounts of the farmers themselves, the story of late-nineteenth-century American agriculture, in all regions save the old cotton South, would be one of triumph. Grain could be produced in Kansas, shipped to Europe, and sold more cheaply than comparable grain produced there. The volume of agricultural exports grew rapidly. True, there were periods of drought, and by the 1930s, it was apparent that the kind of agriculture carried onto the relatively dry plains could not be sustained. Yet, for farmers living and prospering on the prairies and plains from the 1870s until the troubles of the 1920s and 30s, life should have been good, with new machinery available, relatively easy and low-cost credit, government support from the land-grant universities and their research and extension arms, and rapidly growing markets here and abroad.[10]

Why, then, were the farmers so unhappy with their lot during this period, and, specifically, why were they unhappy with the railroads? And, finally, how did this unhappiness affect the way in which the story of Standard Oil came to be told in the popular national narrative?

In part the farmers were unhappy with the railroads because they had been granted land to encourage construction of rail lines in areas of as yet sparse settlement. These grants, which to the twenty-first-century reader will look very much like the kind of encouragements to local development that have become commonplace (though still controversial), enraged the farmers who found, after the promise of the Homestead Act, that the land in closest proximity to the rail lines, those lines that made settlement and commercial agriculture in the frontier regions possible, had to be purchased from the railroads. As Fred Shannon notes, almost all of the land taken by the railroads, an amount equal to "nearly a tenth of the area of the United States," was patented to them after the passage of the Homestead Act (Shannon 1945: 65). This was a bitter turn indeed, for the promise of the Homestead Act, despite the continuing myth of its great importance in textbooks and official stories, contrasted with the reality that good arable land west of the Mississippi most often had to be purchased. Further, in some areas, farmers who leased land from the railroads and made improvements upon it were then further outraged when they found that the railroads wanted a much higher price than originally proposed for the land in its unimproved state. It was this turn of events that prompted the shootout that plays a central role in *The Octopus*, and such events and their telling certainly added to the view of the railroad magnates as evil and conniving masters. However, both in Norris's novel and in myriad accounts of the day, there were other causes of anger with the railroads, causes shared with their allies in towns and in the oil-producing regions.

These causes had to do both with the railroad rates and with the high expectations that the railroads brought as they created a greatly modified economic system, one in which truly millions of farmers and thousands of merchants seized on new opportunities. Response to these opportunities increased the quantity of goods available. The resulting fall in commodity prices was itself a matter of great concern, especially to farmers, but what was perhaps even more important was the new role that prices, and prices determined far away and somewhat mysteriously, played in determining the welfare and status of the farmers and small-town merchants.

Before it was possible to transport a piano to put in a parlor, and, indeed, before it was possible to have a real parlor at all, a farmer could be judged successful by relatively simple standards. If his family was fed and clothed in homespun, he and his farmwife were doing their jobs as well as their neighbors were. The railroads changed the measure of success and introduced new uncertainty. Now a farmer might well grow a bumper crop, but if the prices he received were not as great as in the previous year, or not as great as he had (in some cases quite literally) banked on, then financial ruin could follow, and social status would plummet.

The sad McLane family in Hamlin Garland's widely read story "Up the Coolly" illustrates well what could happen when easily available, land-secured debt was not repaid. When the successful brother returns from the city and asks why the "old farm" has been sold, with the family relocated to an inferior location, the bitter brother who is still on the land responds:

> "How'd we come to sell it?" said Grant with terrible bitterness. "We had something on it that didn't leave anything to sell. You probably don't remember anything about it, but there was a mortgage on it that eat us up in just four years by the almanac. 'Most killed mother to leave it."
>
> (Garland 1891: 85)

The availability of mortgages, which followed the rails and the growth of market opportunities, was an advantage to farmers who had eagerly sought credit to buy land and equipment, but commercial failure could result in loss of both land and status. Nor was loss of land the only failure that could afflict a farm family, for now the measure of success was the ability to plant crops that would grow well, provide high yields, and sell at prices sufficient to cover the growing level of monetary commitments that a successful farm family could and would acquire in the new railroad age.

What the railroads did, then, was to convert American family farming in areas far beyond the reach of water transport into commercial farming. Before the railroads, farmers tried to sell some of their output if they could get it to market, but a good portion of what they produced was for home consumption. And, even more importantly, most of home consumption was what was produced on the farm. The standard of living depended on the soil, the weather, and the work of the farm family itself. Now, with the railroads and the possibility of shipping grain from the prairies of the upper Midwest to the Atlantic seaports and beyond, the standard of living depended upon many others as well and upon forces far from the farmer's control but clearly not beyond the suspected control of others. Middlemen, railroad magnates and their agents, bankers and mortgage holders, and far-away consumers, all now played a role in how successful the farmer and his family were. This was a profound and not always comfortable change, and it is little wonder that much of the literature about farmers written during this time is markedly plaintive even as it is increasingly set in prosperous homes with pianos in the parlors. As Hamlin Garland told it, an old order was passing and a scary, if often prosperous, one was taking its place.

Further, it was not only the farmers who were affected. In making the point that there were casualties among both small and more traditional firms when P&G introduced their new mass-produced and mass-distributed products, Charles Morris cites a passage from an 1884 issue of the *American Journal of Pharmacy* lamenting the fact that "competition and the inability of the public to discriminate between a well-made and a common soap" has led to a drop in the production and purchase of the "best soaps" as "cheaper kinds" have taken their place (Morris 2005: 164). This is surely a trivial complaint, but magnified by the number of small firms, the number of new products, and the number of distributors affected by the new order, it was not.

It is easy to overlook the significance of the sheer and new *disorder* that the rail network introduced among producers of consumer goods. Lebergott's "millions of farmers, thousands of small manufacturers, and dozens of giant trusts [who seized] the opportunity to expand their sales (and profits)" by producing for and selling in markets that were often quite distant were caught up in a stupendous change, the equivalent of an economic earthquake of magnitude eight or more on an economic Richter scale.

Description and analysis of this economic earthquake has been rendered less clear than it might have been because it is all too easy to imagine the United States before the railroads as a land of small producers who operated in a highly competitive market. Nothing could be further from the truth. Limitations on transport of goods, and even in cities where there might be multiple sellers but relative immobility of populations who depended heavily on their own two feet when they shopped, meant that most producers and sellers (and often they were one and the same) were in effect monopolists in their local markets. A major result of rail construction in the US, which, to borrow Lebergott's great phrase, "had been pock-marked by local monopolies," was increased competitiveness. Lowered freight costs, rising real incomes, and a growing population all increased demand for goods shipped over the new rail system, but these were not the only reasons why shipping increased. According to Lebergott's estimates, "[t]he tonnage of raw material shipped into factories, and final products shipped out from 1859 to 1879, rose four times faster than the volume of GNP they produced" (Lebergott 1984: 281). The country shipped more to produce more but also shipped more relative to final output. Put slightly differently, many more goods were being produced, and a greater proportion of those goods reached their final destination far from the point of production.

Using the language of economics, we can say that demand schedules for the local producers prior to the coming of the railroads had been relatively stable, known, and manageable for most producers and distributors. New families might move in or populations shift, but this could be handled by changes in the level of production and in the sales expectations. Production was on a small scale, and the costs of increasing output were largely variable so that anticipated increases in sales revenues from a growing local population could serve as a reliably anticipated source of funds for the additional costs. Expansion of capacity and of associated fixed costs did not require a major gamble. Economic life was orderly.

As the railroads moved in, new markets became available, but they became more or less simultaneously available for all who were paying attention to the schedules of trains and the fares charged for movement of goods. In Alfred Chandler's words:

> For ... small firms [making relatively standardized goods] the coming of the railroad had in many cases enlarged their markets but simultaneously brought them for the first time into competition with many other companies. *Most of these firms appear to have expanded production in order to take advantage of the new markets.* As a result, the industries became plagued with overproduction and excess capacity; that is, continued production at full capacity threatened to drop prices below the cost of production. So in the 1880's and early 1890's, many small manufacturers in the leather, sugar, salt, distilling and other corn products, linseed and cotton oil, biscuit, petroleum, fertilizer and

rubber boot and glove industries, joined in large horizontal combinations.

(Chandler 1959: 10, italics added)

The lack of drama in Chandler's words should not deceive us about the actual unhappiness involved for the small producers who, like the farmers, saw the hope of greater markets and wealth arrive almost simultaneously with the often crushing reality of competition in that market. And, of course, what drove the initial consolidation, as we have already seen in the case of oil production and refining, was the very disorder that apparently shifting, and hard to gauge, demand schedules brought. Chandler's work on the emergence of large-scale firms in the consumer goods industries, and especially in those producing standardized goods, makes it abundantly clear that the initial advantage for larger operations came not from economies of scale in production but, rather, from organizational advantages in eliminating the disorder that accompanied competition among many producers competing for unknown and unknowable market shares:

> In most of these industries, combination was followed by consolidation and vertical integration, and the pattern was comparatively consistent. First, the new combinations concentrated their manufacturing activities in locations more advantageously situated to meet the new growing urban demands. Next they systematized and standardized their manufacturing processes. Then ... the combinations began to build large distributing and smaller purchasing departments. In so doing, many dropped their initial efforts to buy out competitors or to drive them out of business by price-cutting. Instead they concentrated on the creation of a more efficient flow from the producers of their raw materials to the ultimate consumer, and of the development and maintenance of markets through brand names and advertising.

(Chandler 1959: 10)

Order, as John D. Rockefeller famously said of the petroleum industry, was restored in many industries, but in the meantime hundreds and thousands of producers of consumer goods saw their local advantage disappear and watched as well as millions of consumers purchased goods that they themselves might have made and sold.

The dramatic exchange between Silas Lapham, a manufacturer and distributor of paint, and his wife, in the classic W. D. Howells novel of the era, *The Rise of Silas Lapham*, can be taken as a national refrain:

"The new house [which was to have been their ticket to Boston upper-class respectability] has got to go," he answered evasively.

She did not say anything. She knew that the work on the house had been stopped since the beginning of the year.... She saw that he did not eat, and she waited for him to speak again, without urging him to take anything. They were past that.

"And I've sent orders to shut down at the [paint] Works," he added.

"Shut down at the Works!" she echoed with dismay. She could not take it in. The fire at the Works had never been out before since it was first kindled. She knew how he had prided himself upon that; how he had bragged of it to every listener, and had always lugged the fact in as the last expression of his sense of success. "Oh, Silas!"

"What's the use?" he retorted. "I saw it was coming a month ago. There are some fellows out in West Virginia that have been running the paint as hard as they could.... Besides, the market's overstocked. It's glutted. There wasn't anything to do but to shut *down*, and I've *shut* down."

(Howells 2002: 286)

What happened to the farmers and to the small-scale producers like Lapham and to local distributors of consumer goods was in some ways different. The producers and consumers had been thoroughly commercial in operations before the railroads. What did them in was competition – competition, according to Lebergott, "...to a degree never seen outside the textbooks of classical economists" – that led to new ways of organization of markets, ways that gave advantage to those who seized control of throughput and then reorganized accordingly (Lebergott 1984: 281). Most farmers, on the other hand, were brought fully into the nexus of commercial production for the first time. And, to the farmers and local producers and distributors, the railroads clearly appeared to be at the epicenter of the upheaval, an upheaval that involved the railroads playing favorites in a highly destructive manner.

The railroads saw it quite differently. Building and operating railroads involved problems and opportunities quite unlike those involved in earlier transportation enterprises or in manufacturing. Finance, management, cost accounting, and pricing all required innovation because practices that had been developed for earlier business operations simply were not suitable for the railroads. Chandler provides the canonic explanation of the combined effects of size and complexity:

The men who managed ... [the railroads] became the first group of modern business administrators in the United States. Ownership and management soon separated. The capital required to build a railroad was far more than that required to purchase a plantation, a textile mill, or even a fleet of ships. Therefore, a single entrepreneur, family, or small group of associates was rarely able to own a railroad. Nor could the many stockholders or their representatives manage it. The administrative tasks were too numerous, too varied and too complex. They required special skills and training which could only be commanded by a full-time salaried manager.

(Chandler 1977: 87)

The challenges were many and the innovations of profound importance for American industrial management for decades to come.

What users of the railroads, the farmers, and the businesses that were succeeding, as well as those that weren't, were most concerned with were the rates that the railroads charged, and this was a particularly complex issue for railroad management. Chandler notes that the fundamental innovations in financial and capital accounting that were to be used and further refined after the Civil War were actually developed in the 1850s during the great boom of railroad construction east of the Mississippi. What was harder to develop was cost accounting, which is to say the procedures for figuring out how much it cost to move goods and people over different routes. For small local firms whose costs were primarily variable, cost accounting was simple. For large firms that had to allocate the costs of building hundreds or thousands of miles of rail, depots, administrative offices, as well as the costs of borrowed money (primarily interest on bonds), the problem was much, much more complicated. And, the task was made even more complex for the railroads because traffic could be light over some stretches of rail, stretches that were nevertheless required for the entire system to work, and then much heavier over shorter stretches of line.

Daniel C. McCallum, who worked originally for the Erie, developed a general scheme for management and accounting, and did so in response to pressure put on the Erie by competition from the New York Central, an amalgam of shorter competing lines. He developed general principles and an organizational scheme that were widely admired and copied, but it was Albert Fink, a civil engineer, working at the Louisville & Nashville, who, according to Chandler, made McCallum's scheme for cost accounting an operational tool that could be used in control of a complex organization.

An idea of the complexity of the cost accounting comes through from detailed accounts provided by Fink. Detailed accounts of costs (say, of the cost of ballast or the salaries of watchmen and switchmen or stationery and printing) were put into four categories. The first two categories involved costs that did not vary in any direct way with the volume of traffic (maintenance of roadway and general superintendence and interest charges). The third category varied directly with volume (station expenses per train mile), and a fourth (movement expenses per train mile) varied with the number of trains run over what distance. These costs, which were to be carefully compiled by the different divisions of the L&N, could then be used to evaluate the effectiveness of the operating executives of the branches and, very importantly, to establish cost per ton-mile, which could then be used to set what the railroad believed to be fair but profitable rates. The formula for determining the total cost per ton-mile (reproduced in greater complexity in Chandler's book) was a + b + c + d where a was the movement expenses per train mile divided by the average number of tons of freight in each train; b was the cost of handling freight at both forwarding and delivery stations divided by the length of the haul; c was the product of cost of maintenance per mile per year and a ratio of total miles run by freight-trains per year to total revenue trains (passenger and freight) per year; and d was the ratio of freight to revenue train miles times the cost per mile times the rate of interest to average tons of freight carried over a mile in a year (Chandler 1977: 118–19).

Fink's formulas allowed him to calculate the percentage of total finance and fixed costs associated with hauling freight, taking into account the very different conditions that affected those costs on different lines. Movement expenses would be a higher portion of total costs per mile on more heavily used lines, but the overall costs per ton-mile could be considerably lower. This would suggest pricing that would vary from place to place. And, to pick up on a thread from our earlier description of the early petroleum industry, it would also suggest that the costs per ton-mile could be strongly affected by guaranteed shipment of goods.

It is not difficult to see how pricing that could look quite reasonable to the railroads would appear highly discriminatory to farmers and manufacturers. Although not mentioned by W. D. Howells as a factor in the shutting down of Silas Lapham's fictional paint works in Vermont, it is easy enough to spin his tale a bit further and imagine Lapham's frustration had freight rates been lower from the West Virginia suppliers than from his own plant, and not in any obvious way related to the distances involved. We do not need to rely on fiction to know that this is the kind of thing that happened in real life.

The major complaint against Standard by both the oil producers and rival refineries was that through a system of rebates, Rockefeller's company was able to get favorable rates while rivals and suppliers were disadvantaged. Tarbell and others, including those in Congress who pursued complaints about rail rates, compiled abundant evidence that the railroads were indeed offering drawbacks, and it was obvious to all that the pattern of such rebates could make or break individual firms and cities. The advantage of refining in Cleveland, a place that, as Tarbell said, in expressing sympathy for the oil-producing regions, was "more than 200 miles from the spot where the oil was taken from the earth," lay in transportation rates, and it was an advantage that could be readily and swiftly taken away (Tarbell 1904: Vol. 1: 38). Little wonder that Rockefeller and his staff devoted such attention to negotiations with the railroads, and also little wonder that many others resented their success. Nor is it any wonder at all that the businessmen who had occupied Lebergott's pock-marks of monopolistic power across the country vented their anger against the railroads.

But the anger of the farmers with the railroads was even greater, and they had the advantage of numbers in the many states where farm and small-town inhabitants were still the overwhelming majority. Arthur T. Hadley, who was among the first to write analytically about the railroads, explained the situation quite clearly. After an early period in which legislation was designed to get the railroads built as quickly as possible, attention turned to control of railroad charges, and the proposed solutions were simple. The charges should be proportional to distance, but, said Hadley, "it does not cost a railroad anything like twice as much to carry goods two hundred miles as to carry them one hundred miles" (Hadley 1885: 130). Regulatory efforts grew more sophisticated over time, but farmers continued to denounce short haul rates that were higher than those for longer hauls and to see in all differential rates the intent to discriminate in favor of Eastern capitalists. Hadley wrote that it was easy to blame the railroads for all evils that befell the farmers and especially so because

> these capitalists were living in the Eastern States or in Europe, and were regarded by the farmer as the absentee landlord is regarded by the Irish tenantry. Whatever was paid to the railroad owner seemed like so much direct drain on the resources of the community.
>
> (Hadley 1885: 135)

The California farmers about whom Frank Norris wrote certainly saw differential pricing over different lines and for different products as proof of evil intent and as serious grievances to be piled on to anger over land ownership. The ranchers who were growing vast acreages of wheat were acutely conscious of the effect that differences in rates had on their own prospects for profit, and, in fact, Norris's novel revolves around their efforts to capture (unfortunately for the good standing of the central figure, by bribery) the regulatory commission so as to ensure a favorable outcome for their cause. However, Norris's most vivid example of the power of the railroads as they set their rates comes with the ruin of one of the saddest characters of the novel. Dyke, formerly an engineer on the P. and S. W. rail line (the rather transparent pseudonym for the Southern Pacific) loses his job in a wage dispute, but moves with enthusiasm to growing hops, a crop on which he expects to earn a handsome return because of recent crop failures elsewhere. Dyke, a somewhat foolish optimist in Norris's telling, is warned by the ranchers to "look up the freight rates" and "have a clear understanding with the railroad first about the rate" (Norris 1986: 73). As the reader can anticipate, however, Dyke fails to secure such an understanding, and too late he finds himself reading "Tariff Schedule No. 8," which decrees that the rate for hops between his fields and San Francisco has been raised from two cents on the pound to five cents. This is a ruinous rate for Dyke who has mortgaged all to bring in his first crop, and he winds up driven by the "tentacles of the octopus," the P. and S. W., into life as a highwayman and criminal. Some sense of the actual and infuriating phrasing of the railroad documents that caused such anguish is provided by Norris when he describes the tariff schedule handed to Dyke when he goes to arrange for shipment of his crop:

> The following rates for carriage of hops in car load lots ... take effect June 1, and will remain in force until superseded by a later tariff. Those quoted beyond Stockton are subject to changes in traffic arrangements with carriers by water from that point.
>
> (Norris 1986: 346)

This ruinous state of affairs is enough to drive Dyke to drink and beyond, and his situation is presented by Norris in stark contrast with the dining room of a railroad magnate where, in a room with a sideboard of gigantic size that once had adorned the banquet hall of an Italian palace of the late Renaissance, "a dinner of many courses and many wines" is served. In the eyes of Presley, the observer-writer of the saga, it was for this opulent setting and feast that "Dyke had been driven to outlawry and a jail" and the ranchers shot dead or ruined (Norris 1986: 604).

A lot of Norris's fellow citizens saw it the same way as stories of extravagant spending and financial corruption on the part of railroad owners spread throughout the land. According to Charles Perrow,

> the nineteenth-century counterpart of the Internet and fierce investigatory journalists existed in the numerous pamphlets and tear sheets of the time. [They] thundered, in wonderfully colorful language, against the railroad monopolies and their control of the political process.
>
> (Perrow 2002: 144–5)

For all of the appearance of their sheer venality, the reality was that in spite of ostentatious expenditures by some of the railroad barons, the railroad companies were themselves being wracked by competition. Part of the problem, as has often been told, was a consequence of the way in which they had been built. "Construction" companies formed specifically for the purpose of overseeing the building of a rail line were created often with board members who also served as officers of the rail lines. These construction companies charged prices that were, or at least were alleged to have been, higher than necessary. The consequence was that the indebtedness of the new rail line was higher than it needed to be, with the result that revenues required to cover costs, including interest payments on the debt, were greater than they might otherwise have been. What was even more important, however, was the competitive pressure that developed, especially from 1873 onwards. As new lines were built and alliances among existing lines shifted, railroads frequently found themselves unable, or close to being unable, to meet all costs.

It was in this climate of distress that rail lines attempted to set rates that would serve the interests of the industry and ensure some degree of freedom from threat of bankruptcy. What made the situation much more complex were the high barriers to interfirm cooperation, cooperation that was needed in a number of areas. In the earliest years of railroad construction, neither the gauge of the lines nor the equipment itself was standardized. This required unloading and reloading, a process also necessary where bridges had yet to be constructed. Chandler uses Taylor and Neu's estimate of an average cost of seven to twenty-five cents a ton and a day's delay for a single transshipment in the late 1850s (Chandler 1977: 122–3). Even after standardization, there were other issues that required close cooperation among the rail lines if freight was to move easily and efficiently. It is worth stressing that many of the people, including Fink, who worked out the processes for interfirm cooperation were "engineers," a newly important and rapidly professionalizing occupation. They, and not the owners, the hated capitalists, were the professional railroad managers who were trying to make the different rail lines work as a coherent national system.[11]

However, even for these professionals, setting uniform classifications for the variety of products shipped, uniform freight rates, and ticket prices and schedules for passengers, as well as agreed upon allocation of the proceeds when freight or people traveled on more than one line to complete the journey, proved a lot more difficult than standardizing the physical plant. And, the difficulty was compounded by the contentious public character of decisions taken. To illustrate, during the 1850s at railroad conventions, an agreement was reached to charge on the basis of the market value of the product rather than the actual cost of transportation. The rationale for adopting this principle, first put in place by the canals, was that charges would otherwise be prohibitively high for bulk freight. To the railroads, this was good business and seemed fair; to the farmers of California and of the Midwest and to many others, it was a hated policy of "charging what the traffic will bear," all in the interest of funding yet more opulent dining rooms and decadent multi-course feasts.

In their negotiations with each other, the representatives of the railroads left room for the separate rail lines to be flexible in dealing with specific circumstances. One important circumstance had to do with the direction of shipment. The rate per ton of freight (of whatever classification) could be much lower if the freight was being sent against the normal flow on a train that would otherwise be traveling empty. But, once again, pricing that was entirely sensible for the railroads look discriminatory to shippers. Why should Eastern establishments get lower rates on goods shipped to the middle of the country when farmers there felt themselves squeezed to cover the costs of shipping their corn and wheat eastward to market?

The advantages to the railroads of doing business with Rockefeller offer a dramatic example of how good business practice for the railroads equated to discrimination against others. Consider the case of the negotiations with General J. H. Devereux, a trained civil engineer who was also vice president of the Lake Shore Railroad, itself part of the New York Central system. In partial exchange for an agreement that allowed them to ship crude to Cleveland and refined products on to New York at a discount of roughly one-third the officially listed rate, Rockefeller and Flagler promised daily shipments of sixty carloads (Chernow 1998: 113). The advantages of guaranteed regular shipments to the railroad were huge and justified the rebates against which Tarbell and rival refineries railed. The problem was, as with different rates for different products and short and long haul differentials, that this looked for all the world like the rich aiding the rich, simply for the sake of further impoverishing the poor.

Whatever the justification for differential pricing and discounts, however, the master popular narrative that emerged from the triumphs of such as Cather's Alexandra Bergson and from the sadness and tragedy of Howell's Silas Lapham, Hamlin Garland's McLanes, and Norris's ranchers, as well as from Fink, Flagler, Rockefeller, and other real personalities of the era, was one that focused on the darker side of the gilded age. The story most often remembered is one in which the railroads and the trusts, exemplified by the granddaddy of them all, Standard Oil, conspired to defraud a great number of Americans of what should have been theirs. They used the new and wonderful technology of rail and oil (and steel and more) to enrich themselves and impoverish the masses.

The dominant theme of this narrative of the gilded age is that large numbers of Americans were seriously deprived of both the good things, and sometimes of the necessary things, of life while the highly successful few engaged in orgies of conspicuous consumption. The photographs taken by Jacob Riis and others of children and their hard-pressed parents in the tenements of New York, set against the photographs and drawings of the summer "cottages" in Newport and the cartoons of railroad and other business barons lighting their cigars with currency of large denomination, have become part of our shared history because they seem to sum up what went wrong. And in fiction, as in Norris's *The Octopus* and in Sinclair's *The Jungle*, starvation occurs in proximity to opulence. The farmers, as we have already seen, were convinced that they were being taken and so needed to "raise more hell and less corn."[12] And, this seems to be the not quite fully articulated conclusion of standard interpretations of American history as well. Consider the words of a leading historian, Alan Brinkley:

> remarkable growth did much to increase the wealth and improve the lives of many Americans. But such benefits were far from equally shared. While industrial titans and a growing middle class were enjoying prosperity without precedent in the nation's history, workers, farmers, and others were experiencing an often painful ordeal that slowly edged the United States toward a great economic and political crisis.
>
> (Brinkley 1997: 487)

While Brinkley's choice of the word crisis may be overly dramatic, it is true that by the beginning of the twentieth century widespread anger and concern led to a period of substantial reform in aid of achieving greater economic and social justice. The Progressive reforms of the years before World War I addressed many such issues, most of which were related in one way or another to the inequality of income distribution.[13] Although from the perspective of economic statisticians and economic historians the charge that "workers, farmers, and others" had not shared in the growing prosperity of the last three decades of the nineteenth century must be judged unproven and, indeed, considered highly doubtful, there is no doubt whatsoever that there had been a highly skewed distribution of that output. There is abundant evidence that the rich had gotten richer faster than the poor got better off.[14]

Further, the growth of ostentation for which the period has been named took place at a time of high hopes which often failed to materialize. The farmers, even if better off, still had hard lives made even harder by the additional uncertainty that participation in an international market entailed. Urban workers, even if materially better off in their new nation, were still subject to the terrors of unemployment and deprivation. And, throughout the country, as Robert Wiebe has put it:

> A pall of thwarted opportunity, of frustrated dreams, hung over large parts of the nation. Innumerable townsmen had been looking to the railroads as their avenues to greatness.... Towns that had tied their future to a local line almost never owned it. Nor did they have any part in deciding the rates charged, the services offered, the distant connections made or not made. That power lay elsewhere, in "alien" hands. Moreover, crops were increasingly processed well beyond the farmer's ken, and the goods he needed came more often from strange, remote places.
>
> (Wiebe 1967: 7)

Blame for this unhappy state of affairs in the minds of a large part of the public lay squarely upon those who had the power to manipulate the railroads for their own economic advantage, and prime among them was John D. Rockefeller. In summing up her account of *The History of The Standard Oil Company*, Tarbell concluded that "the crucial question now, as always, is a transportation question" and, more specifically, profit:

> today, as at the start, the purpose of the Standard Oil Company is the purpose of the South Improvement Company – the regulation of the price of crude and refined oil by the control of the output; and the chief means for sustaining this purpose is still that of the original scheme – a control of oil transportation giving special privileges in rates.
>
> (Tarbell 1904: 256–7)

"And what," she asked, "are we going to do about it? ... it is *our* business. We, the people of the United States, and nobody else, must cure whatever is wrong in the industrial situation, typified by this narrative of the growth of the Standard Oil Company" (Tarbell 1904: 292).

That was the question that those who studied the industrial situation needed to answer. The Progressive Movement brought new urgency to the efforts of economists and lawyers in the new field of regulation to find a satisfactory answer, one that made sense within their own intellectual traditions and could, at the same time, address the issues of the narratives of Tarbell and her fellow muckrakers. How they reacted will be the subject of Chapters Four and Five. For now, we come forward a hundred years to a not dissimilar story, in which once again the themes are appropriation of a new technology in apparent aid of a skewed income distribution.

Sam Walton's context

The years of Walton's and Wal-Mart's rise were years in many respects like that of the Rockefeller era, a period of rapid growth in total population and in total output. The baby boom that followed World War II and, as the birth rate leveled off in the 1970s, high rates of immigration (both legal and otherwise), especially in the years since 1990, have caused the US population to grow rapidly, with a doubling once again between 1950 and sometime in 2007. Both per capita and per family gross domestic product (GDP) and personal disposable income have also continued to grow, and at a rate that makes, by standard measures, Americans some three times better off than they were in 1950, and 1950 was not a bad year at all by comparison with the past. In that same year of 1950, some 29 percent of workers were employed in manufacturing; by 2000, the percentage was only 13 percent while over the period the percentage of the employed who worked in trade (both wholesale and retail) and in services had grown from 42 percent to 52 percent. The Wal-Mart era has also been one of increasingly skewed income distribution, with, by one measure, the share of income going to the top 10 percent of the population rising from roughly 33 percent in 1982 to over 40 percent by 2002 (Atkinson and Piketty 2007: Figure 1).

The Walton era was not only a period of massive shifts in employment, in this case from primary production and manufacturing to services; it was also a period of great geographic expansion of integrated markets, and of very considerable economic insecurity during a time of rapidly growing national output. Each of these trends and their multiple causes have become intertwined with the popular Wal-Mart narrative, much as the stories of the railroads were intermingled with Rockefeller's rise to riches. Rockefeller was charged with using the railroads to gain unfair advantage, an advantage that deprived farmers, workers, and competitors of a fair share of the growth dividend of his era. In like manner, Walton has been blamed, though not in parallel fashion to Rockefeller, for nefarious use of the computers and containerized shipping that have been the railroads of the more recent era. Instead, and for reasons peculiar to the Wal-Mart story, the main charge against Walton and his associates is that they brought into the American mainstream a Southern and small-town emphasis on low wages and low costs that has sabotaged more respectable American patterns and dreams. One passage from a paper prepared for a conference specifically about Wal-Mart will serve as an example of this often repeated charge:

Wal-Mart's mastery of information technology and the logistics revolution explains but a slice of the company's success. Equally important, Wal-Mart has been the beneficiary and a driving force behind the transformation in the politics and culture of a business system that has arisen in a southernized, deunionized post-New Deal America. The controversies sparked by Wal-Mart's entry into metropolitan markets ... embody the larger conflict between what remains of New Deal America and the aggressive, successful effort waged by Sunbelt politicians and entrepreneurs to eviscerate it.

(Lichtenstein 2006: 13)

By some accounts, including his own, Walton was a true rural hick; in others an "unadulterated innovator" whose "carefully cultivated traditionalism itself represents a radical new creation" (Moreton 2006: 61).[15] However, there is general agreement in most popular accounts that Walton personified a disturbing trend in American business practice.

In the popular press and in a number of books, as well as in the movies, including *The High Cost of Low Prices*, Wal-Mart has been described as unfair to its employees, as anti-union, as a poor community citizen, as exploiter of foreign labor, and, like Standard Oil, as a vicious and probably unfair competitor. Newspaper stories such as "Inside Wal-Mart's Bid to Slash State Taxes," an account in the usually pro-business *Wall Street Journal* of efforts to evade taxes, paint the picture of a rogue company that seeks more than others to bend the law unfairly to their advantage (Drucker October 23, 2007). These charges and more are available on a web site entitled Wal-Mart Watch (http://walmartwatch. com). At the same time, however, Wal-Mart has been widely praised for bringing low prices and a wide choice of goods to consumers outside of major urban areas and to those with limited incomes, as a leading innovator of modern supply chain management, and as a force for creation of a more, and often beneficially, integrated world economy. While more nuanced and scholarly treatments note that Wal-Mart has been more successful than most in developing tools and business approaches that are at the core of much praised new business practices, attacks that are shriller in tone ignore the context and see Walton as a more or less free-standing importer of Southern backwardness into a once-thriving America. Low wages both at home and abroad are described as the central aspect of this imported Southern tradition, as is the emphasis on cheap goods and slightly tatty taste. Above all, however, the deeply felt charge in most quarters is that Wal-Mart has sabotaged America by providing cheap goods but not good jobs:

Who among us does not crave a bargain? But we Americans – including the financially strapped folks Wal-Mart claims as its own – are not defined by how much money we save down at the Supercenter. We are a nation of workers *first* and shoppers second.

(Bianco 2006: 3)

In spite of what Bianco says about America as workers first, it is important to note that Americans as shoppers have been a key element in the growing importance of Wal-Mart and of the ambivalence toward the firm. It is an astounding fact that even as American per capita income more than tripled (in constant dollars) between 1950 and 2005, American consumption of goods and services kept pace. In the 1930s, John Maynard Keynes, Alvin Hansen, and others thought that as purchasing power rose, people would spend less on consumer goods. The post-war spending boom that was associated with recovery from the miseries of the 1930s and the pent-up demand of the war years, in combination with new family formation and the baby boom, relieved economists of the worry that such dampened consumption expenditure would contribute to continued economic depression. Even so, when John Kenneth Galbraith wrote *The Affluent Society* in 1958, he spoke of the "declining marginal urgency of goods" as a fact of American existence and was concerned with ways of ensuring income for individuals whose productive efforts were no longer needed (Galbraith 1958: 334).

But, the "marginal urgency of goods," or at least of goods and related services, did not decline. Purchase of services as a whole grew (in dollars not adjusted for price changes) by just over eighty times between 1950 and 2005, and total consumption expenditures increased ninety-fold. An even clearer picture of the role that consumption, and Americans as shoppers, has played in the evolution of the economy comes from noting that as a percentage of disposable personal income, personal consumption expenditures have risen from roughly 90 percent in 1950 to 97 percent in 2005. Of course, it is true that as more Americans have purchased more durable goods, some of what is counted as consumption expenditure is in reality a form of saving for the future by way of acquisition of durable goods that can be used for a long time, though it is also the case that goods tend to become technologically obsolete more quickly. This additional reality runs in a counter direction and tends to decrease the proportion of consumption that might legitimately be counted as a form of saving. However one views it, the continued expenditure of ever higher incomes has been nothing less than astounding.[16]

If Americans have enjoyed the fruits of this consumption binge, they have at the same time been unhappy with some aspects of it and deeply ambivalent about others. And Sam Walton and his Wal-Mart are most often mentioned in discussions of the darker side. Much as Rockefeller was held responsible for malfeasance in connection with the complex issues of railroad rate setting, so Walton has been held individually accountable for the explosion of low-cost consumer goods that characterized late-twentieth-century America and culpable for what seems to have gone wrong with the American dream.[17]

It is not difficult to see how a complex story of global economic integration and mass consumption has been told in simpler and perhaps more emotionally satisfying form as a story of Walton's success and one of immiserization for many others, both in the US and abroad. The notion that Walton's success was founded on cut-rate pricing derived from practices of the rural South, an area associated with low wages and anti-unionism, has made sense to many. Walton did nothing whatsoever to deny these associations and, in fact, made "everyday low prices" his hallmark and reveled in his role as Southern hick. Nevertheless, to fully understand Walton's context, the simple story needs to be separated into component parts.

Discounting as a retail strategy is a good place to begin. In the years after World War II, a new form of retailing was added to the department stores, which date to the nineteenth century, and to the grocery supermarket chains, large drug stores, and variety stores, all of which date to the 1930s, and, of course, to the mail-order catalogs. Discount merchandising, which, according to Vance and Scott, began as a concept with the supermarkets, where low prices and long hours were characteristic, took root in the 1940s, primarily in large cities, most often in "small, almost secret outlets," where brand-name goods were sold at prices well below those found in other retail outlets. This was possible because of direct supply from manufacturers and low-cost operations in austere settings. What happened next, according to Vance and Scott, is not surprising given the growth of output and consumption expenditure following World War II.

> During the 1950s discounting emerged from the fringe of American retailing and entered the mainstream.... The rapid growth of discounting during the fifties was caused by several factors. One element was the increased supply of consumer products relative to demand.... Manufacturers found that in this buyer's market discounters represented a more effective means of getting products to consumers because their willingness to accept lower margins enabled them to move large quantities of goods more rapidly than conventional retailers, who required higher markups.
>
> (Vance and Scott 1994: 24–5)

It was also important that in the post-World War II era, the rapid spread of television with its national commercials as well as the consumption illustrated on the hundreds of sitcoms and dramas represented a powerful new forum for creation of emulation-driven wants. These wants, and the purchases that followed, were as keenly felt in rural areas and in small towns as in urban areas, and the desirability of the goods offered by the Sears and Montgomery Catalogs that, even into the 1950s, had been satisfactory sources began to pale. Because automobiles, cheap gasoline, and the expansion of systems of paved roads running through the countryside meant that almost all people could, at least on occasion, go to larger towns and cities and enjoy what was rapidly becoming the national pastime of shopping, catalog shopping lost its luster.[18] Sam Walton saw the opportunities, and it is this small-town beginning that is most often mentioned in accounts of the creation of Wal-Mart.

One of Walton's contributions was to bring variety and discounted prices much closer to people who lived in small towns. He also generalized a process of discount pricing that had begun in cities and turned it into "every day low pricing" rather than sale pricing. This process was not unique to Walton; what he did was put his stamp on it. Looked at from a broader perspective, it is difficult to see how the second consumer revolution could have unfolded as it did without an emphasis on affordable pricing. The enormous expansion in consumption expenditure rested not upon persuading a narrow elite of the population to purchase luxury goods but, rather, upon rapid commodification of new goods and variations upon old goods. The presence of shrink-wrapped personal computers in Sam's discount stores not so many years after they became available for home purchase is illustrative of the process.

If the shrink-wrapped computers are a sign of the democratization of consumption, there were also downsides. By bringing big stores with discounted prices into rural America, Walton helped to hasten a process that had begun much earlier in the twentieth century, the physical deterioration, and often abandonment, of small towns and especially of their retail centers. Automobiles, interstate highways, suburban shopping malls had all contributed to continuing decline, but in many cases it took the arrival of a Wal-Mart on the edges of town to finally force local merchants to close. In the movie *Wal-Mart: The High Cost of Low Price*, the story of a family firm, H & H Hardware of Middlefield, Ohio, gives personal and dramatic form to incontrovertible evidence that Wal-Mart often delivers the final blow. Sad accounts by the father and son who founded the hardware establishment that has been part of a small town are followed by scenes of abandoned stores in multiple towns across the country. Even though the survival of a small town may hinge upon its ability to gain a

Wal-Mart, and in spite of the possibility of increased tax revenue and opportunities for service providers, the pain of many local merchants has been real.[19] Add to this nostalgia for small-town ways, especially among those who have never lived in one, and the result has been that the destruction of small-town America has been a telling point against Wal-Mart.

There were, however, even more serious charges, and prime among them was the complaint that Wal-Mart had led the way in reducing the availability of full-time, well-paying jobs for the American labor force. What Wal-Mart did was to extend the managerial practices developed for its suppliers to those who worked in the stores. Workers became just-in-time suppliers of hourly labor, wages were kept low, and benefits minimal. Computer tracking of hourly sales volume in the different stores made very close management of hours worked technically feasible, and the drive to sell goods as cheaply as possible provided the imperative. From the standpoint of workers, this has meant part-time work for those called by Wal-Mart "peak-time associates," with schedules built around in-store demand rather than accustomed rhythms of life as dictated by school schedules, social obligations, and family life. To an extent not fully implemented in many other places in modern capitalist societies, labor has been successfully transformed by Wal-Mart into a commodity just like any other. Rather than hiring people, Wal-Mart have successfully hired units of labor in quantities that they can vary with the need of the company and have done so on a large scale. This in combination with explicit opposition to unionization and an increased need to hire workers who are not as amenable to "company spirit" and low wages as were the original small-town and rural employees has led to growing criticism of what, in managerial textbook terms, appears an ideal of effective management. Walton himself provided the statement that critic Anthony Bianco used to sum up the impact and dilemma of Walton's hiring strategy:

> There was no way – short of relocating Ozarkers en masse – that Wal-Mart could have maintained the homogeneity and docility of its workforce as its expansion carried it from its natural rural habitat into urban America. Walton conceded as much in his autobiography, which was completed just before he died. In cities, he acknowledged "we have more trouble coming up with educated people who want to work in our industry, or with people of the right moral character and integrity. Folks in small towns in Iowa and Mississippi are more likely to want to work for what we can pay than folks in Houston or Dallas or St. Louis. And, yes, they're probably more likely to buy our philosophy in the country than they are in the city."
>
> (Bianco 2006: 77)

Had Wal-Mart begun operations in an urban area in another part of the country, it is possible, but by no means certain, that their labor practices would have been different. In point of fact, the move to outsourcing (as with janitors and other service workers), part-time scheduling, low wages, and minimal benefits has characterized a considerable part of the American economy in the Wal-Mart era. Whether because of international competition brought about by labor out-sourcing, by changes in public policy that have been permissive, or by technological change, or, more likely, by a combination of all three, employment and employment practices across the country and in many firms (and, for that matter, many public sector organizations) have come to look much like that to be found at Wal-Mart. Wal-Mart was early in the process, they were good at it, and they have made an excellent lightening rod for anger about the growth of part-time employment.

Other employment practices at Wal-Mart have been equally unattractive in the public mind. Among these are the use of undocumented workers, inhumane practices, and discrimination. In a widely publicized story that appeared in 2005, Wal-Mart paid $11 million to settle a federal investigation into the use of undocumented workers who were employed "off-clock" to clean stores (Barbaro 2005). In 2004, there was widespread publicity, including a front-page story in *The New York Times*, which described how workers were locked into stores to clean overnight, a practice that is also recounted in the film *Wal-Mart*. The $11 million settlement was in response to only one of many complaints, lawsuits, and investigations into use of undocumented workers, unsavory practices, and both racial and gender discrimination, all highly publicized (Fishman 2006: 27). Stories about these practices and well-publicized efforts to defeat efforts to organize workers in the stores have made Wal-Mart the poster-firm for bad labor practices and for the stagnant wages that have characterized the US economy in recent years. As Paul Krugman wrote in 2005, Wal-Mart has become "the symbol of the state of our economy, which delivers rising GDP but stagnant or falling living standards for working Americans."[20]

Wal-Mart became this symbol not simply because of labor practices at home but also because of the importation of so many of the goods they sell, often, it is widely alleged, from countries where workers produce the goods under miserable conditions and for very low wages. Ironically, Sam Walton garnered good publicity for himself and his firm when he announced a "Buy American" plan in 1985. Vance and Scott attribute this plan, which involved invitations to 3,000 US manufacturers to supply goods, some of which were to be replacements for imports, to Walton's realization that imported goods did not appeal in small towns in the South that had been damaged by loss of textile employment and to "a strain of old-fashioned patriotism" (Vance and Scott 1994: 111).

Whatever the motives, Wal-Mart was not willing, as Vance and Scott also note, to pay higher prices for domestic goods than for imports, and it is a notorious and widely recognized fact that the Chinese (and other foreign) goods that have become the subject of great American concern stock a good portion of Wal-Mart shelf space. Further, the same just-in-time policies and tight management of relationships with suppliers that led to Wal-Mart's success have made them suspect players in a world where concern over working conditions abroad, free trade, and the safety of imported goods have all become matters of wide concern. Wal-Mart is certainly not the only firm that now sells goods manufactured outside of the US, but they are the largest such firm and the symbol for much that concerns Americans in these early years of the twenty-first century. Stories about the miserable conditions, including twenty-hour days and near-slavery in factories created in part in response to free trade agreements with the US in countries such as Jordan, may begin by noting production for "Target, Wal-Mart and other American retailers," but it is almost inevitably Wal-Mart that takes center place in the accounts (Greenhouse and Barbaro 2006).

These concerns have not only to do with small towns, employment conditions, and imports but also include environmental and health issues, and here, too, Wal-Mart's practices have been widely and unfavorably reported in the national press. In the film *Wal-Mart*, the practice of storing bags of pesticides and insecticides on parking lots is noted, and, in a world of growing concern about the environmental effects of such practices, it is little wonder that the nation's largest retailer gets blamed. So, too, with the lack of sufficient health insurance for workers, a point of major emphasis in the film and in the many newspaper accounts. It is little wonder that the announcement of new Wal-Mart locations has become a cause for protest in many communities. To these and other related charges against Wal-Mart, we will return in Chapter 6. For now, however, I turn to a narrower focus, which is to say the stories that economists have created to deal with the causes and consequences of big business in general.

4 Economists, trusts, and big business

Chapter 3 explored the ways in which the American public, guided by journalists, novelists, short story writers, movie makers, and other molders of general opinion viewed the rise to power of Standard Oil and Wal-Mart. In this chapter, the focus shifts to economists and the ways in which they, sometimes in collaboration with lawyers, have explained the rise of big business. Both the traditions of economic analysis and growing public concern about business giants meant that economists of the late nineteenth and early twentieth centuries had little choice; they had to confront the growing clout of Standard Oil and the railroads. In more recent times, recurrence of worry about skewedness of income distribution in a land that prides itself on equality of opportunity has also forced the attention of at least some economists to the questions raised by public reaction to Wal-Mart.

Indeed, the stories about industrial organization that economists in the US have told both themselves and the public over the past century and a quarter have their origin in the struggles to explain the railroads, Standard Oil, and the other "trusts" of the late nineteenth century.[1] As was true of the angry public, and the journalists and novelists, economists based their stories on their own inherited ideas and on the evidence at hand about the new kinds of firms that were emerging. The new firms were very much larger than any that had existed before and their power to control the markets in which they operated vastly greater. The conviction of economists that competition was essential to control the power of these firms conflicted with evidence that competition was not working as the books they had read suggested it would. New theories were required. This chapter delves more deeply into what may appear in places to be arcane aspects of this theory, but the subtleties do, in fact, matter a lot for the world in which we now live. The following timeline of developing ideas and policies will serve as a guide to the discussions in this and the following chapter.

Timeline of ideas and actions, 1776–1914: old discussions, new theories, public reactions

1776   Adam Smith describes labor specialization in a pin factory
1817   David Ricardo's *Principles of Economics* published
1835   Charles Babbage elaborates on pin factories
1848   John Stuart Mill in *Principles of Political Economy* compares large and small Productions; calls water works a natural monopoly
1867   Karl Marx defines the capitalist firm as M→C→C′→M′
1869   Charles Francis Adams joins newly created Massachusetts Railroad Commission
1887   Passage of the Interstate Commerce Act
1889   Benjamin Andrews reports on the Report for the Committee on Manufactures of the US House of Representatives
1890   Sherman Antitrust Act is passed
        First edition of Alfred Marshall's *Principles of Economics*
1899   John Bates Clark takes a leap of reason at the Chicago Conference on Trusts
        Henry Carter Adams takes a different view at the same Conference
1901   John Bates Clark publishes *The Control of Trusts* (reissued with John Maurice Clark in 1912)
1904   John Bates Clark talks of the importance of "the size of the mill" at Cooper Union
        Thorstein Veblen publishes *The Theory of Business Enterprise*
1911   Standard Oil and American Tobacco dissolved by Supreme Court
1914   Passage of Clayton Antitrust and Federal Trade Commission Acts

Theorizing the railroads

To understand how explanations of the trusts and other large firms unfolded, it is necessary to begin with the reaction of economists to the first large-scale business organizations in the US, the railroads.[2] Even though they were not organized as "trusts," all of the discussion that was to follow about Standard Oil and other large firms was shaped by the initial responses to these emerging giants.

In the years following the Civil War, it became obvious that the railroads would not only contribute mightily to economic growth and opportunity, but would also command the attention of policy makers at both the state and Federal levels. As the individual railroad firms struggled to cooperate with each other or fail, and as the farmers and local businessmen became ever more angry about both cooperation and the consequences of failure, state legislatures moved to create railroad commissions. The laws creating the commissions varied considerably. Midwestern commissions, created as part of the third-party Granger movement, were empowered to set and limit railroad rates. At the other extreme of state-granted power was the "sunshine" approach of Massachusetts, which relied on transparency of rate setting to ensure fairness. The Federal agency created by passage of the Interstate Commerce Act of 1887 (after the Supreme Court declared state control of interstate lines illegal) was a combination of the purposes and tools that had been written into a variety of state acts. In all cases, however, the new state regulatory commissions represented a significant departure in American public policy and represented an intellectual challenge for the American economists who had been the keepers of Adam Smith's legacy of the invisible hand of competition, a hand until then deemed sufficient to control business in the public interest.

To understand the strength of this challenge, it is important to recognize the power of traditional British political economy in American thought. In spite of the fact that the economies of the two countries were different in many important ways, and especially so during the early years of the nineteenth century, the economic treatises of the United Kingdom remained the texts of the United States until well after American literature in other areas had broken from the traditions of the mother country. A central feature of much of English economic theory and debate had to do with the threat of rising grain prices given limited supplies of land and a growing population, and so the easy transfer of traditional analysis seems very odd, for in the US quite different conditions prevailed. In fact, American economists remained so true to the word from England that an American economist of the twentieth century, Wesley Mitchell, likened them to an earlier group of "American poets who wrote many verses to the skylark without observing that the skylark is not an American species" (Mitchell 1969: 234).

In part the power of British political economy in its former colonies derived from the essentially theological nature of American instruction in matters economic throughout most of the nineteenth century. But, it was also the case that there was not much that stood in the way of a smooth translation of Adam Smith's ideas about the virtues of competition, as Smith's recommendations, though written for a different place, fit well into the freewheeling and rapidly expanding antebellum economy of the US. Smith's rosy vision and his emphasis on individual responsibility for safeguarding economic welfare provided an ideal platform for the Americans of the Jacksonian era. Here is how Joseph Dorfman described it:

In substance, the Jacksonian era marked the culmination of the attack on the tradition of a feudal, aristocratic society of privilege and perquisites bestowed by law on the few at the expense of the many. It marked the triumph of the idea that, in the absence of law-created privileges, most men could acquire a competence by industry and could become politically independent. The diffusion of property was the safeguard of democratic society. The moral duty of self-assertion became embedded in the principle of competition, for – so it was thought – only the nerveless, parasitic, aristocratic-minded Tory wanted the security of legal monopoly in order to filch an income from the industrious.

(Dorfman 1969: 3)

When faced with the realities of the railroads, however, American economists had to reinterpret this tradition in an entirely different context, and they did so by casting their justification for state control in terms that were also inherited, both for better and for worse, from British traditions.[3]

Among the earliest and most influential creators of a new American tradition of social control via regulation as a substitute for competition was Charles Francis Adams, who became a member of the Massachusetts Railroad Commission in 1869.[4] Adams led the way in advocating state regulation, rather than competition, as the solution to the problems presented by the railroads, and in so doing began to weave a story that drew from empirical observation about the character of the railroads, from American legal tradition, and, most especially, from a classificatory system created in England.

What was particularly important to Adams – as it was to Albert Fink, the accounting innovator with whom Adams worked as an arbitrator with the Eastern Trunk Line Association – were the presence of fixed costs and of variation in costs over different miles of track, which, in combination, meant that competition among railroads could not lead to the cheapest transportation (McCraw 1984: 9). Because the railroads had to set prices for their services so as to cover all of their costs (as per Fink's formula described in Chapter 3), if they were to stay out of bankruptcy, some degree of cooperation among them was required. Unfortunately, this would have every appearance, and probably the reality, of conspiratorial collaboration to those who paid for the services.

Adams saw consolidation as necessary, but he also held that the cheapest transport was likely to be gained by "directing the largest possible volume of movement through the fewest possible channels." Of course, this was exactly what John D. Rockefeller also understood, and it certainly appeared to vocal members of the public to be an argument that favored the moneyed interests. That the commissions had a legal right to regulate was not difficult to establish because railroads were chartered by state legislatures and longstanding practice encumbered such charters with the right to regulate, and in 1876 in Munn v. Illinois this right was upheld for railroads. The really difficult question was how to set rates or, as Adams preferred, how to guide the railroads themselves to set rates that were indeed in the public interest and could be shown to be so.

What Adams set forth as a basis for understanding and for policy was the proposition that railroads were "natural monopolies" because, in his words, "the cost of the movement of goods is in direct inverse ratio to the amount moved" (McCraw 1984: 9). One way to understand this statement is as an observation about the railroads, an observation that could be said to rest squarely upon Fink's formulas and his careful accounting of the costs of moving goods. Another way to understand the statement is to put it in the context of economic thought and say that unlike other industries where, with a fixed plant capacity, one observed rising costs and diminishing rates of increase in output as volume of output was increased, railroads were an industry wherein returns increased and costs decreased as output increased. In this form, Adams' statement becomes a rejection of the applicability in the case of railroads of the "law of diminishing returns" that had been articulated by David Ricardo and others during debates over agricultural tariffs in the United Kingdom at the end of the Napoleonic Wars.[5] This law held that when variable inputs, primarily labor in the case of early eighteenth-century agriculture, were added to a fixed quantity of land, output would increase but at a decreasing rate, and the average cost of output would, therefore, rise.

As Adams saw the railroad problem, the issue was that as variable inputs, in the form of labor, coal, water, etc., were added in order to carry more freight over fixed track and rolling stock capacity (which could not be quickly or easily varied in quantity), average costs per ton-mile would tend to decrease. Hence, one had the reverse of the case that Ricardo had made for agriculture in the United Kingdom. And, this would be true, in the view that Adams adopted, whether or not the fixed railroad capacity was already in place, as it was when he began his work as a commissioner, or whether or not it was part of planned expansion. The high fixed costs of laying track and adding rolling stock would mean that returns to variable inputs would increase and costs decrease. In the inherited language of economics, about which more will be said shortly, this meant that the railroads were "natural monopolies" because falling costs associated with larger size would make the existence of competition among enough rival firms to protect the public interest impossible to achieve and sustain. State regulation was required if the public interest was to be protected.

The challenge of the trusts

The argument made for railroads being a special case was a persuasive one, but matters soon became more complex and confusing. Even as Adams was developing his model of railroads as natural monopolies, a cohort of prominent economists was confronted with a new problem, the problem of the trusts.[6] As odd as it may seem, these and other leading economists of the day offered little or no support for the politically popular cause of a national antitrust law that would replace and supplement the variety of state antitrust laws already on the books in fourteen states. In the words of Hans Thorelli:

> It is indeed remarkable that of the several university-affiliated economists and political scientists setting forth their views on the trust problem in writings published before 1890 apparently no one favored the enactment of general antitrust legislation of the specific preventative-prohibitory type represented by the Sherman Act.
>
> (Thorelli 1955: 121)

The Sherman Antitrust Act, which was passed with an overwhelming majority in Congress in 1890, was not greeted with enthusiasm by economists for the simple reason that most of those who spoke or wrote on the topic approved of the trend toward consolidation, and did so because they saw considerable evidence of decreasing costs associated with size.[7] Direct opposition to the Sherman Act would have been futile in the face of strong antitrust sentiment in the country, but there can be no doubt that the economists opposed it. In their view the trusts were largely beneficial, even though they had no obvious and inherited way of explaining why.[8] This was new territory, and it took a while for a consensus story to be developed.

Benjamin Andrews, another prominent economist, reporting on an 1889 Report for the Committee on Manufactures that had been requested by the US House of Representatives, wrote that competition could often be wasteful: "Competition is by no means always a good. It is, indeed, never so for its own sake, but only as a means to keep lowest possible cost plus normal profit the law of price" (Andrews 1889: 136). And, even though Andrews noted that "trusts" came in a bewildering variety, having in common "only the single feature of excluding more or less perfectly old-fashioned individualism of management," he felt comfortable in concluding that "[t]he aggregation of capital and the centralization of management are often incalculable benefits" (Andrews 1889: 136). As to the effects on price in individual cases, Andrews was unable to reach a clear conclusion from his detailed studies, though he did note that in the case of Standard

Oil, the prices of petroleum fell after the trust was formed, and the margin between crude and refined prices remained roughly the same.

What is particularly noteworthy, in light of the leap of reason that was to occur at the end of the century, was that Andrews found the source of the advantages enjoyed by the new trusts, the advantages that allowed them to enjoy "normal profits" while lowering costs to consumers, to be cooperation itself. Unlike the railroads, for which the advantage of size came in large measure, as Charles Francis Adams had insisted, from the technology of the industry, the advantages of the trusts came from organizational coordination of output itself. Here is how Andrews described it:

> Competition ... may abnormally raise cost and prices both. Different manufacturers start their machinery in ignorance of each other's aims, and crowd the markets with a stock too heavy to be taken off. While the strife is on, prices are low; and for this felicity, people bless competition. The failures which ensue, the stoppage of work, the decay of mills and machinery, and the rise of prices entailed by all this, often making the average costs of goods for the period far higher than was necessary, these things few refer, as all should, to competition. The giant style of undertaking is, in part at least, a wholesome movement away from this evil. By it, the field of industry in question can be mapped out, careful estimates made of the probable demand, and production adapted to this in both place and time, all with thoroughness impossible so long as competition was unbridled.
>
> (Andrews 1889: 136–7)

The major question for Andrews was whether or not prices would be maintained at no more than cost plus "normal profit," and this he took to be an empirical question. He thought it quite possible that this would be the case with the trusts, though he did express concern at the end of his report about the political power of large firms, for he noted that "the witchery of the Standard Oil interest has penetrated even the political world," and he also noted that dealing with such power in the public realm would require "the nation's arm," as state governments had shown themselves unable to provide the needed control (Andrews 1889: 149–50).

On the question of economic consequences, then, Andrews thought the trusts beneficial, *though not because their operations were characterized by increasing returns to scale and decreasing average costs of production.*

The contrast between the trust-tolerant attitude of the economists and the concerns of the public at large came to a head, not with passage of the Sherman Antitrust Act in 1890, but, rather, with the renewed public fury about large businesses at the end of the century. The need to speak on "the trust question" had become sufficiently pressing to call forth responses from economists, which, if substantively the same as that of Andrews and the others who spoke favorably of the trusts, did address more directly the concerns of the public. And in addressing these concerns, the dominant voice of the economists moved away from Andrews' conclusions about the advantages offered by the trusts and significantly conflated the separate stories of the railroads and the manufacturing trusts. There then occurred a leap of reason that finessed the need for the kind of detailed empirical work that Andrews had offered in his report on official investigations of trusts, and that converted the trust question into one that could be treated as a variation on the theme of natural monopolies.

The record of the Chicago Conference on Trusts, which was convened in 1899 by the Civic Federation of Chicago, documents the leap.[9] This was an event attended by a long list of governors, members of state legislatures, members of the bar, economists and statisticians, among others. In his introductory remarks, Franklin H. Head, President of the Civic Federation, said that the meeting was "not a trust or an anti-trust conference, but a conference in search of truth and light." Perhaps so, but the impassioned oratory offered by Dudley G. Wooten, a member of the Texas legislature, in his introductory remarks, suggests otherwise. Mr. Wooten, we are told, "was the first speaker on the uncompromising anti-trust side of the debate. The gallery audience was in sympathy with his views, and, carried away by the eloquence of the gifted orator, punctuated his address with salvo after salvo of applause" (Civic Federation of Chicago 1900: 42). The tenor of Wooten's remarks can be gained from these brief passages, which are representative of the whole of his speech:

> In the Constitution under which we in Texas live – handed down to us by the heroes of the Alamo and San Jacinto – we are taught that "monopolies are contrary to the genius of a free government, and shall never be allowed"; and we adhere with unhesitating loyalty to both the letter and the spirit of that declaration. In the Federal Constitution under which we all live – handed down to us all by the heroes of Lexington and Saratoga and Yorktown – we have been taught that "all rights not delegated to the United States, nor prohibited to the States, are reserved to the people"; and among the most valuable of those reserved rights we esteem the traditional freedom of trade, contract and labor that has been cherished and defended by Anglo-Saxon yeomen in every age since their history began.
> [...]

Would that some second Lincoln could arise, with the sublime courage and majestic patriotism of that splendid seer, to tell this generation of Americans that the Union cannot endure nor its freedom be insured half composed of natural citizenship and half of artificial citizenship. Nay, the condition is even worse than that. Under the sinister conditions brought about by the inordinate growth and overshadowing power of private corporations, the division is not even in equal portions, for the government-created citizens completely dominate their natural rivals and crush out the divinity and the manhood of the individual sovereigns of the nation.

(Civic Federation of Chicago 1900: 43 and 49)

Henry Carter Adams, Statistician for the Interstate Commerce Commission and Professor of Political Economy at the University of Michigan, and Jeremiah W. Jenks, Statistician for the United States Industrial Commission and Professor of Political Economy at Cornell University, also made opening remarks that were, as one might expect, of a more measured tenor. Jenks emphasized that there was much that was as yet unknown about the causes and consequences of the trusts, and raised a series of questions that needed to be answered, suggesting, in the spirit of reconciliation that the organizers hoped for, that "suspicion and denunciation" be replaced by "fair dealing and mutual respect" (Civic Federation of Chicago 1900: 34–5).

Adams suggested that questions of policy toward "the combinations generally called trusts" required answers to several questions: What was the effect of consolidation on costs? To what degree did trusts protect against panics and depressions? And, what was the effect of such organizations on the democratic organization of society? To the first question, he offered what he called a "curt answer to a profound question" and said that

"manufacturing combinations ... contribute nothing to the reduction of the cost of manufacturing beyond what would be contributed should each of the industries continue its independent competitive existence.

(Civic Federation of Chicago 1900: 37)

Nor did Adams find favorable answers for the trusts when he turned to his other two questions. Instead, he stressed undesirable railroad discrimination and opportunism in the face of purely local jurisdiction over activities undertaken in national markets as causes. Control of business combinations at the national level would be required but could not be based upon the treatment of all large consolidations as being of similar cause:

Some [industries] tend toward consolidation and combination, while others are well fitted by their character to continue a separate and a competitive existence. The manufacturing industries are, speaking generally, of the latter class. Railways by their very nature tend toward combinations and consolidation. The biscuit industry, the manufacture of nails, the refining of oil, on the other hand, are well fitted for individual management and administration.

(Civic Federation of Chicago 1900: 36)

Adams' call for national policies to ensure that competition was maintained in those industries that did not tend naturally toward consolidation and combination became one part of the consensus about the trusts that had begun to emerge. If he was less dramatic in his call to action than were Wooten, William Jennings Bryan and others at the Chicago Conference, he was in agreement that unfair practices that facilitated consolidation could and should be prevented through legal action.

A second, and in the end much more important, strand of the emerging consensus was offered by John Bates Clark, who had emerged as a leader of economists and, as will be explained more fully a bit later on, was the creator of an American neoclassical synthesis of classical English thought and new and specifically American concerns with income distribution. In his comments at the Chicago Conference, Clark began by defining the trusts as "any combination so big as to be menacing." However, Clark then went on to argue that trusts were not monopolies:

If it were impossible to have capital in great masses without having true monopolies, I would favor a heroic effort to stem the current of natural progress, and keep the general capital of each branch of business in the shape of separate smaller and competing capitals. Monopoly is evil, and almost wholly so; and if the massing of productive wealth necessarily means monopoly, farewell to centralization. We shall do our best to get rid of it, and shall suffer the loss of productive power that this entails, as the price that we are willing to pay for being rid of a great evil.

(Chicago Federation of Chicago 1900: 405)

But, said Clark, the massing of productive wealth need not mean monopoly. If the laws of the land are such that "predatory competition" is prevented, then producers who have a "right to survive" will be protected from discrimination and will serve the public interest:

With a fair field and no favor the independent producer is the protector of the public and of the wage-earner; but with an unfair field and much favor he is the first and most unfortunate victim. Save him, and you save the great interests of the public. You can do this if you find or make a way to success in that type of legislation that will prevent the single evil, discrimination in the treatment of customers.

(Chicago Federation of Chicago 1900: 409)

What is key here is Clark's notion of the "right to survive." The leap of reason that had been taken by Clark was to assume that if manufacturing firms grew, whether through some form of consolidation or by internal growth, and if they survived, then the mere fact of survival indicated that they were not monopolies. Monopoly meant, to Clark, the act of restricting output to raise prices and, with a "fair field," independent producers could enter the market, and because they would survive, failure of the monopolistic firm to secure its ill-gained advantage would be guaranteed. Adam Smith's invisible hand of competition would, therefore, be sufficient to control firms in industries with a "fair field."

Although Clark did not say so explicitly, survival would mean that the firm had found a legitimate (which is to say non-monopolistic) way to produce at lower cost. This could be because of the nature of the technology used, as in the case of the railroads, or, presumably, because of organizational coordination, which is perhaps what Clark meant when he said that "without sacrificing the prosperity that a high organization of industry assures," simple dependence on "economic law" would be sufficient to keep prices and wages "at or near their natural level" (Clark 1900: 409). The implicit plea for patience in the face of "trust" formation made sense given a high rate of failure of combinations in a number of industries.[10] At the same time, however, a number of other firms were, through internal growth and merger, growing steadily larger, and it would only be by an extension of his argument that Clark would be able to maintain his optimistic view that monopoly power would not result from this growth.

In a series of lectures delivered at Cooper Union in 1904, Clark explained his emerging views a bit more fully. The lectures were published under the title *The Problem of Monopoly: A Study of a Grave Danger*, which suggests that Clark had modified the generally optimistic views that he expressed at the Chicago Conference, for at the Cooper Union he began with these words:

I know of no more startling and disquieting tendency of recent times than the growth of these great corporations which have gathered to themselves, each in its own field, nearly all the business that is there transacted. They look like all-consuming monopolies and we regarded them at first with an alarm which has partly subsided as we have gotten more and more used to them. That alarm, however, was not ill-grounded.

(Clark 1904: 3)

Nevertheless, and in spite of the somewhat different tone, Clark again lays out two ideas that were to become permanent features of the stories of most economists. The first of these ideas involved the notion that "economies of scale" (where scale is what Clark would refer to as "the size of the mill") were in some considerable measure responsible for the development of the trusts. (I will have much more to say about the meaning of "economies of scale" below.) The second was that even with a concentration of production, a form of competitiveness could continue to protect the public interest, and especially so if governments acted to prevent unfair practices. Here are Clark's words:

All this brings us clearly face to face with a very serious problem – whether we possibly can control the great political forces which economic forces have created. For the whole political and moral evolution was inherent in the machines that replaced the hand labor of former times. You would not have had the trusts in a regime of hand labor; you would not have had the enormous mills that united to form the trusts. *It is the machine that has made the size of a mill so important and has made it impossible for any but the big one to survive.* The fact that only a few did survive first caused those few to compete so vigorously with each other that they made almost no profits, then enabled them to save their profits by consolidating and finally incited them to seek, besides legitimate profits to which they had a perfect right, an income not founded in justice and one to which a harsh term may correctly be applied.

(Clark 1904: 21, italics added)

If Clark was prepared to apply the harsh term "monopoly profits" to the income of trusts, he also, however, retained his faith that "[i]f the market is open to competitors ... in spite of the trust, prices will be low" (Clark 1904: 32).

In a slightly earlier book published in 1901 entitled *The Control of Trusts*, and in the revised version of the book that he published with his son John Maurice Clark in 1912, Clark laid out the actions that were required to prevent the trusts from unfairly excluding efficient competitors. These were actions that were incorporated into the Clayton Act and the Federal Trade Commission Act, both of which became law in 1914.[11] Although these Acts were relatively mild in effect, and provided large loopholes for corporations to argue that their behavior would not have anticompetitive consequences, the Acts did add to the limited regulatory options available under the Sherman Antitrust Act and did so in a way that was consistent with Clark's desire to allow great corporations to retain their efficiency while taking from them their power of oppression.[12]

However, what is most important for our analysis of the stories (and I again emphasize the plural) told by economists is what had been tacitly excluded from Clark's account. By identifying the source of the efficiencies of the large corporations as attributable to "the size of the mill" and to the machines that replaced hand labor, Clark had thoroughly conflated the source of efficiencies in the railroad industry with those found in manufacturing. This he had done by resort to the test of survival rather than any direct evidence as to the relationship of "the size of the mill" and survival rates.

This was a conflation that made considerable common sense when you looked at, for example, the evolution of Carnegie Steelworks into United States Steel. Large plants and large-scale equipment were rapidly becoming the picture that people, economists included, had of the ever more efficient American producers. What got forgotten, however, was that not all of the advantages and causes of consolidation were attributable to economies of scale in production or to unfair exclusion of competitors. Neither economies of scale in production nor clearly unfair exclusion of competitors could account for the rise of the first and biggest trust of them all, Standard Oil. In that case as in others, what was far more important than size of plants (as opposed to firms), and what will be discussed in much greater detail in the next chapter, were the successful consolidations followed by cooperation in planning and execution that turned manufacturing and distribution into a flow-like process. Expansion of "the size of the mill," which is to say the adoption of new technologies, often followed rather than led this process, as it did in the case of Standard Oil.[13] However, because of the emphasis on the size of the mill, both the adoption of new technology and the cooperation in planning and execution that Andrews had observed were not given their due. This left ample room for a reasonable alternative story. However, before that alternative can be told, it will be useful to carry forward the story of the emerging policy consensus that was based to a large extent upon the "size of the mill" version of what had happened to American industrial organization.

With passage of the Clayton and FTC Acts in 1914, there was at least the appearance of a new start on the perplexing problem of how America, through its Federal government, would tame and cope with the large industrial firms that were rapidly coming to dominate production and distribution. It took some time, however, before a consensus view among economists was fully developed and some time as well before public concern was quieted. The Sherman Act itself had produced mixed results no matter the stand from which judgment was made. And public concern with apparent abuses of corporate power continued to be a major political factor, even as there was growing acceptance of large business firms.

The struggle to write laws and have them interpreted so as to distinguish between "good" and "bad" trusts was a recurring theme in political campaigns throughout the early years of the twentieth century and was made more important by the Supreme Court's adoption of the "rule of reason" in the Standard Oil and American Tobacco cases, which were decided in 1911. The Court held that both of these companies should be broken apart because they, in the words of Chief Justice Edward White, restrained trade "to the prejudice of the public interests by unduly restricting competition" (US v. American Tobacco). The Sherman Act, White argued for the majority, should be understood not as preventing all restraints of trade but only those that unreasonably restricted trade, something of which he and the majority of his colleagues found both American Tobacco Company and Standard Oil of New Jersey guilty. Although these decisions appeared to some to be a dramatic departure from a stricter interpretation of the Sherman Act, little was actually changed, and uncertainty as to the actual effect of the law remained. In the words of William Letwin:

> White ... left the Act largely unchanged in its practical effects, though he established a doctrine which somewhat stretched the precedents. That doctrine recognized, as none of the previous interpretations had recognized quite so clearly, the obvious fact that some or many combinations took place innocently, being aimed not at all at monopoly control – and coming nowhere near it – but aimed merely at achieving an economically efficient scale of production.
>
> (Letwin 1965: 265)

Of course, this begged the question of what combinations were innocent and undertaken in pursuit of efficiency of production and by what means, and the Court decisions of 1911 neither ended concentration of power in the petroleum industry nor in the production of cigarettes, nor did they end debate as to appropriate public policy.[14] However, there seems little doubt that a fairly large majority of the public had come to accept that large firms once established were indeed a permanent feature of the American scene, but that additional legal specificity and administrative power were required to keep them in check. The results were precisely the Acts that created the Federal Trade Commission, which was charged with preventing specified unfair practices, and data collection, and the Clayton Antitrust Act, which specified practices deemed unfair and anticompetitive.[15] Not only did the passage of these Acts reflect a reasonable political consensus; they also reflected fairly well the opinions of professional economists who had come to view large concerns as inevitable consequences of economies of scale, with, however, acknowledgment of some egregious cases of unfair practices that could and should be controlled by law and commission.

An associationist detour

World War I created a hiatus in the ongoing discussion about large firms and took the nation on what turned out to be something of a detour in both discussion and policy making. Experience during the War with a dysfunctional rail system and with increased utilization of industrial capacity in aid of the war effort led to post-war interest in improving efficiency and to ensuring that productive capacity continued to be fully exploited. Among the manifestations of this carryover were the efforts of engineers, under the leadership of Herbert Hoover, as the first president of the Federated American Engineering Societies (FAES), to combine in "the service of the community, state, and nation" to eliminate waste. As Hoover put it, engineers were assuming the responsibility to "visualize the nation as a single organism," with the goal of maximum production (Knoedler and Mayhew 1999; Stabile 1986; Layton 1969; Barber 1985). When, in 1920, Hoover became Secretary of Commerce, he sought to implement ideas developed as part of his collaboration with fellow engineers, and he became a strong advocate of trade associations, an advocacy that brought him into conflict with the Department of Justice, which saw such associations of firms in the same industry as inconsistent with the provisions of the antitrust laws (Barber 1985: 8–13).

Trade associations and other business organizations designed (as Hoover and his many allies hoped) to gather industry-wide data and to share it in the interests of maximum and efficient production were in apparent conflict with the antitrust goals of minimal contact among competing firms. Many were supportive of Hoover's efforts to promote standardization of such goods as automobile tires, but not so supportive when information about costs and prices was shared by producers who were supposed to be competing with each other. To Hoover, it looked like cooperation in the interests of efficiency; to many others, it seemed another route to business collusion against the public interest, and over the course of the 1920s, these conflicting views came to be seen as, on the one hand, pro-competitive support of antitrust and, on the other, a cooperative and associationist alternative that might or might not serve the public as well as private interests. In some ways the lasting importance of the 1920s enthusiasm for such associations was that they were seen to be in opposition to strong antitrust measures when, in the 1930s, the program of which they had become part was decisively rejected.

The move toward decisive rejection began when, in 1931, Gerard Swope, president of the General Electric Company, proposed a program whereby firms with fifty or more employees would be *required* to join trade associations (Barber 1985: 121). Trade associations, which had seemed merely a good idea in the early 1920s, now were seen, in the depths of the depression of the '30s, as a way to achieve agreement among competitors that could prevent further price declines, bankruptcies, and loss of jobs. Hoover, by this time President of the US, was not receptive to the planning envisaged by Swopes, and, more importantly for this account, neither were most economists. In 1932, Frank A. Fetter organized economists to support antitrust planks that were being urged on the political parties. Included in the Fetter statement was the proposition that prior failures to enforce the Sherman Act had led to "the control of large areas of the industrial field by great combinations and by monopolistic practices having neither legal or economic justification" (Fetter 1932: 468). As the economic depression of the 1930s worsened, debate between those who advocated coordination among firms in the same industry and those who did not was sharpened. The debate was brought to prominence and then effectively ended by the creation and rapid demise of the National Industrial Recovery Act (the NIRA).

The NIRA, signed by President Franklin Roosevelt in 1933, was designed to do many things, but, most controversially, it was an enactment of "associationism," with provision for codes of fair conduct that would maintain prices (thereby halting, it was hoped, the ongoing decline that was for many both manifestation and cause of the depression) and would establish minimum wages, maximum hours, and other protections for workers. The Act revealed, says William Barber, that "enthusiasts for 'concentration and control' – as opposed to 'competition and conflict' – were riding the crest of the wave." To Rexford Tugwell and others in the New Deal administration, it was "a sea change in the functioning of the American economy" in which "[a]t last it had been officially recognized that faith in the social benevolence of free markets was out of touch with the reality of mature industrialism" (Barber 1996: 53). The change did not last long. On an issue having to do with taxation and not with the larger issues involved, the Supreme Court declared the NIRA unconstitutional in 1935, but by this time, Tugwell's pro-planning view was on the way to being completely discredited. The NIRA had not led to rapid recovery from economic depression, and those who had disliked the "structuralist" agenda of the planners and regulators from the beginning were now empowered.

The invisible hand returns

By 1937, Tugwell and Adolph Berle, both of whom had urged planning, regulation and acceptance of the inevitability of industrial concentration, were no longer part of the New Deal. In the meantime, however, the antitrust approach had been significantly strengthened by the appointment of Thurman Arnold, an active and able advocate, as Director of the Antitrust Division of the Department of Justice. What made this turn of events particularly important for the evolution of the stories of economists were two other background events. One was the development of the idea of intermediate structures between "perfect competition," on the one hand, and "pure monopoly," on the other. When economists began to wrestle with the railroads and then the trusts, they had only these opposing poles with which to work. Creation of theories of intermediate economic forms was thus both a logical result of changing economic reality and of the need to accommodate economic discourse to the political compromises that both resulted from and helped form that reality.

The contributions of Edward Chamberlain and Joan Robinson are the best-known examples of this work. Working independently, Chamberlain and Robinson expanded the theoretical language of economists to include "monopolistic competition" and "imperfect competition" as tightly defined types. Their theories retained the Smithian ideas as they had been formalized diagrammatically by Alfred Marshall and other "neoclassical" economists, and allowed economists to incorporate reasonable characterizations of large industrial firms in standard textbook accounts.[16] The older ideas of competition and monopoly as opposite poles in a spectrum of desirability were maintained but with new terminology and tools for analysis of the mid-range.

Added to this theoretical development, which took place largely in the two Cambridges, Cambridge Mass. and Cambridge UK, was what has been described, by Robert Bork, as a "religious conversion" of bright young economists-in-training at the University of Chicago in the 1930s. Central to this conversion was Henry Simon's *Positive Program for Laissez-Faire*, a work that was interpreted by one young disciple, Milton Friedman, as the basis for use of antitrust laws to achieve a state in which competition would play a much more important role than active government in ensuring socioeconomic well-being.[17] In the words of Steven Medema, a scholar who has written extensively about the Chicago economists:

In simple terms, proponents of the early Chicago approach generally accepted the propositions that had been at the heart of economics since the writing of Adam Smith: In a liberal democracy, the rational pursuit of economic self-interest by economic actors was taken as given, competition was seen as inherent in and intrinsic to economic life, and market-generated outcomes were thought to be superior to those resulting from government interference with the market mechanism. Although during the 1930s these propositions (the later two in particular) were increasingly called into question within the profession at large, their continuity within the Chicago school set the Chicago perspective apart from much of the rest of the economics profession.

(Medema 1998: 210)

By the end of the 1930s, a canonic work by Edward Mason had been published that laid out industrial structure, conduct, and performance on a spectrum from highly competitive to monopolistic. This, in combination with the new vision of a better world to be created through antitrust enforcement that came both from Chicago and, ironically, given that he was a liberal advocate of active government, from Thurman Arnold's leadership, revolutionized and focused the views of a great many economists. At the beginning of the decade, there had still been considerable distance between two camps. On the one hand, there were those that thought assurance of a "fair field" and fairly non-intrusive prohibitions on a limited range of practices would suffice to ensure competition. On the other were those, such as Tugwell and Berle, who, very much in the spirit of Hoover when he was Secretary of Commerce, wanted full-bore cooperation among large firms in combination with government oversight that would be required to prevent unfair practices.

In the years following World War II, the intellectual foundation that had been laid for a revitalized antitrust approach and the legacy of the New Deal had been reformed by the compromises of the late 1930s. Now the goal was limited control of the modern "trusts" (a word that had largely disappeared from public discourse) rather than planned and cooperative management. Together the elements that revitalized the invisible hand as the public protector had also helped create a vested interest in antitrust practice that certainly did not diminish the enthusiasm of most economists for the new view that monopolistic competition and oligopoly were manageable industrial forms that could be nudged away from monopoly and toward the ideal of perfect competition. George Stigler and Donald Dewey have presented the Whiggish view that the new acceptance of the importance of antitrust law and policy by the majority of economists at mid-century was a consequence of greater learning. In their version of the history of thought on the subject, it had simply taken some time for economists to develop the scientific understanding that allowed them to recognize monopolistic competitors and oligopolists for what they were, which is to say legitimate forms of business organization on the spectrum that Mason delineated. Both also argued, as in somewhat different terms has Craufurd Goodwin, that the employment opportunities offered economists by antitrust enforcement may also have played a role in the transformation of the way in which economists viewed antitrust laws (Stigler 1982; Dewey 1990; Goodwin 1998).

Whatever the case may have been, whether through collective wisdom or by individual recognition of economic advantage or both, the majority of economists had changed their minds. Whereas the Sherman Antitrust Act had initially been viewed by prominent economists as a somewhat embarrassing, and certainly irrelevant, product of public hysteria, by the time World War II was over, the majority were enthusiastic supporters. There were skeptics and critics of the underlying reasoning, but it would be fair enough to say that, as of the 1940s, the standard view was that some combination of not-quite-fair practices and "economies of scale," such as those that produced the peculiar challenge of the railroads, had conspired to create new industrial structures. And, in spite of the existence of some monopolistic elements in these structures, most economists were reasonably certain that they had the tools to mitigate the influences of these undesirable elements. This was the consensus that became the core of what was widely known as the sub-discipline of Industrial Organization.

Crucial to this consensus was the implicit agreement that price of products produced and sold was the crucial measure of how well society as a whole was served by firms brought under scrutiny by the antitrust and fair trade laws. Given this agreement, the task of economic analysis was to show how, even under conditions in which monopolistic elements mixed with those of greater competitiveness, all firms, large and small, were driven by competition to offer the lowest possible prices. With the addition of transaction cost analysis (about which more in the next chapter) as an additional explanation of the size of firms, most economists have been confident since the late 1930s that they have theories sufficient to account for the industrial and distribution structure of the American economy. They have also been generally content that these theories promise consistency between that structure and the larger public interest.

But, there were other stories.

5 Alternative stories

An alternative story that explains the growth and consequences of large firms has long been told by economists in sub-disciplines that lie outside of the mainstream of economic theory. Because there has not been a shared terminology among all who have told it, it has been a fragmented story, one in which the common elements were not always clearly recognized as such. In this chapter, the accounts of several writers who may at first glance appear to be unlikely bedfellows indeed will be pieced together in an alternative account against which, in Chapter 6, both the popular stories of Standard Oil and Wal-Mart recounted in Chapter 3, as well as the economic theories that have been spun off those stories in Chapter 4, will be compared. The authors of the alternative account include, among others, Thorstein Veblen, best known as the acerbic author of *The Theory of the Leisure Class;* Bela Gold, an economist who trained first as an industrial engineer; the business and economic historian Alfred Chandler, who remade the field of business history; Armen Alchian, a widely respected economic theorist associated with the Chicago School; and Ronald Coase, also a member of the Chicago School, who is generally credited with being one of the major creators of transaction cost theory.

Seeing the firm whole

The most important common feature of the alternative views is that they have all been based on an effort to analyze the entire range of activities of the modern firm. The consensus view of the firm described in Chapter 4 is based upon the long-standing practice among economists to think of the firm as a place in which raw materials are transformed into goods. What matters to the firm so conceived is that inputs (of required quality) be acquired as cheaply as possible and transformed with efficiency so that the price at which output is sold will cover the costs of inputs and yield a reasonable return to the owner(s) of the firm. The great task of the firm in this standardized view is to use the minimum of resources to produce the maximum possible output. In this view the firm is an organization or place where production takes place, with the transactions required to initiate that production, including acquisition of money used to purchase the inputs, and the management of sales of output given relatively little attention. The important, or at least legitimate, activities of the firm in this standard view can be described as $C \rightarrow C'$, which is to say that the firm is an organization or place where inputs of commodities (including units of labor), designated as C, are transformed into other commodities, designated as C'.[1]

The alternative view of the firm that will be explored in this chapter is one that requires the phrase $M \rightarrow C \rightarrow C' \rightarrow M'$ to describe activities. In this alternative view there is no presupposition as to which of the steps takes precedence in determining the success of the firm and all parts are interrelated. In this view the goal of the firm is to ensure that M', total receipts, exceeds M, total outlays, and this may be accomplished by minimizing C but there are other ways to achieve the goal as well.

When Adam Smith began his career as founding economist, and certainly in earlier decades and centuries, commercial business was dominated by banking and commerce, which is to say by the processes of provision of M and, even more importantly, by transport and distribution of both C and C'. The actual production process rested in the hands of craftsmen and was not the stuff of economic analysis. That changed with Smith, whose major goal in *The Wealth of Nations* was to show that governments were not well advised to control trade in order to achieve that wealth. Rather, they should do what they could, which would be mostly to stay out of the way, to ensure that production of goods was as efficient as possible.

What interested Smith was the way in which the transformation of $C \rightarrow C'$ could be made better, meaning more productive, by allowing businesses freedom to acquire, produce, and distribute as they wished without the mercantilist restrictions on trade that had characterized the nations of Western Europe from the sixteenth through the late eighteenth centuries. As Smith put it in the first pages of his famous book, *The Wealth of Nations*, labor was the "fund" which supplies the nation. It was not, as the mercantilists had mistakenly thought, a fund of money that controlled the process but, rather, labor. He went on to argue that labor's ability to supply the nation could be augmented by specialization (division of duties) that increased the dexterity of the workman, the organization of related work in the same "workhouse," or at least nearby, and application of proper machinery (Smith 1937: Book 1, Chapter 1). If governments gave businessmen and craftsmen freedom to do as they would, all three of these augmentations would continue apace, and the wealth of the nation would grow. This argument was a powerfully reasonable one in 1776, for much of government policy had been based on the notion that money was the wealth of the nation, so that both production and trade, though mainly trade, needed to be controlled to allow acquisition of silver and gold. Smith turned the argument on its head and treated money as the "wheel of circulation" but as otherwise immaterial to national wealth. Smith's emphasis, both as he worried about the collusive tendencies of merchants of the same trade, and as he praised the advantages of *laissez faire*, was on the limited range of control available to the individual businessman that could enhance the wealth of the nation, which is to say on $C \rightarrow C'$. Put simply, Smith moved analysis of those parts of economics having to do with money to the margins.[2]

By mid-century, when the industrial revolution had changed much, Karl Marx expanded the theoretical structure created by Smith and described business activity as involving a process of $M \rightarrow C \rightarrow C' \rightarrow M'$. He did so to show how the transformation of money to commodities to money was critical to an understanding of capitalism as it had evolved.[3] Marx contrasted the household that would purchase corn for use and not be concerned with converting it into more money with the successful business firm that would by sale of transformed corn acquire additional funds that would be accumulated and used again to buy still more corn. Marx emphasized and, in fact, built his whole model of the economy on this process of accumulation: the excess of M' over M (for successful firms) is used to purchase goods to be transformed and sold for more accumulation.

This understanding of what makes capitalism work as a system of ever increasing output has become commonplace. In the parlance of modern business schools and executive suites, firms add value to the purchased inputs by manufacture and distribution, and use accumulated funds to reinvest. As will become clear, the now standard business school view of firms is much closer to Marx's view of the firm as a process of $M \rightarrow C \rightarrow C' \rightarrow M'$ than it is to that of Smith who emphasized the importance of $C \rightarrow C'$, though it was Smith's focus that dominated discussion of the big new firms of the late nineteenth century. This was so even though Marx's expanded formulation would have been quite useful to organize and articulate some of the most important observations about the transformation of American business firms at the end of the nineteenth century. The conclusions about the direction of the economy would not have been those that Marx might have reached, but the vision of the firm that he proposed to be of capitalist essence would have been a better framework for the observations of Benjamin Andrews, both Adamses (Charles Francis and Henry Carter), and their economist colleagues than was the one inherited from Smith.

As noted in Chapter 4, when the respected Benjamin Andrews summarized the results of the congressionally mandated investigations undertaken in the late 1880s into the economic impact of trusts, he listed several advantages of "the giant style of undertaking," including the ability to "map out" demand and by doing so preventing "the stoppage of work, the decay of mills and machinery, and the rise of prices" (Andrews 1889: 136). These advantages were difficult to fit into the Clark-led consensus about costs of production but could easily be described as ameliorative actions taken by large firms to coordinate the output of C' with transformation into M'. Among others who looked more broadly at the effects of the trusts was Henry Carter Adams, who, it will be remembered, had spoken at the Chicago Conference in 1899, suggesting regulation of unfair practices but also denying that greater size through consolidation led to reduced costs of production in manufacturing industries.[4] Adams, writing in 1903, for the sixteenth annual meeting of the American Economic Association, began by noting his disagreement with what he described as a "discussion designed to reconcile us with the existence of exclusive industries" and with the view that potential competition could be a satisfactory substitute for actual competition. Most importantly, he disagreed with the proposition that trusts were productive by virtue of their ability to increase output beyond what would have been achieved with active competition. He found no evidence that consolidation and increase in size of firm produced the same kind of increased returns to inputs that Charles Francis Adams had documented for the railroads. Rather, such evidence as he could find suggested constant returns. He did say, and this is a point to be taken up in more detail a bit further on, that observed growth in plant size had indeed been associated with adoption of new inventions, but, he insisted, that for any given state of the manufacturing arts, an increase in size of firm was unlikely to bring additional output.

Adams wrote:

> It may be urged that I overlook the savings incident to great organizations. No, I do not overlook the possibility of savings. Savings incident to great industries are of two kinds: first, the production of by-products in sufficient quantities to make their collection and preparation for the market profitable, and second, the avoidance of unnecessary expense in the administration of the business *and in the sale of the product.*
>
> (Adams 1904: 101, italics added)

In short, Adams thought there could be savings from economies of scope, meaning by production of by-products, and from a reduction in unit cost in the $C' \rightarrow M'$ portion of the activity of consolidated firms. However, he saw no evidence for advantage in the $C \rightarrow C'$ portion. He was, in other words, in agreement with Benjamin Andrews, but he did not buy Clark's argument that there were genuine and substantial economies of scale in manufacturing.

A more general statement of this proposition was offered in 1904 by Thorstein Veblen in *The Theory of Business Enterprise*. In the Preface to this book, Veblen made clear that his intent was to develop a theory of business enterprise from the standpoint of businessmen operating at the beginning of the twentieth century. Veblen was trying to abandon preconceptions inherited from earlier theories of the role and function of firms and to begin anew, using the new businessman's perspective as the starting point.[5] What had changed, said Veblen, that made much of the prior theory of business behavior irrelevant was "the machine process," a phrase that he used to describe "something more comprehensive and less external than a mere aggregate of mechanical appliances for the mediation of human labor" (Veblen 1975: 5). The new processes that were described in the *Report of the Industrial Commission* and the other sources upon which Veblen relied were

> two well-marked general characteristics: (a) the running maintenance of interstitial adjustments between the several sub-processes or branches of industry, wherever in their working they touch one another in the sequence of industrial elaboration; and (b) an unremitting requirement of quantitative precision, [and] accuracy in point of time and sequence.
>
> (Veblen 1975: 8)

Further, said Veblen,

> [e]ach industrial unit, represented by a given industrial "plant," stands in close relations of interdependence with other industrial processes ... from which it receives supplies ... and to which it turns over its output of products and waste, or on which it depends for auxiliary work, such as transportation.... By virtue of this concatenation of processes the modern industrial system at large bears the character of a comprehensive, balanced mechanical process.... Any degree of maladjustment in the interstitial coordinations of this industrial process at large in some degree hinders its working.... [The] work of interstitial adjustment, and in great part also the more immediate supervision of the various industrial processes, have become urgent only since the advent of the machine industry and in

proportion as the machine industry has advanced in compass and consistency.

(Veblen 1975: 15–18)

The interstices that required adjustment in Veblen's view were the consequence of an integration of new physical processes with existing legal and commercial organization. To illustrate: in the 1880s, the distribution of kerosene to consumers on the east coast required movement of crude oil from production in the Oil Regions of Pennsylvania to refineries in, let us say, Cleveland and then shipment either in barrels loaded onto box cars or, increasingly, in tank cars built for the purpose. Separate ownership of oil wells, of refineries, of the railroads, and of the distribution network created legal and commercial spaces, or, to use Veblen's preferred term, interstices across which coordination was required, and this coordination created new opportunities, ones seized as we have seen by Rockefeller. Oil refining may have remained a batch process in production through the nineteenth century, but Rockefeller turned it into a flow-process business. The revolution was in management of, as Veblen would have put it, the interstices, something that Rockefeller understood very well.

In a way these observations seem so ordinary that the modern reader may wonder why Veblen took such care to begin his work with them. What he was doing, however, was, as he said, beginning from a different point of view than that adopted in the more typical views of the firm where the focus was on the individual firm in competition (or not, as with "trusts" and monopolies) with other firms. The firms of classical inheritance were focused on their own production, which is to say on $C \rightarrow C'$, whereas Veblen's firms were part of a larger system of production and flow of goods. It was a system in which $M \rightarrow C \rightarrow C' \rightarrow M'$ of one firm linked with the process of other firms; one firm's inputs were another firm's outputs, and any break in the interconnections threatened a failure in the required acquisition of an M' that was greater than M. Such failure had dire consequences in the new world of harsh and immediate competition.

Certainly, it had long been true that the outputs of one firm or farm were the inputs of another so that the work of managing interstitial adjustment had always been there, but both urgency of completing the transactions and opportunities for exploiting them were not as great. Farmers hauled their produce to markets and sold it; craftsmen and factory owners also sold output. The new firms of the late nineteenth century were still the firms of old in their commercial patterns; they bought and sold with the time-honored goals of ensuring the greatest possible difference between receipts and outlays, or, in the worst case, of avoiding receipts that were less than outlays.[6] What had changed, however, was that new processes and technologies, particularly in iron and steel and the refining industries, meant that a disruption of supply became a much larger threat that it could have been in an earlier time. Physical damage to plant capacity in some industries such as iron and steel could result from a failure of raw materials to arrive in a timely manner, and commercial damage was an ever present danger. If the crude oil did not arrive at the refinery or the tank cars were not available for shipping the refined products, then M′ would not exceed M by an anticipated or sufficient amount and other firms might do better. The possibilities of integration over a larger area provided new opportunities for firms that could ensure reliable and rapid movement of goods from one place to another and from one unit of production to other units. Effective integration made the task of predicting and controlling when goods would move across the commercial spaces represented by the arrows between M and C and C′ and M′ much more important. And, the ability to disrupt the flow became a much more vicious form of economic warfare. Rockefeller could do a lot more harm over a much larger region than any single merchant or farmer could have done in an earlier time, and he could also achieve wonders that they could not, but it did require close management of the interstices.

As Veblen saw it, the outcome of the combination of new industrial processes and the inherited forms of organizing production and distribution were new opportunities for efficiency, but not so much because of reduced costs of production (C→C′) as because of savings in the other parts of the process, namely M→C and C′→M′. New commercial opportunities opened by industrialization changed the older business structure to make close management of the ends of the process advantageous. It is worth quoting Veblen at some length:

> As regards the economies in production effected by ... consolidations, there is a further characteristic feature to be noted, a feature of some significance for any theory of modern business. In great measure the saving effected is a saving of the costs of business management and of the competitive costs of marketing products and services, rather than a saving in the prime costs of production. The heightened facility and efficiency of the new and larger business combinations primarily affect the expenses of office work and sales.... The amount of "business" that has to be transacted per unit of product is much greater where the various related industrial processes are managed in severalty than where several of them are brought under one business management. A pecuniary discretion has to be exercised at every point of contact or transition, where the process or its product touches or

passes the boundary between different spheres of ownership. Business transactions have to do with ownership and changes of ownership. The greater the placement in point of ownership, the greater the amount of business work that has to be done in connection with a given output of goods or services, and the slower, less facile, and less accurate, on the whole, is the work. This applies both to the work of bargain and contract, wherein pecuniary initiative and discretion are chiefly exercised, and to the routine work of accounting, and of gathering and applying information and misinformation.

(Veblen 1975: 46–7)

It was, said Veblen, the standardization of industrial processes that facilitated this reorganization of the businessman's work. The result was that "[t]he heroic role of the captain of industry is that of a deliverer from an excess of business management. It is a casting out of business men by the chief of business men" (Veblen 1975: 49).[7]

For Veblen, then, business consolidation was an inevitable consequence of industrialization. Although he did not share the concerns of those who worried about the effect of consolidation on prices (and I will say more about this later), what he did have to say to the small-scale producers who were the leaders of public outrage could not have been comforting to those who hoped for a return to the patterns of nineteenth-century American life.

Modern circumstances do not permit the competitive management of property invested in industrial enterprise, much less its management in detail by the individual owners. In short, the exercise of free contract, and the other powers inhering in the natural right of ownership, is incompatible with the modern machine technology. Business discretion necessarily centres in other hands than those of the general body of owners. In the ideal case, so far as the machine technology and its business concomitants are consistently carried through, the general body of owners are necessarily reduced to the practical status of pensioners dependent on the discretion of the great holders of immaterial wealth [the financial shares]; the general body of business men are similarly, in the ideal outcome, disfranchised in point of business initiative and reduced to a bureaucratic hierarchy under the same guidance; and the rest, the populace, is very difficult to bring into the schedule except as raw material of industry.

(Veblen 1975: 266–7)

High monopolistic prices would not be the necessary or worrisome consequence of consolidation in this view, but a totally altered economic structure would.[8]

Veblen's theory of the consolidation movement made considerable sense, and it was not unknown to either of the Clarks or to the other economists who were struggling with the trusts.[9] However, it did not lend itself to policy prescriptions that fit within any of the political possibilities of twentieth-century America. And, the tide of thought about the trusts, especially as public concern waned, was directed by a growing belief that there were indeed economies of scale in production that could account for the growth of megabusinesses. The problem came to be seen as one of preventing capture of these savings by firms that would be in a position to take advantage of monopoly power, and the solution as one of ensuring John Bates Clark's "fair field" of competition. Neither the dissenting arguments of Benjamin Andrews, or of Henry Carter Adams, nor Veblen's alternative vision could withstand the visual evidence that seemed to come from the steel mills and the new automobile assembly lines. Nor could their views withstand the political and social readiness on the part of the public and their political leaders to reach a tentative peace with the once-hated trusts through the mechanisms of antitrust and prohibition of unfair practices. Veblen's analysis was put on a little-noticed shelf only to be resurrected, as we shall see, in a quite different form a few decades later.

Alfred Chandler's stories

After years in which the stories of the industrial tycoons were most often told as tales of immorality and evildoing *or* as stories of brilliance and courage, a new and discipline-changing book was published in 1977. The story of the rise of big business in America that Alfred D. Chandler provided in *The Visible Hand: The Managerial Revolution in American Business* changed the field of business history and dramatically altered understanding of the rise of big business, at least for economic and business historians if not for economists in general. Chandler brought the approach of a social scientist to a sub-discipline that had been dominated by largely admiring biographies or muckraking denunciations.[10] Whether with praise or denunciation, the emphasis among those who did history had been on individuals rather than systems. And, while economists had paid little or no attention to actual individuals, neither did they seek a historically grounded account of the rise of big business; for them, a stylized, theory-derived account sufficed. With Chandler's work, emphasis, at least for business historians, shifted from the morality or immorality and the achievements of individuals to a social scientific search for common patterns in the records of the past.

By careful review of the records of firms with assets of $20 million or more in 1917, Chandler discovered such patterns. Among the general propositions that he gleaned from the various histories were these:

- Firms grew and mergers succeeded when administrative coordination allowed increased productivity, lower costs, and higher profits than could be achieved through market coordination.
- A managerial hierarchy was required if the benefits of administrative coordination were to be achieved.
- New technology and expanding markets caused the increased economic activity that made administrative coordination advantageous to some firms.
- Once successfully established, an administrative hierarchy became itself a source of permanence for administrative coordination. That is, an administrative hierarchy became itself a source of growth, efficiency, and profitability.
- Those who managed the hierarchies were technically and professionally skilled bureaucrats.
- A separation of ownership and control resulted from the creation of administrative coordination managed by technically skilled managers.[11]

The first and third of these propositions (which are listed here in the order in which Chandler presented them) are of greatest interest, for they contrast with the story that economists had woven together by the middle of the twentieth century. True, the first proposition is, in one sense, a return to John Bates Clark's notion that some of the "trusts" would have a "right to survive" and would serve the public interest by their survival. Remember that those that did survive, according to Clark, would not be monopolies, meaning that they would not restrict output to raise prices, and, so long as a "fair field" was preserved, competitors could enter the industry and succeed if the large firm did not produce and sell at a lower cost than could achieved by smaller firms.[12] Clark's proposal was, in a sense, a revolutionary one when it was offered to the Chicago Conference on Trusts, for it moved the public debate away from concern with the essential unfairness of large firms when seen from the standpoint of rival producers and toward judging fairness solely by the effect on consumers. Chandler's argument was a continuation of this part of the political consensus to which Clark was an early contributor.

In another sense, however, there was a marked difference between

Clark's argument as it became part of the later consensus and Chandler's evidence. Clark's proposition about the "right to survive" served to embed analysis of the effect of large firms in the inherited notion that technology had created economies of scale in production that then dictated large size. Although he did not make this explicit at the Chicago meetings, Clark did state the proposition quite directly in his 1904 Cooper Union speeches when he said that "[i]t is the machine that has made the size of a mill so important and has made it impossible for any but the big one to survive" (Clark 1904: 21). This was the railroad argument applied to manufacturing: economies of scale *in production* created bigness.

Chandler, on the other hand, did not attribute lowered costs to more efficiency in the C→C′ transformation. His argument was closely akin to that of Benjamin Andrews, who, in his 1889 Report for the Committee on Manufactures for the House of Representatives, had found that the advantage of the trusts derived from organizational coordination of output rather than from the machinery used in producing that output. His conclusions, as were those reached by Chandler almost sixty years later, were based on analysis of firms, including Standard Oil. Chandler also sounds the same note as did Henry Carter Adams when he told the American Economic Association that "savings incident" to large firms were a product of efficient use of by-products and of "avoidance of unnecessary expense in the administration of the business and in the sale of product," not from "size of plant" or "density of traffic" as with the railroads (Adams 1904: 99 and 101). And, Veblen, who based his conclusions on testimony that was part of the *Report of the Industrial Commission*, found the advantages that could be gained by large firms to lie in the "work of interstitial adjustment" through which "there is a saving of work and an avoidance of that systematic mutual hindrance that characterizes the competitive management of industry" (Veblen 1975: 48).

Chandler also concluded that it was new technology and expanding markets that made administrative coordination advantageous in some industries, and in offering richly detailed accounts of how this happened for individual firms, he coined a new phrase, "economies of speed." Three passages from *The Visible Hand* will serve to explain the concept and the central role that it played in Chandler's explanation of the rise of big business. The first concerns the revolution in mass distribution that came as a result of the interactive process of westward movement and the development of the telegraph and railroad systems:

The mass marketers [wholesale jobbers, department stores, retail chains] replaced merchants as distributors of goods in the American economy ... because they internalized a high volume of market transactions within a single large modern enterprise. They reduced the unit costs of distributing goods by making it possible for a single set of workers using a single set of facilities to handle a much greater number of transactions within a specific period than the same number of workers could if they had been scattered in many separate small facilities. At the same time, high-volume stock-turn assured a steady cash flow that permitted the enterprises to purchase larger quantities in cash and so greatly reduce the cost of credit needs and finance distribution of goods. Such savings were, however, possible only if the flow of goods through the enterprise was carefully coordinated. The internal transactions had to be made more quickly and at a greater volume than if they were made in the external market. *Economies of scale and distribution were not those of size but of speed.*

(Chandler 1977: 236; italics added)

Even more to the point of the difference between John Bates Clark's theoretical view and the observations of Andrews-Adams-Veblen is this passage about Standard Oil:

Increased size of still, intensified use of energy, and improved design of plant brought rapid increase in throughput. Early in the decade, normal output was 900 barrels a week; it reached 500 barrels a day by 1870. Large refineries already had a charging capacity of 800 to 1,000 barrels a day and even more.... The size of establishment was still small, in terms of capital invested, costing no more than two miles of well-laid railroad track. *But the economies of speed were of critical importance. And one does not need to be an economic historian to identify the senior partner of the fastest refinery in the west in 1869.* The high speed of throughput and the resulting lowered unit cost gave John D. Rockefeller his initial advantage in the competitive battles in the American petroleum industry during the 1870s.

(Chandler 1977: 256; italics added)

Finally, in summarizing the history of distilling and refining industries, Chandler wrote this about "the basic axiom of mass production":

Economies and lower unit costs resulted from an intensification of the speed of materials through an establishment rather than from enlarging its size. They came more from organization and technological innovations that increased the velocity of throughput than from adding more men and machines.

(Chandler 1977: 257)

Chandler provides the detailed descriptions that Veblen's theoretical treatment lacked, but he was saying the same thing. By minding the interstices, some, such as Rockefeller, were able to take advantage of the opportunities offered by the new technologies and they did survive, but not for the reasons that John Bates Clark thought.

A search for theoretical consistency

If Chandler's conclusions were consistent with an earlier evidence and reasoning about large firms, they were not consistent with the received stories of a majority of economists, for their theories had no place for economies of speed. This reality brought adjustments in the way in which Chandler presented his argument about the growth of firms, though they did not change his central conclusion. In 1990, Chandler published a second massive volume, *Scale and Scope*, in which he further systematized the regularities described in *The Visible Hand*. And, with that systemization he both clarified and, in some ways, obfuscated the significance of speed of throughput as a crucial advantage for firms that grew large. First, Chandler noted that in one set of industries, one that included natural fiber textiles, lumber, furniture, printing and publishing, production had remained labor-intensive. In these industries, the advantages of size were not great. In the second set of industries, new or vastly improved processes of production were introduced, and in these industries the ratio of capital to labor rose. These industries included petroleum, iron and steel, chemicals, and many others.

What set these industries apart, aside from the higher ratio of capital to labor, Chandler now said, was that the "cost per unit dropped more quickly as the volume of materials being processed increased" (Chandler 1990: 23). This is to say, of course, that these industries shared, after all, the tendency of unit costs to decline with volume and, in Clark's words, with "the size of the mill." But, Chandler went on to say this:

> These potential cost advantages ... could not be fully realized unless a constant flow of materials through the plant or factory was maintained to assure effective capacity utilization. If the realized volume of flow fell below capacity, then actual costs per unit rose rapidly. They did so because fixed costs remained much higher and "sunk costs" (the original capital investment) were also much higher than in the more labor-intensive industries. *Thus the two decisive figures in determining costs and profits were (and still are) rated capacity and throughput, or the amount actually processed within a specified time period.* (The economies of scale *theoretically incorporate* the economies of

speed, as I use that term in the *Visible Hand*, because the economies of scale depend on both size – rated capacity – and speed – the intensity at which the capacity is utilized.) In the capital-intensive industries the throughput needed to maintain minimum efficient scale requires careful coordination not only of the flow of processes of production *but also of the flow of inputs from suppliers and the flow of outputs to intermediaries and final users.*

(Chandler 1990: 24; italics added)

Two things seem clear. One is that Chandler continued to think that management of throughput was essential to the growth and survival of large firms. The second is that exclusive focus on the transformation of $C \rightarrow C'$, which is to say on actual production as opposed to acquisition of inputs, production, and distribution of output was not sufficient to describe either the advantages of size or the tasks necessary to maintain Clark's "right to survive." Nevertheless, Chandler did, both with the title of the 1990 book, and by explicit statement, subsume his earlier "economies of speed" as part of "economies of scale." This served to make his story seem much closer to the stylized consensus story of economists, but it also brings into relevance another aspect of the evolution of the stories told by economists about big business and takes us to the work of both Armen Alchian and Ronald Coase.

Economies of scale and speed: the modern firm in abstract

Although the phrase "economies of speed" that Chandler gave to the phenomenon was new, he was by no means the first to suggest that management of throughput was part of what economists have called "economies of scale." There are, however, both conceptual and measurement difficulties with the notion that rapidity of throughput is key to volume-related reductions in cost per unit of output. The first is that "economies of scale," strictly defined as it is in economic theory, must for reasons of history refer only to economies in production, but logic makes the matter tricky.

Consider first the history of the idea that size brings cost advantages. The survival test that John Bates Clark suggested for the "trusts" was one whereby only those firms that could produce goods using fewer resources, which is to say at lower cost per unit, would survive. On the level playing field that FTC-guaranteed competitiveness was supposed to ensure, large firms would not survive simply because they could use their power to buy cheaper inputs or prevent competitors from sharing the market for outputs.

Clark would not have wanted to appear before the Chicago Conference on Trusts and explain that some large firms might survive because of either of these aspects of market power. Many of those in attendance were upset precisely because they saw, or thought they saw, such power as the cause of trusts. Clark's claim had to be, and was, different. He said there were sometimes advantages in large-scale *production* that, in turn, made some large firms advantageous to society as a whole.[13]

When, however, this idea is put into the logical terms of economic theory and analysis, trouble starts. While the explanation that size alone can confer such advantage is an intuitively appealing one, identification of the source of that advantage within the framework of economic analysis is more difficult. To understand why this is so difficult, it will help to sort through some of the confusion that has long surrounded efforts to understand the apparently simple notion that big factories produce cheaper goods.

The idea that increasing the size of the productive unit would lead to lower costs is often traced back to Adam Smith and his claims for the virtues of specialization in production (Vassilakis 1987: 761). When Smith wrote about the ways in which the wealth of a nation could grow, prime among his list was labor specialization, which he illustrated with a kind of pin assembly line that would result, he said, in ten persons making "upwards of forty-eight thousand pins in a day," whereas a single worker doing all of the separate tasks would not make as many as twenty, and "perhaps not [even] one whole pin in the same period. Such division of labor "so far as it can be introduced, occasions in every art, a proportionable increase of the productive powers of labor" (Smith 1937: 4–5). This is clearly an assertion of the economy introduced by scale and Smith went on to make the argument even more explicit by arguing a few pages later that it was "the extent of the market" that would limit the division of labor and the economies that could result. The idea that size of operation led to inexpensive production became, with these arguments, a standard part of the economists' toolbox. However, labor specialization in and of itself is a weak argument for very large establishments for there are a limited number of ways in which to subdivide tasks. Ten workers may be, as Smith said, far more productive than one person who does the entire job, but why would you need 100 workers in a plant?[14]

Of course, in Smith's largely pre-industrial world, the only real source of advantage in size in manufacturing would have been specialization of labor and it was true, as Charles Babbage explained some sixty years after Smith wrote, that such specialization would introduce "indivisibilities" or "lumpiness" in production that could require larger factories. Organizing pin production into ten specialized tasks meant that efficient plants would have to employ multiples of ten (Babbage 1963: Chapter XXII). This would have been the case when Smith wrote, but Babbage also found other explanations for large (by the standards of the 1830s, when he wrote) establishments. He observed that the cost of moving heavy materials could be reduced by localizing production within a limited area, and in the case of steam-powered looms by having several looms in one place so that one workman could attend them all. What Babbage did not do was to confuse a concentration of steam-powered looms in comparison to hand-looms as evidence of economies of size alone. He was careful to avoid the confusion between the effects of different technologies and size on costs of production, a confusion that unfortunately became more common later.

In the meantime, however, yet another aspect and advantage of size of firm became part of the discussion. John Stuart Mill, in his enormously influential *Principles of Political Economy*, first published in 1848, devoted a chapter to a comparison of large-scale and small-scale production in which he reported a somewhat abstracted version of Babbage's arguments and also stated, quite explicitly, the survival test upon which John Bates Clark was later to rely. He also foretold Veblen's point that savings could result from fewer businessmen: "A considerable part of saving of labour effected by substituting the large system of production for the small, is the saving in the labour of the capitalists themselves" (Mill 1878: 84). Most notably, though, for what was to come later, Mill argued that in some cases, as with the provision of water in London, it made sense to treat a supplying firm as a "natural monopoly" because to do otherwise and encourage competition would encourage wasteful duplication of the basic infrastructure (in this case, iron pipes and steam engines for pumping).

By decreeing water works to be natural monopolies, he established the concept and terminology that Charles Francis Adams needed to describe the railroads, but he did not state the case for increased returns to scale in production where everything other than size remained the same.[15] Rather, it was the need for substantial investment and the waste of competing infrastructure in such undertakings as a city water system that recommended large size to Mill.

Charles Bullock observed that in the years after Mill's *Principles*, it was common for works on economics to include discussion of the effect of size of establishment on production, and with this discussion there came increased insistence that the notion of economies of scale was something quite distinct from "the law of diminishing returns" to a fixed input. Remember that Charles Francis Adams in writing about the railroads in effect took the track, engines, and rolling stock to be fixed inputs so that reduced costs associated with volume could be understood to be a result of the reverse of diminishing returns, which is to say the result could be described as increasing returns to a fixed input.[16] The question of the effect of size itself on costs of production was, however, a real and new one: did modern manufacturing technologies mean that production on a very large scale would be required to take advantage of all possible efficiencies in production? If large-scale fixed infrastructure was not already in place and there were alternative techniques of production available, was there some law, different from the law of diminishing returns but of equal binding power in the economic and physical realm, that gave rise to economies of size? Mill's proposition that there were some utilities that were natural monopolies could be, and was, extended to the railroads without difficulty and for reasons of necessary size of infrastructure and waste involved in duplication. And, the detailed work of Fink on freight costs per mile made it relatively easy to justify this extension, for costs did, with sensible accounting, fall with more freight carried. The case was, however, simply not so clear in manufacturing.

One might think that Alfred Marshall, the man who synthesized and took the initial steps toward formalization of neoclassical economics, a formalization upon which much of twentieth-century microeconomics has rested, would have sorted things out. However, as Spyros Vassilakis says in the *New Palgrave Dictionary of Economics*, Marshall did not have a formal theory for increasing returns to scale although he "relentlessly applied 'the principle of Increasing Returns'" to assert that "almost every kind of horizontal extension tends to increase the internal economies of production on a large scale" (Vassilakis 1987: 764). Marshall was led to this somewhat odd action because he was an acute observer of late-nineteenth-century economies and industries and knew that increased size of firm or plant did not entail maintenance of inputs in the same ratios that characterized smaller operations, nor did it usually entail use of the same techniques of production as would be required if economies in production were to be attributed to size alone. Most often reductions in unit costs of output were associated with new techniques of production, but in the static system that Marshall was building, there was no room for changing technology.[17]

Marshall could have argued on the basis of logic that a proportionate increase of inputs would result in a more than proportionate increase in outputs, or he could have argued that the observed increase in output was due to organization rather than production itself and so moved out of the narrow $C \rightarrow C'$ conception of the firm. Instead, he left the cause of economies of scale undefined, at least in any way that could be said to be central to his analytical system.[18] Marshall's admirable reluctance to abandon observed patterns in favor of a more complete formulation of his static theory was not, unfortunately, part of his legacy that was carried forward by the neoclassical economists who became the dominant voice in the discipline at the end of the interwar period.[19] With the growing acceptance of large firms as at least a necessary, and probably a desirable, feature of the modern economy, there also came a growing acceptance among economists of the proposition that size of the producing unit (the $C \rightarrow C'$ part of the firm's processes) was cause rather than consequence of efficient firm size. Gold observes that "widespread faith in 'economies of scale' has not gained much support from the relevant theoretical and empirical literature," but nonetheless "[t]he theory of scale effects continues to be taught" (Gold 1981: 5, 19).

This was so even though empirical evidence was lacking, as Gold says. To repeat: the difficulty was not that advantages that accrued to large-scale operations were hard to find. Marshall and many others had noted that discounts were to be had for large purchases of inputs, that selling costs could be reduced by large organizations, and that it was most often cheaper for big firms to borrow money. Legitimate explanations for decreases in costs of production in large firms can certainly be found. The difficulty is that even while wanting evidence for genuine economies of scale, economic analysis has been steadfastly focused on the $C \rightarrow C'$ portion of firm activities, and there evidence is hard to find. Studies that compare costs as between plants that differ only in respect of size are difficult to carry out for the simple reason that firms with plants that differ *only* in respect of size are difficult to identify, and there are always many things other than size that can account for variations in cost of production.[20]

Investigations into the advantages of size in the $C \rightarrow C'$ process, which is to say investigations of the importance of scale in plant as opposed to firm size, in the relatively few cases in which they have been attempted have not been strongly supportive of size as cause of lowered costs. Not only have tests of the proposition that there are genuine economies of scale been rare and difficult to pursue, but when they have been done, what they reveal is a lack of clear evidence that size of manufacturing plant is sufficient to explain the size of firms. Bain concluded that "production economies of plant scale" in the seventeen concentrated industries that he studied exhibited no single pattern and that such economies "were not sufficient to explain the existing sizes of larger firms in these industries, as they ordinarily have grown to scales much larger than those of minimum optimal plants" (Bain 1956: 337).[21]

Where evidence of beneficial effects of size on production costs has been found, it is very difficult to determine whether the requirements of the formalized and restrictive definition of economies of scale have been met.[22] Once again, I quote Bela Gold's words:

[The] requirement of fixed factor proportions [if the restrictive theory of scale is to hold] is seldom encountered in actual cases involving substantial increases in scale, precisely because such restrictions tend to minimize or prevent the benefits whose expected realization is a primary motive for considering increases in scale.... And its correlative requirement of unchanged technology is likewise contrary to most experience.... [Moreover, and] contrary to their casual treatment in discussions of scale by many economists, further "increases in specialization" that yield significantly increasing returns are seldom readily available for the taking.[23]

(Gold 1981: 14)

In the face of such skepticism and the lack of clear evidence that size of plants alone is an important determinative factor in explaining the advantages of large firms, economists have been able to rationalize continued acceptance of the idea only by renaming and reclassifying advantages that might be thought to lie outside narrowly defined $C \rightarrow C'$ transformation and by employing the highly unrealistic assumption that all else could remain the same while size of productive unit varied.

One way to appreciate how this is done is to consider this passage from Joaquim Silvestre's entry on "Economies and Diseconomies of Scale" in *The New Palgrave Dictionary of Economics:*

Decreasing returns imply that duplicating *all* inputs yields less than twice the amount of output.... The failure to double the output suggests the presence of an extra input, not listed in the production function that cannot be duplicated. This idea goes back to Ricardo's rent as based on the impossibility of duplicating land of a given quality. Alternatively, the extra input can be interpreted as managerial skill.

(Silvestre 1987: 81)

If we turn from the decreasing returns that Silvestre is describing and back to increasing returns, it appears that the process that he describes is one that both Gold and H. H. Liebhafsky found common in explanations of increasing returns to scale. Such returns, which is to say declining costs with size, are attributed, though without hard evidence, to "learning," or "increased specialization."[24] Both Gold and Liebhafsky are skeptics who argue that the desire to find that there are economies of scale in large firms derives from the need to show that large business firms are not, at least with some degree of legal oversight, inconsistent with the requirements for a competitive economy such as that envisioned by Adam Smith. Certainly, it seems reasonable to conclude that economists have incorporated a number of explanations for the advantages that size gives that should not, strictly speaking, be attributed to size of production units. It also seems reasonable to conclude that the phrase "economies of scale," while convenient for justification of large firm size, has remained either rigorously defined, in which case rarely observed, or loosely defined, in which case capable of being used to cover a wide variety of cases.

Such was the rather messy but usually ignored state of affairs in the discipline when Chandler redefined his "economies of speed" as an aspect of "economies of scale." Given the common looseness in use of the term, at least where observation of actual processes was involved, Chandler's suggestion makes sense. Chandler was working very much in the way that Alfred Marshall, the observer, had worked. But, Chandler's classification does raise the question of how "speed" can be used as an explanation of large *firm* size if the firm is to be understood in the economic theory of which economies of scale is part. That is, if the firm is seen as a unit of production, concerned only with $C \rightarrow C'$, what role can speed play? Of course, if "economies of scale" are understood in the loose sense to mean that big firms survive, then there is no special need to worry about what speed in production entails. However, it seems only fair to consider the question, and especially so given Chandler's insistence on the importance of speed of throughput, an insistence that continued even after he abandoned the term "economies of speed."

Fortunately for the task of understanding the relationship of "speed" to "scale," we have the work of Armen Alchian who, in a very carefully constructed essay published in 1968 under the simple title "Costs and Outputs," observed that "obscurities, ambiguities, and errors" continued in spite of the immense literature dealing with the relationship between the two crucial concepts of his title (Alchian 1959: 23). Using both logic and empirical evidence from the literature of production engineering, Alchian considered several commonly assumed relationships, and with respect to speed of production, a concept that, he notes, is frequently confused with volume of production, found that the actual effects are the opposite of those most often assumed to hold. That is, with a given production technique, a technologically determined optimum rate of throughput will exist, and increases or decreases from this optimum rate will increase rather than decrease unit costs. A machine, let us say a copying machine for this is the example that Alchian uses, may be used over more hours of a day (so that volume of production increases) but there is no sensible way to speed the working of the machine. As a matter of logic, which is the way that Alchian approaches it, speeding up production, even if technically possible, which is what one might think is meant by "economies of speed," doesn't pay: speed increases cost. So, what does this mean for Chandler's analysis?

To answer this question a closer look at Alchian's argument is required. He begins his analysis by assuming that there are no sunk costs, which is to say that the hypothetical firm of Alchian's reasoning is free to choose any production technique available, with the costs of choice varying. The choice of method of production will be driven by the volume of output to be produced, and there are often economies to be found from choosing "more durable dies," which is to say more expensive "dies" (by which he means the totality of production equipment):

> The method of production is a function of the volume of output, especially when output is produced from basic dies – and there are few, if any, methods of production that do not involve "dies." Why increased expenditures on more durable dies should result in more than proportional increase of output potential is a question that cannot be answered, except to say that the physical principles of the world are not all linear (which may or may not be the same thing as "indivisible"). Different methods of tooling, parts design, and assembly is the usual explanation given in the production engineering literature.
>
> (Alchian 1959: 29)

In other words, there may indeed be economies of scale associated with greater initial investment in "dies," a statement that can be translated as saying that more expensive plants (dies) are likely to lead to reduced costs of output because of superior engineering and construction.

However, the most important point that Alchian makes is that in a world of no sunk costs, efficient planning for production requires that the volume to be produced be determined, and with that determination in hand, the most efficient die can be chosen, and once chosen, the rate of efficient production is given. Even if one drops the assumption of no sunk costs in recognition of the reality of actual firm and plant management, Alchian's point would be that variation in speed from the optimal rate, even if technically possible, would increase unit costs. Of course, in response to increased or decreased inventories, managers might add shifts of workers or close production on some lines for a time, but this is an adjustment in volume of output and not of rate of use of the existing dies. You can hire people to work another shift and use the copier all night, but you can't make the copier go faster or slower. And, as with copiers, pace of work is built in to the machines, which is to say to the dies.[25]

While Alchian's deconstruction of the ongoing confusion between rate and volume in the economics literature is valuable, it does not, of course, directly address Chandler's notion of the importance of speed. In part this is the case because Chandler's descriptions apply to the entire

$M \rightarrow C \rightarrow C' \rightarrow M'$ process rather than the $C \rightarrow C'$ component with which Alchian is concerned. For Chandler, the issue was as much or more whether or not firms could manage the acquisition of inputs ($M \rightarrow C$) and sale of outputs ($C' \rightarrow M'$) expeditiously. Recast in Alchian's terms, the firms that Chandler found to benefit from speed were those that could maintain a volume of production that could be produced with the most efficient dies available, thereby taking advantage of true economies of scale where such existed by "running full."

Consider this passage from one of Chandler's essays:

> The economies of speed resulting from ... administrative coordination are central to an understanding of what economists have called the economies of scale. The economies of scale are, in fact, much more the result of speed than size. In modern business enterprise the reductions of per-unit cost made possible by increasing the size of the establishment (that is, by adding more men and equipment) are tiny compared to the economies made possible by making a more intensive, steadier use of personnel and facilities.... To illustrate, until total capacity is reached, the flow through a tunnel can be increased at much less cost by speeding up and scheduling traffic than by widening the tunnel.
>
> (Chandler 1988: 402)

The issue, Alchian would say, is to make sure that the capacity of the tunnel is appropriate to the volume of traffic, and Chandler would say that the real issue for most firms was to be able to control (and predict, but mainly to control) the volume to fit the capacity.

It may appear, therefore, that by emphasizing economies of speed as the most important element of economies of scale, Chandler was simply restating what a good many critics of large business firms had been saying all along. Strategic actions in the form of trust formation, mergers, and discriminatory pricing were used to ensure that the plants could run full, which is to say at the optimal capacity. Further, and once again using Alchian's formulation, it becomes possible to recast the familiar argument that trust formation, mergers, and internal growth grew out of the tendency, especially in new industries and expanding markets, to overestimate demand, with the result that too many plants were built with optimal volumes of production that could not be sustained.[26] Incorporating the Alchian proposition that there are indeed economies of scale that result from non-linearity in the productive characteristics of dies, we get this further restatement: production at lower cost was possible using the "more durable dies" that new technologies made possible, but these dies required careful management of the $C' \rightarrow M'$ portion of firm processes to ensure that the plants ran full, a task made more urgent by the tendency to overestimate demand in an expanding market.

Restated this way, Chandler's argument is made consistent with Alchian's theoretical formulation of the firm, but it remains unclear as to whether or not we are left with economies to society, which is to say real economies, or simply advantages to individual firms, that is, pecuniary economies. The two are, as Bain (1968) reminded us, not at all the same thing. The advantage to economists of a strict notion of economies of scale derives from the proposition that only those firms that use fewer scarce resources because of the available economies will survive. If prices are raised above the "cost plus normal profit" level then others will enter the industry and drive prices back down. The advantage of the economies of scale will accrue to society and not be diverted via "monopoly profits" to the owners of the firm. However, if it is necessary for the firm to manage disposal of output, which is to say to manage the $C' \rightarrow M'$ transformation, then the fears of the antitrusters at the Chicago Conference become real again, an issue that will be dealt with at much greater length in the next chapter.

For now, however, consider the work of Ronald Coase and its relevance for the evolution of economic thought about the benefits of large firms. What Coase did in a now famous article published in 1937 was to deal in rigorously deductive theoretical fashion, by far the preferred fashion of most economists, with the question of why some business transactions are handled externally by buying from and selling to other firms while others are internalized. Some firms may outsource accounting services, others set up their own full-service accounting departments. Wal-Mart runs its own trucking fleet; other retailers hire trucking services. The question is why, and more specifically, the question is why firms have tended to grow large by bringing a wide range of activities under one administrative umbrella.[27]

At issue, said Coase, was the definition of the firm, a definition that he proposed to establish using "the most powerful instruments of economic analysis developed by Marshall, the idea of the margin and that of substitution, together giving the idea of substitution at the margin" (Coase 1937: 386–7). "Those," said Coase, "who object to economic planning on the grounds that the problem is solved by price movements can be answered by pointing out that there is planning within our economic system," planning that takes place within the firm rather than through market allocation. This fact, he said, had not been ignored by earlier economists, for John Bates Clark, Frank Knight, and D. H. Robertson had all pointed to organizations, or entrepreneurs, and managers as planners who occupied, in

Robertson's phrase, "islands of conscious power in this ocean of unconscious co-operation like lumps of butter coagulating in a pail of buttermilk" (Coase 1937: 388). Why, Coase asked, did these lumps exist when market transactions between firms could be used instead? Put simply, Coase's answer was that there are costs of using the price mechanism, costs such as that of discovering what prices are, as well as costs of negotiating and contracting, and costs associated with an inability to know the future.

Coase's argument, which by now has been restated and reformulated many times, especially in the work of Oliver E. Williamson, can be used here to restate the arguments of Andrews-Adams-Veblen-Chandler-Alchian.[28] The railroads and the telegraph, in combination with new methods of production and new industries, altered the costs of internalization versus externalization of transactions. The costs of finding what prices were and of contracting became much more complicated as markets expanded geographically and in complexity. Both expansion and complexity, as Chandler describes in detail in his chapter on "Mass Distribution" in *The Visible Hand*, increased the need for standardization of products and for new forms of contract and finance. As Veblen put it, though without Chandler's detail, "standardization of industrial process, products, services, and consumers" serves the businessman's purposes "by permitting a uniform routine in accounting, invoices, contracts, etc" (Veblen 1975: 47). This standardization was part of the dynamic interaction between organization and technology that Chandler saw as central to the rise of the new large firms. It was this interaction that encouraged and allowed increases in the "die," to use Alchian's term, or fixed plant capacity to use a more familiar term, that had to be fully utilized to minimize costs. Put in Coasian terms, the costs of relying on market coordination increased, and the costs of internalization decreased. There was, to put it mildly, considerable substitution at the margin.

The appeal of Coase's analysis for economists is that it allows the dramatic changes that occurred in the organization of the American economy after 1870 to be treated as part of the $C \rightarrow C'$ transformation. What might quite reasonably be described as costs of managing throughput by management of $M \rightarrow C$ and especially by management of $C \rightarrow M'$ are reclassified in Coase's analysis as transaction costs that can be treated as part of the costs of production. Oliver Williamson wrote that "the transaction cost economics approach to the study of economic organization can be infectious" and explained this infectiousness as a consequence of the "core commitment" of transaction cost economics to economic "orthodoxy," which he identifies as a "combination of a 'rational spirit' with a 'systems' perspective" (Williamson 1996: 8 and 18).[29] I would restate this only slightly by saying that rationality as defined in economic orthodoxy is a commercial rationality, in which minimizing costs for any given quantity and quality of output is the measure of success. By translating organizational maneuvering and advantage into the language of costs, long-observed facts about concentration of business were tamed and incorporated into economic orthodoxy. If the administrative coordination that Chandler saw as arising from the new technologies of the late nineteenth century can be described as part of the $C \rightarrow C'$ process of production of goods, then Coase has provided a way of seeing size of firms, and not just size of plants, as advantageous. In like manner, Veblen's understanding that management of the interstices provided a wealth (quite literally) of new business opportunities for a few can be tamed if restated in Coase's terms by simply saying that interstitial management was internalized because, given costs, it was more efficient that way. For economists this restatement has many advantages.

There are, however, some major disadvantages. What, after all, does all of this have to do with Wal-Mart, or even with Standard Oil? If the goal of economic theory is abstraction and elegance, then a translation of the struggles of such as Charles Francis Adams, Benjamin Andrews, Henry Carter Adams, John Bates Clark, John Maurice Clark, Thorstein Veblen, and Alfred Chandler into the simple and elegant terms of Ronald Coase signals mission accomplished. If, however, the goal is to understand the distress that was clear at the Chicago Conference on Trusts and is today evident in multiple protests against Wal-Mart, then the Coasian formulation is less useful. And, if the goal is also to assist in crafting policies and procedures to address public concern, then the Coasian translation is even less helpful, for it essentially amounts to saying, with room for elegantly expressed regret, "que sera sera." The problem is not that the Coasian formulation is wrong; it is that it allows no room for negotiation about the legitimacy and control of the many different kinds of power that are exercised by large firms. Power over price is not all that matters. What also matters is economic power, and economic power, in several forms, will be the topic of the next chapter.

6 Supply chains and $M \rightarrow C \rightarrow C' \rightarrow M'$

Even with the addition of transaction cost analysis to its inventory, modern economic theory does not provide a ready-to-use language for talking about the entire range of firm activity. Discussion of many kinds of power is effectively put off limits by defining its exercise as that which is to be prevented by antitrust or other regulation of price-setting abilities. While there is an instinctive distrust of public bureaucracies in their exercise of a wide range of discretionary powers, the same lack of confidence is not generally extended to the private sector except where pricing is concerned. Not only is power in its many manifestations largely missing from discussions of firm behavior, so too are a wide variety of ways in which firms interact with other firms and with their employees, suppliers, and customers. While it is true that modern transaction theory allows a variety of factors such as treachery and trust in negotiation and enforcement of contracts to be brought into analysis by rendering them as costs, a wide range of activities that influence the lives of workers and consumers are excluded from analysis.

The omissions are serious because negative public reactions to both Standard Oil and Wal-Mart, two firms who did, after all, lower costs to consumers, show clearly that people care about far more than the prices of products produced. People are part of the production and distribution processes as much as they are consumers. They live in communities with others whose well-being affects their own. Standard Oil, by its power over the location of refineries, its differential treatment of railroads, and its decisions about distribution affected where people could live and prosper. Wal-Mart, in like manner, determines the commercial landscape of great portions of America. Decisions made in Bentonville, Arkansas, determine not only whether or not a particular small town will be one of reasonably prosperous service establishments, while a neighboring town will die, but also much else about the lives of those who supply the Wal-Mart stores and work there. This is the exercise of power that must be incorporated into the discussion of big firms if that discussion is to have relevance in public discourse. Americans may have accepted the reality of large firms, but they continue to worry over and discuss their impact, often in a fragmented way for want of a clear framework of reasonably objective analysis.[1]

Fortunately, business strategists have supplied the needed framework. Those who advise and instruct in what is required for successful management of modern firms will recognize that the expanded view of the firm as an organization that must engage in $M \rightarrow C \rightarrow C' \rightarrow M'$ bears a close relationship to the formulation of those who write of "value chains" or "supply chains."[2] Beginning in the 1980s, Michael Porter and other scholars of business strategy began to talk of these chains as key to good management. In Porter's words, a value chain is a tool that can be used "to disaggregate buyers, suppliers, and a firm into the discrete but interrelated activities from which value stems," with value being "prices lower than competitiors' for equivalent benefits, or the provision of unique benefits that more than offset a premium price" (Porter 1985: xvi).

Although Porter did not cite Chandler's descriptions of the strategies of Standard Oil, he might well have done so, and his notion of a "value chain" might also have been used to describe the development of the integrated rail systems as well. Indeed, Marx's capitalists of the mid-nineteenth century could be said to have been successful if they managed well their value chains, and Wal-Mart has clearly succeeded in the twentieth and twenty-first centuries by similar control. It is this control that can be used most effectively to explain both the heroic side of the achievements of Rockefeller and Walton and to explore the darker side as well. To that end, we need to deconstruct the supply chains of each. We will begin with the acquisition of M and the transformation of M into physical inputs ($M \rightarrow C$), proceed to the acquisition and production process itself ($C \rightarrow C'$), and finally move only to the sale of output, or $C' \rightarrow M'$. Although Porter does not use exactly this same terminology, his illustration (Porter 1985: 5) of the five competitive forces that determine competitiveness contains the same vector, with the addition of potential entrants into the industry and potential substitute products or services.

$M \rightarrow C$

Both Rockefeller and Walton understood the importance of a sufficient source of finance from the very beginning. Rockefeller, when he first moved into the oil industry with the establishment of the Excelsior Works in 1863, had already established a network of relationships with Cleveland bankers. He used funds from his successful commodity business to take his first step into the oil business when, with his partner, Maurice Clark, he invested $4,000 to establish the partnership with Samuel Andrews, a man who knew how to turn crude oil into kerosene (Chernow 1998: 105). However, it was Rockefeller's network of banking connections that quickly became crucial to his success.

> It is impossible to comprehend Rockefeller's breathtaking ascent without realizing that he always moved into battle backed by abundant cash. Whether riding out downturns or coasting on booms, he kept plentiful reserves and won many bidding contests simply because his war chest was deeper.
>
> (Chernow 1998: 105)

By way of illustration, Chernow quotes from Rockefeller's own reminiscences:

> It [the purchase of a refinery] required many hundreds of thousands of dollars – and in cash; securities would not answer. I received the message at about noon, and had to get off on the 3 o'clock train. I drove from bank to bank, asking each president or cashier, whomever I could find first, to get ready for me all the funds he could possibly lay hands on. I told them I would be back to get the money later. I rounded up all of our banks in the city, and made a second journey to get the money, and kept going until I secured the necessary amount. With this I was off on the 3 o'clock train, and closed the transaction.
>
> (Chernow 1998: 105)

That Rockefeller was good for the borrowed funds was crucial in his expansion of sources of funding, and the expansion of lines of credit also served him well in becoming more and more successful. This rather obvious fact makes clear the importance of viewing the firm as an evolving entity. Success bred success. It also serves to emphasize the importance of the bargaining power of the borrower. The recent history of the firm and of those associated with it means that not all firms enter the M→C phase of the value chain on equal footing, with price of money the only important variable.

A not dissimilar story can be told about Sam Walton. In Chapter 2, I noted that Walton, through marriage, gained his first connection to a bank, but it is obvious from his own autobiography and from other accounts that he also went about establishing a network of bankers. And, like Rockefeller, he appreciated the importance of taking on debt even as he continued to live frugally and put his own funds into Wal-Mart. Here are his own words:

From the time I took out my first bank loan ... I was never really comfortable with debt. But I recognized it as a necessity of doing business, and I had gotten pretty good at accumulating it. For a while, I would just go down to the local bank and borrow whatever I could to build a store or buy something we needed to grow the business. That practice had gotten me in debt to practically every bank in Arkansas and southern Missouri ...[;] sometimes I would borrow from one to pay the other.

Walton goes on to say that along the way he bought a bank and studied bankers and "how they liked to do business." And, he continues,

I struck up a relationship with a guy named Jimmy Jones at Republic Bank down in Dallas, and he loaned us a million dollars. And, of course, I had tried all along to attract some equity investment from our store managers and a few relatives. So by 1970, we had seventy-eight partners invested in our company, which really wasn't one company, but thirty-two different stores owned by a combination of different folks.

(Walton 1992: 92–3)

By 1970, Wal-Mart had gone public and thereby gained additional funds to continue expansion. Although Walton, in his autobiography, adopts an "aw-shucks" and disapproving tone about debt and incorporation as a public company, it is very clear that he, like Rockefeller, understood the need to have always at hand a line of credit with which to expand the supply chain.[3]

Although the acquisition of funds has not been a direct focus of protests against Wal-Mart, nor was it in the case of Standard Oil, expanded treatment of the firm reveals the importance of power gained in both cases by a combination of the luck of being in the right place at the right time, the skill of Rockefeller and Walton in human relations, and their intelligence in money management, as well as the sheer chutzpah of both in being willing to take on enormous amounts of debt. Recognition of the role that power in the market for funds actually played in both cases serves to cast doubt upon two enduring stories about the finance of big business in the US, stories that have served to quiet concern about these firms.

The first story, and one that requires a bit of a detour in the deconstruction of the supply chains, is that great inequality in the distribution of income was not only a consequence of the growth of the large-scale business firms of the late nineteenth and early twentieth centuries but also in itself an engine of further growth and remains so even today. Crucial to this story is the notion that the capitalists who create large firms – in our case Rockefeller and Walton – get their start and perpetuate their enterprise through their own frugality and by plowing revenues back into their businesses. That both Rockefeller and Walton were thrifty and perhaps even stingy men lends a kind of surface credence to this version of events. More important support comes, however, from the long and serious intellectual pedigree of the notion that capitalist accumulation by the capitalists themselves is essential for economic growth.

A recurring justification of a highly skewed income distribution derives from the argument that profits are reinvested and lead to growth that is good for all. In Adam Smith's version of the good economy, normal profits, augmented by the services of bankers who would make the capital (meaning in this case money) of a nation "active and productive" would be used by thrifty businessmen to engage more employees and purchase more physical capital and so enhance the output per unit of labor. Thus would nations grow. Karl Marx thought much the same thing would happen but with a twist: an inexorable process would lead to an eventual replacement of labor by accumulated capital (meaning in this case physical capital in the form of machines) with resulting impoverishment of workers and eventually revolution. Following Smith and Marx, economists have created hundreds of variations on these themes, with the common element of most being that without disparity in income distribution a sufficiency of saving would not be possible to finance economic growth.

The reality is that Walton and Rockefeller borrowed almost all of the funds that were required for growth of their firms. They borrowed those funds from banks that were, in the modern parlance, leveraging debt in anticipation of repayments to come. It is the ability of borrowers to repay out of earnings that determines the ability of banks to continue such leverage, not a squirreling away of funds prior to the bank funds being lent. Prior saving, whether directly by the individuals who created the large firms or by others, was simply not a necessary condition of the growth of businesses.[4] Nevertheless, the beat for inequality as a necessary condition of further growth goes on. In an article on "The Inequality Conundrum" in *The New York Times*, Roger Lowenstein asks, "how can you promote equality without killing off the genie of American prosperity?" (Lowenstein: June 10, 2007).

A variation on the theme that the inequality of income distribution is itself a cause of economic growth comes in the argument that great incomes are the reward for extraordinary ability (comparable perhaps to that of highly paid star athletes) and risk taken. In "The Richest of the Rich, Proud of a New Gilded Age," a story about the super-rich of the current era, Louis Uchitelle, another *New York Times* reporter, wrote:

Other very wealthy men in the new Gilded Age talk of themselves as having a flair for business not unlike Derek Jeter's "unique talent" for baseball, as Leo J. Hindery Jr. [creator of a cable television sports network] put it. "I think there are people ... who because of their uniqueness warrant whatever the market will bear."

The new tycoons describe a history that gives them a heroic role. The American economy, they acknowledge, did grow more rapidly on average in the decades immediately after World War II than it is growing today. Incomes rose faster than inflation for most Americans and the spread between rich and poor was much less. But the United States was far and away the dominant economy, and government played a strong supporting role. In such a world, the new tycoons argue, business leaders needed only to be good managers

Then, with globalization, with America competing once again for first place as strenuously as it had in the first Gilded Age, the need grew for a different type of business leader – one more entrepreneurial, more daring, more willing to take risks, more like the rough and tumble tycoons of the first Gilded Age.

(Uchitelle: July 15, 2007)

The arguments of the "new tycoons" can be found in drier form in the literature of economics where, going back at least until the time of the older tycoons of the 1880s and 90s, similar arguments were put forth.[5] And, in the absence of any independent measure of the "extraordinary ability" relative to sheer luck of highly successful entrepreneurs, it is hard to gainsay the claims of the new tycoons. To this one may add the powerful argument put forth by yet another economist, Joseph A. Schumpeter, who argued that even if not fully justified by the effort involved, large fortunes were the prize required to call for the efforts of entrepreneurs in our pecuniary society. "Plausible," as opposed to idealized textbook capitalism, in Schumpeter's words, is a system in which promises of wealth are

not proffered at random; yet there is a sufficiently enticing admixture of chance: the game is not like roulette, it is more like poker. They [the pecuniary rewards] are addressed to ability, energy and supernormal capacity for work; but if there were a way of measuring either that ability in general or the personal achievement that goes into any particular success, the premiums actually paid out would probably not be found proportional to either. Spectacular prizes much greater than would have been necessary to call forth the particular effort are thrown to a small minority of winners, thus propelling much more efficaciously than a more equal and "just" distribution would....

(Schumpeter 1994: 73–4)

Surely Schumpeter's point does seem to apply to both Walton and Rockefeller, men who were driven to success, but it is worth stressing that it was the possibility of the big pecuniary prize rather than their own frugality or the prior existence of income inequality that would in a Schumpeterian world explain their success in acquiring the M of the $M \rightarrow C$ portion of the value chain.

There is, however, a second story about finance of big business that should be considered. This is the story of the textbooks in economics, a story in which the funds required for establishment of large-scale business enterprise were beyond those that could be amassed by an individual or a small group of individuals organized as partners. The story continues that "the size of the mill" dictated by technological advance was such that a pooling of funds from many individuals was required, and the modern corporate form of business organization was created to meet this need. Unfortunately, the textbook story simply does not fit very well what happened in the cases of Standard Oil or Wal-Mart.

During the crucial decade of the 1870s, and, in fact, up until the creation of the Standard Oil Trust in 1882, the refineries that Rockefeller controlled were in reality "a far-flung patchwork of firms, each nominally independent," and the funds that had been raised to create this patchwork had, as in the case of the parent company, Standard Oil of Ohio, come from small groups of investors usually organized as partners (Chernow 1998: 224). When the original Standard Oil was incorporated in 1870, shares were closely held by the original partners (Rockefeller, Andrews, and Flagler) and a few others. Not only were outside investors scarce, but the intent of raising additional funds was less to afford new and expensive equipment than to take advantage of their already existing control over some 10 percent of American refining capacity in order to "devise a comprehensive solution for the industry" (Chernow 1998: 130). Although Chernow writes that Rockefeller "needed money to create economies of scale," he goes on in a somewhat more descriptive vein to say that he also needed money "to endure downturns" and, in Rockefeller's own words, "to buy in the many refineries that were a source of overproduction and confusion" (Chernow 1998: 130–2).

When the Standard Oil Trust was formed, the total capitalization was some $70 million, and it controlled 90 percent of refining capacity and the same group of Cleveland insiders owned most of the shares. Chernow's description of the effect of the creation of negotiable securities, something new when the Trust was formed, is interesting:

For the first time, the trust's formation created negotiable securities, and this profoundly affected the Standard Oil culture. Not only did Rockefeller urge underlings to take stock but made money abundantly available to do so. As such shareholding became wide spread, it welded the organization more tightly together, creating an esprit de corps that helped in steamrolling over competitors and government investigators alike. With employees receiving huge capital gains and dividends, they converted Standard Oil into a holy crusade. Rockefeller hoped the trust would serve as a model for a new populist capitalism marked by employee share ownership. "I would have every man a capitalist, every man, woman and child," he said. "I would have everyone save his earnings, not squander it: own the industries, own the railroads, own the telegraph lines."

(Chernow 1998: 227)

A fine vision, to be sure, but there is little in Chernow's account that upholds the view that such investments by the masses, or even by the few, were required to build the basic refining capacity. That was financed through the short-term borrowing already described.

Wal-Mart's story is similar in that it was a highly successful company well before it went public. Walton describes how he and his associates restructured the debt of the company in 1969, securing a large loan from Mass Mutual, but concluding that "I was tired of owing money to people I knew, and was even more tired of begging money from strangers" (Walton 1992: 95). However, in going public, Wal-Mart, like Standard, remained closely held by long-time associates and, like Standard, was already well on the way to its dominant position by the time shares were publicly issued. And, even though Wal-Mart is not thought of as operating in the kind of high-fixed-cost industries said to have required the corporate revolution of the late nineteenth century, the pattern of their incorporation bears close resemblance to the common pattern of that period. Based on a study of the financial histories of the meat packing and sugar refining industries, William Doyle concluded that

[t]he new financial developments which accompanied the corporate revolution of the late nineteenth century, in fact, had far less to do with obtaining funds from savers than with changing, establishing or formalizing relationships within and between existing businesses. These new relationships enabled business to manage their internal affairs and coordinate their activities with other firms in ways that would have been impossible before.

(Doyle 1993: 223)

From reconstruction of late-nineteenth-century accounts, Doyle concluded that, at least in meat packing and sugar refining, two industries that became highly concentrated, the personal resources of a small circle of owners in combination with "the use of commercial bank credit, single name commercial paper and borrowing on open account from suppliers" plus quick turnover of working capital was sufficient to fund expansion of productive capacity (Doyle 1993: 226–7). Going public after large size was achieved allowed owners to liquefy portions of their equity and to manage debt more effectively. And so it was with Standard and with Wal-Mart.

Return now to the $M \to C$ portion of the supply chain and the analysis of power as exercised by large firms. The assertion at the end of Chapter 5 was that concentration on $C \to C'$ only leaves out a lot of the power of large firms that concerns the public. It seems clear enough from the descriptions given here of the way in which Standard Oil and Wal-Mart were financed, and from the apparent typicality of that finance, that the ability of highly successful businessmen in America, even today, does not depend so much upon an impersonal stock market as upon connections and networks. It remains unproven here how seriously tilted by gender, ethnicity, race, class, or other factors John Bates Clark's desired level playing field may be in the first phases of the supply chain, but it does seem pretty clear that power is required to produce the kind of well-plowed field that yields ready money.[6] Even though it is not exactly news that power, whether it derives from force of personality, from skill, or factors perhaps less justifiable, matters in getting started, it is a reality that needs to be acknowledged.

There is an added twist to concerns about equality of business opportunity in the world in which Sam Walton and his associates have operated. Beginning in the 1930s, some economically depressed towns in the South began to raise money from the public to help underwrite the costs of building new factories. In some cases, those who would be employees agreed to deductions from their pay checks in order to establish "building funds.[7] These highly local efforts became more sophisticated and more lucrative to would-be investors after World War II and played at least some role in the economic growth of the US "Sunbelt." Whatever their initial justification and importance, such subsidies continue today, and Wal-Mart is one firm that has benefited substantially. By one account, over $1 billion in state and local subsidies, in the form of free or reduced-cost land, tax reductions, infrastructure assistance, job training and recruiting funds, and assorted other assistance programs, were granted to Wal-Mart prior to 2004 (Feder: May 4, 2004). Such programs differ in range from the nineteenth-century land grants to railroads but not in their effect of offsetting the need for funds. Where they do differ from those earlier subsidies is that they are now available to a range of industries and from a variety of governments at various levels. Those who can court local and state officials as well as bankers will find it easier to get the required M to make the first $M \rightarrow C$ steps, and this makes access to the playing field an even more complicated one for would-be players.

$C \rightarrow C'$

Considerable attention, acrimony, and analysis have been focused on the $C \rightarrow C'$ portion of the supply chains of Standard Oil and Wal-Mart, and for good reason. A realistic diagram of both firms would show multiple arrows, each representing a separate and subsidiary supply chain, feeding into the C of our simplified supply chain. Acquisition of C then led to the actual transformation of C into C', which is the phase of the supply chain in which economies of scale are supposed to operate. Comparison of this phase of the supply chain for two firms as different as Standard Oil and Wal-Mart might seem impossible. Standard Oil was a manufacturing firm; it took crude oil and turned it into other products. Wal-Mart, on the other hand, is, above all, a retailer, a firm that acquires already manufactured goods and puts them on shelves for purchase by end users.

What makes comparison of $C \rightarrow C'$ of the two firms more reasonable is that Wal-Mart is not the retailer of old who purchased goods from independent producers, and perhaps from independent wholesalers, and then put the goods on the shelves. As Nelson Lichtenstein, in summarizing the work of Bonacich, has written about the containers that bring goods across the Pacific to the Wal-Mart distribution centers:

> these containers are "pulled" across the Pacific, not "pushed." In a push system, characteristic of manufacturing in the last century ... [goods were] pushed out to retailers.... But under the pull system, the retailer tracks consumer behavior with meticulous care and then transmits consumer preferences down the supply chain. Replenishment is put in motion almost immediately, with the supplier required to make more frequent deliveries of smaller lots. This is just-in-time for retailers, or "lean retailing." To make it all work, the supply firms and the discount retailers have to be functionally linked, even if they retain a separate legal and administrative existence. Wal-Mart is therefore not simply a huge retailer, but increasingly a manufacturing giant in all but name.
>
> (Lichtenstein 2006: 11–12)

The fundamental difference between Standard Oil and Wal-Mart is in the legal forms of organization, about which more will be said later in this chapter, and not in the nature of what they did as firms. And, for both firms the acquisition of C and the transformation of C into C′ blur together and require more than a simple arrow of movement through the chain.

For Standard Oil the most important arrow would have been the one that ran from the oil-producing regions, but there would have been other arrows indicating acquisition of the chemicals used to "clean" (refine) the oil, the barrels used for storage and shipping, the tank cars, the railroad services, and the labor involved to put all of these together. Much of the story of Standard that has already been told in Chapters Two and Three involved the way in which Rockefeller was able to use his negotiating skill and power to make arrangements for acquisition of these inputs that were advantageous to Standard Oil. These are the stories that would fit into the space between the suppliers and the firm/industry box in Porter's diagram. I shall not repeat the details of these stories here but will use a brief review to note that Standard's advantage was, as Veblen would have emphasized, one of management of the interstices between the suppliers and Standard. Further, the way in which Rockefeller and associates managed the C→C′ portion of the supply chain illustrates Chandler's proposition that "once successfully established, an administrative hierarchy" becomes "itself a source of permanence for administrative coordination." It also illustrates Porter's point that strategy makes the structure of the market. The same points will become obvious as we review Wal-Mart's story as well.

Rockefeller began his march to almost total control of the American petroleum industry by working with the railroads to secure favorable rates in exchange for guarantees of large daily shipments of refined oil from Cleveland. He then moved on to "bring order" (his phrase) to the chaos that threatened the entire industry in the early 1870s, as ease of entry into both refining and drilling resulted in falling prices and widespread business failure. In this he was guided, in the words of Chernow, by a vision of the industry "as a gigantic, interrelated mechanism" (Chernow 1998: 130). Having secured control of competing refiners in Cleveland, and in the process secured contracts that would prevent their later reentry into the industry, he shut down less efficient refineries, coordinated production in those with then up-to-date facilities, and began expansion to take advantage of such economies of scale in production as were possible with the batch technology that continued to prevail in the industry.[8] And, he moved to purchase, either with cash or Standard Oil stock, control over refineries elsewhere, a move that was made more urgent by recurring "overproduction" of both crude and refined products.

Only by limiting production of crude and by ensuring that control over refining capacity, once obtained, would remain in effect when the spread between crude and refined prices increased and made reentry into refining a serious temptation could Rockefeller ensure himself a steady profit on his large volume of output. Already regarded as an evil force in the oil-producing regions, Rockefeller had in 1874 put together a network of short-distance pipelines to move crude from well head to railroads in the producing regions, and this system, in combination with storage tanks, allowed tight control of whose oil could be moved from well to market. As new fields were discovered and output expanded, his restrictive actions in taking oil caused a massive uproar.

It was clear that Rockefeller had by this time put in place an administrative hierarchy that enabled him to move quickly and decisively. Chernow tells us that when a torrent of new oil was brought into production in the Bradford, Pennsylvania, area in 1875–6, Rockefeller was able to expand tank capacity in the region from one million to 4.5 million barrels in only eight months and was able to hook up five new wells a day to the network (Chernow 1998: 197–8). This took ready finance and administrative coordination, two elements in place for Rockefeller but not for the competitors who had been left in the shade. It also extended the power of Rockefeller and his associates, especially when Standard's United Pipeline, the feeder lines from wells to railheads, refused to take oil not already sold. This forced producers to sell to Standard, or, rather, to the purchasing agent for Standard, Jebez A. Bostwick & Company, at what were often ruinously low prices (Williamson and Daum 1959: 384). According to Williamson and Daum:

> By refusing to run crude from the wells unless it was sold, United forced many producers into distress sales, primarily to Standard agents, at prices ranging between $2\frac{1}{2}$ and 25¢ a barrel below the prices quoted in the oil exchanges, which by 1879 averaged below $1.00 per barrel.
>
> (Williamson and Daum 1959: 384)

To the producers, who paraded in protest at night covered with sheets even as they negotiated with Standard for shipment of their oil by day, this smacked of high-handed exploitation. It can, of course, also be described as the result of the increased finance and administrative coordination that Rockefeller was using to bring order to the "gigantic and interrelated mechanism" that the petroleum industry had become.

At the same time, Rockefeller's increasingly dominant role in the petroleum mechanism can be described in terms of the effects that it had on the individuals and communities involved in the various parts of the supply chain from M→C→C'. As Rockefeller bought up control in competing refineries, he aroused protest, particularly from those who would later complain that they had been forced to sell out for prices that were unfairly low. As Chernow and others have observed, Rockefeller most likely paid reasonable prices at the time of purchase, in most cases a time of distress in the industry. Whether or not the charges of unfairness that form so much of Tarbell's muckraking account are true or simply a delayed form of seller's regret in the face of the later prosperity of the industry cannot be determined with certainty. What is certain is that Rockefeller's success prevented other owners from enjoying the kind of fortune that he amassed. In the words of Veblen, words similar to those used earlier by John Stuart Mill, Rockefeller assumed the role of "chief of business men" who cast out others.

It was not a pretty process for many. Here is a description from Chernow of the effect on Cleveland society:

> The oil wars of 1872 turned Cleveland society upside down. Many who had made easy fortunes in oil refining and built splendid mansions on Euclid Avenue found themselves bankrupt and forced to sell. Whether it was Rockefeller or the slumping oil market that forced them to sell their refineries at distress-sale prices, they chose to see Rockefeller as the author of their woes. It is likely that in many cases the marketplace would eventually have closed their unprofitable firms, but Rockefeller certainly speeded up the winnowing. Though several independent refiners held on for a few years, in most cases this merely postponed the day of reckoning. Ella Grant Wilson, a social chronicler of nineteenth-century Cleveland, recalled how her father, a partner in the refinery of Grant, Foote and Company, had befriended Rockefeller in various Baptist causes but refused to join Standard Oil, convinced it would fail. When it became impossible to compete with this leviathan, his refinery went bankrupt, and he surrendered his life savings. "Father went almost insane over this terrible upset to his business. He walked the house night and day ... [He] left the church and never entered a church afterward. His whole life was embittered...."
>
> (Chernow 1998: 147–8)

Chernow concludes that, "With so many losers in the struggle – and one shrewd gigantic winner – it comes as no surprise to learn that John D. Rockefeller had made his first group of implacable enemies" (Chernow 1998: 147–8).

There were, of course, others whose prospects for a life of riches were now being ruined, apparently by Rockefeller. The oil producers who banded together in 1872 in one of the early efforts to combat the organizing efforts of Rockefeller are described by Tarbell as a diverse band of men, some of whom were producing thousands of barrels a day while others produced "scarcely ten." Some were "college-bred" and others "signed their names with an effort." Some "came from the East with comfortable sums to invest" while others had "first wells that they had 'kicked down' themselves" (Tarbell 1904: 110). What all had in common was great hope for oil-funded riches:

> If he had been contented to economise and to accept small gains, even the small producer could live on a much lower price than three dollars; but nobody in the Oil Regions in 1872 looked with favour on economy, and everybody despised small things. The oil men as a class had been brought up to enormous profits, and held an entirely false standard of values.... They had seen nothing but the extreme of fortune.
>
> (Tarbell 1904: 112–13)

But they, like Wilson, now faced ruin at the hands, or so it seemed, of Rockefeller. Others, too, were broken. Chernow tells the story of Colonel Joseph D. Potts, whose title came from the Civil War and whose training was that of a civil engineer. He was the creator of a subsidiary of the Pennsylvania Railroad, the Empire Transportation Company, which had five hundred miles of pipeline and a thousand tank cars which, by arrangement with the Pennsylvania Railroad, were to pay a regular toll to use the tracks of Philadelphia & Erie, with the Empire Company to receive a mileage allowance and a drawback of one-third of the toll (Chernow 1998: 201; Williamson and Daum 1959: 174–5). Rockefeller was incensed that the Pennsylvania Railroad, a major carrier for Standard, would allow the Empire Company to enter what he regarded as his territory, buying refineries in New York, Philadelphia, and Pittsburgh, and he went to war with them:

> In spring 1877, Rockefeller told railroad officials point-blank that if Empire didn't retreat from refining, Standard Oil would divert its shipments to other railroads. When they didn't flinch, Rockefeller launched an all-out attack. To starve out the railroad, he idled all his Pittsburgh refineries and ordered corresponding increases in output in his Cleveland refineries.... Turning to the two railroads long solidly in his corner, the Erie and the New York Central, Rockefeller had them trim rates to ratchet up the pressure.... To handle the extra volume expected on these two railroads, Flagler negotiated a deal with William Vanderbilt to build another six hundred tank cars. With blazing speed, Rockefeller was on his way to humbling the world's

largest freight carrier, a company long thought invincible in the business and political world.

(Chernow 1998: 201)

The Pennsylvania Railroad survived, but Colonel Potts, in some ways a bit player in the battle, was left "a broken, humiliated man." Chernow adds that Tarbell romanticized him as "an incorruptible martyr, the Abraham Lincoln of the oil industry," when in reality he was "just an able, aggressive businessman who lost out in a power struggle to a shrewder, bolder opponent" (Chernow 1998: 203). By the 1880s, Potts was a director of a Standard Oil pipeline subsidiary.

These are dramatic and sometimes sad stories. But, from the standpoint of the normal theory of the firm, Rockefeller's actions were simple and straightforward: he lowered costs of C. From the M→C perspective, Rockefeller not only got his crude oil at a good price; he also ensured that his refineries could run full with an assured supply. But to the producers and competitors, Rockefeller destroyed their roles in an industry that might have brought them far greater riches. How they might all have prospered is not, in retrospect, clear, for in the absence of order the petroleum industry would have continued as chaotic and tumultuous as it was in the early 1870s, with alternating periods of prosperity and ruin. What seems more likely is that in the absence of Rockefeller, then someone else, someone whose name is now lost to history, would have imposed similar order.

This deterministic view need not rest upon a notion of history as foreordained but can be drawn from the contingency-based analysis of both Veblen and Chandler, as well as of Michael Porter. The organizational forms in place when the new technologies of drilling and refining were developed were such that the opportunities to bridge the interstices and provide administrative coordination of interrelated processes would have produced supply chains and processes much like those that Rockefeller produced, even if he had not been in Cleveland when the oil industry began. To say this is not to deny either the contingency or the role of social structure in thrusting some individuals and not others into lead roles. All of this is important, but it is even more important to recognize that all of the conditions, the forms of business organization, the way in which finance was organized, the technologies developed in the oil fields and in the centers of refining, as well as the opportunities for use of the final products, shaped John D. Rockefeller and his actions as much as he shaped these circumstances.

It is also worth commenting that there must always be for individuals living through episodes of change such as that which produced Rockefeller and his triumphant firm a disconcerting element of luck in the outcomes of such cumulatively causative processes as the one that produced Rockefeller and Standard Oil. In his novel *The Hazard of New Fortunes*, William Dean Howells tells the story of how otherwise unremarkable people are lifted by sheer luck into positions of great riches. Indeed, the theme is one that resonates throughout the literature of the period. Rockefeller had more than luck; he was without doubt brilliant and hardworking. But, he was also lucky just as others, perhaps also brilliant and hard-working, were not. Such is the messy world of both economic and social reality; it is not the theoretical world of John Bates Clark's fair returns to all.

Nor is the world of Sam Walton well told by use of Clark's model or, for that matter, by use of Coasean elegance. Just as was the case with Rockefeller, Walton took advantage of the opportunities provided by new technologies to assure supplies and to assure deliveries of those supplies at prices favorable to his firms. Some of the ways in which Walton and his associates built their computer network in order to achieve this and the way, as they tell it, that they eased traditionally adversarial relationships between suppliers and buyers were recounted in Chapters Two and Three. With computer tracking of inventories and with Retail-Link, the software that they provided their suppliers for tracking orders and inventories, both suppliers and Wal-Mart administrative staff in Bentonville could move quickly to acquire goods as customers took them off shelves so that "out-of-stock" or "waiting for restocking" signs were not likely to confront the millions who sought the everyday low prices.

There is, of course, a much darker side to this story as well and one that gives further emphasis to two points about the general $M \rightarrow C \rightarrow C' \rightarrow M'$, or supply chain, process. The first has to do with the exercise of power that goes well beyond negotiation of price and time of delivery. The second involves the multiple dimensions of outcomes.

First, consider power. One of the things for which Wal-Mart has been most harshly criticized is the ability of the firm to push costs of holding goods to producers, often small-scale producers. To understand this charge and the importance for Wal-Mart of the process that led to the charges, consider this description by Bianco:

> The leverage that Wal-Mart exercises over its suppliers is grounded as much in its masterful use of technology as its brandishing of the club of foreign sourcing. From the introduction of bar codes and scanning devices to the innovations of electronic data interchange and Radio Frequency Identification (RFIT) tagging, Wal-Mart has blazed the way in using the power of information technology to remake the

entire consumer products supply chain over the last three decades. Tens of billions of dollars of capital investment by Wal-Mart and by other big retail chains has enthroned "just-in-time" or "lean retailing" as the regulator of the U.S. consumer industry.

(Bianco 2006: 178)

Actually, lean production and "just-in-time" inventory management gained its greatest early fame in manufacturing industries when Japanese automobile manufacturers, and later Boeing and Dell and other companies in the US, began to manufacture output in rapid-fire response to changes in demand, thus avoiding the costs of holding inventories. The perception was that such manufacturing would reduce overall costs to the economy because fewer goods would be held in idle status. When, however, this approach is employed in retail and with multiple suppliers, many of them of small scale, the saving is more likely to be to the purchasing firm, Wal-Mart in this case, and the aggregate effect one of shifting rather than saved costs.[9] A simplified example will suffice: If Wal-Mart does not want shipment of shirts until the last possible minute and if those shirts take some days to cut and assemble in a far-away factory, then the factory owner will have to assume the costs of having money tied up in the shirts (money already paid to workers but not yet received from Wal-Mart) and of storage.[10] Speed, be it noted, is indeed important, but it is speed in transformation of M into M' and not of C into C' that matters to Wal-Mart.

The second point, a simple one indeed that is illustrated by looking at the darker side of Wal-Mart's power in dealing with its suppliers, is that there are no easy conclusions to be reached about the advantages and disadvantages that the Wal-Mart system has introduced for mankind. Many commentators on Wal-Mart have noted that it is a terrible thing to be a Wal-Mart supplier but a terrible thing not to be one as well. (The same could be said of the oil producers in regard to Standard Oil, which is why they wore sheets to protest by night but negotiated by day). For producers of goods, signing on with Wal-Mart can guarantee a substantial market, but it will be a substantial market that will be served according to Wal-Mart's dictates, of which the most important is to keep costs to a minimum. The very real threat of finding overseas suppliers has been used to persuade domestic producers to look for ways to reduce costs, and the use of the latest technology for shipping and communication has made that threat real. At the same time, foreign purchases have provided opportunities for sale in the US (and now other Wal-Mart-served) markets but have also entailed cost-containment for the producers.

The Wal-Mart squeeze cycle, as Petra Rivoli and her source in the field, Auggie Tantillo, describe it, goes like this:

Wal-Mart ... supplies about 25 percent of the U.S. apparel market with goods that are virtually all imported from abroad. While Wal-Mart's provision of cheaper and cheaper imports is unquestionably a boon to the apparel consumer and to the economy at large, virtually every aspect of the firm's behavior has drawn protests, and the very behavior that gives consumers a windfall is at the same time the target of critics. Protestors want Wal-Mart to stop their union-bashing, and to improve its pay and benefits for employees. The company is also criticized for its merciless squeeze on supplier pricing, and for its failure to effectively monitor the working conditions in the overseas factories that produce the apparel for its stores. The cheap apparel itself is blamed for the demise of South Carolina textile mills, and the laid-off textile workers complain that the only jobs left when the mills closed were as checkout clerks behind the enemy lines, because Wal-Mart had also squeezed out the smaller stores on Main Street.... Wal-Mart's squeeze on its American suppliers has bankrupted them, and led the firm to China where it squeezes Chinese suppliers, who in turn squeeze their own suppliers as well as their sweatshop workers. At the end of the squeeze cycle, we can buy our T-shirts for 25 cents less, so on average we are richer, but at what cost?

(Rivoli 2005: 150)

And, in China,

Thanks to globalization, the sweatshop, and the race to the bottom, He Yuan Zhi of Shanghai Brightness [a T-shirt factory in Shanghai] doesn't worry about being stuck on the farm anymore. She married when and whom she chose, she makes her own living and her own choices ... she works 50 hours per week and not 80, she can read and write, and her children can too.

(Rivoli 2005: 107)

As Rivoli says, "the bottom is rising" but Americans are buying from that bottom of the supply heap, which is where Walton and associates have led us in spite of their brave 1984 vow to "Buy American," at least when price allowed. The triumph of Wal-Mart over Main Street merchants, South Carolina textile workers, Kmart and other big box firms has a different face than Rockefeller's triumph over the gamblers of the Oil Regions, Potts, and Ella Grant Wilson's father, but it is the same story. The ability to acquire C at low cost counts for a lot in the success of a firm and low cost involves power. It also carries a diversity of outcomes that are not easily summarized by simple consideration of incomes and costs of living of affected parties. It is not therefore surprising that there is a diversity of stories about the multiple ways in which lives were changed by exercise of this power.

It is also important to recognize that both Rockefeller and Walton, along with their associates, were masters in transforming C into C' with enormous efficiency. In Rockefeller's case, we have ample evidence, already mentioned in Chapters Two and Three, that he was an efficiency demon, finding ways to reduce costs of relatively minor inputs (the sealant for barrels, for example) and always alert to waste in production, and we also know that Standard was quick to adopt new technologies. So, too, was Walton keen on finding every cost saving possible as he moved goods from the warehouse to the shopping carts of customers, a pattern that was apparent even before the IT innovations began. Indeed, one analyst noting the remarkable increase in labor productivity in retail trade during recent decades attributes most of it to organizational innovations made by Wal-Mart:

> At least half of Wal-Mart's productivity edge stems from managerial innovations that improve the efficiency of stores and have nothing to do with IT; employees who have been cross-trained, for instance, can function effectively in more than one department at a time. Better training of cashiers and monitoring of utilization can increase productivity rates at checkout counters by 10 to 20 percent.
>
> (Johnson 2002: 40)

Nevertheless, it seems obvious that economies in production as such do not account for the initial advantages that both Rockefeller and Walton created and on which they capitalized as they built their empires. Both were quick to adopt new techniques of production, or, in the case of Walton, new techniques of moving and distributing goods, but their initial advantage did not come from greater efficiency in transforming C into C'. This is a point that deserves emphasis, for the standard story about "the size of the mill" and its relationship to firm size is that technology required a large firm from the beginning. This was true for the railroads, and with John Bates Clark's leap of reason, it came to be assumed that it was true of all successful large firms. While it does seem to have been the case that administratively induced growth in the size of firms led to adoption of technologies that did involve economies of scale, this is a process through time. An explanation of initial advantage must therefore be sought elsewhere, and in the case of Rockefeller and Walton it seems reasonable on the basis of evidence reviewed so far to conclude that what allowed their firms to achieve initial advantage was their ability to harness M in order to acquire C and to acquire both C and distribution of C′ at low cost; this accounted for most of their success. Both were also good at the final step of the value chain.

C′→M′

Before further consideration of the ways in which Standard Oil and Wal-Mart organized marketing of output, some things need to be said about how difficult treatment of this portion of the supply chain is for economists. As recounted in earlier chapters, a major part of the evolution of economic thought about the firm that came with the rise of large business can be explained as an effort to retain the essence of Adam Smith's very powerful argument about the efficacy of the invisible hand of competition even in the face of a radically altered structure of production and distribution. Economies of scale, due somehow to "the size of the mill," and restrictions on unfair practices were called forth as reasons to believe that in an economy of large firms that unseen hand could still serve to preclude unfair manipulation of prices. However, even with those amendments to the Smithian system, faith in the invisible hand would have been severely shaken – and perhaps destroyed – had economists admitted the possibility that firms could significantly determine consumer wants.

If even under otherwise largely competitive circumstances it could be shown that firms affected consumer preferences either by direct advertising or by some other form of social manipulation (for example, in the world of today by sponsorship of entertainment and sporting events that establish what are seen as desirable patterns of behavior), then it becomes much harder to conclude that the best interests of society are necessarily and always served by reliance on an invisible hand. To pick an obvious and perhaps unfair example, if cigarette companies were, let us say, able, by advertising, by distribution of free cigarettes to soldiers during World War II, or by other means of persuasion, to increase the number of smokers, it would not be possible to argue that cigarette use was simply a matter of consumer choice. Firms, even those guided by an invisible hand, could be held accountable for more than pricing policy.

Even for products far less addictive and less obviously dangerous to health than cigarettes, economists shy from allowing for producer effects on consumer choice and consumer spending. In a careful review of the literature on this topic, John Kenneth Galbraith found economists willing to accept that consumers adjust their preferences to changes in the cost functions of producers which are transmitted through the market. That is, if it becomes possible to produce a new product or an older product at lower cost, this information will be transmitted to consumers, who will respond according to their own independently formed tastes and preferences. Using the current language of standard microeconomics, advertising outlays will tend to be optimally (for society) chosen by firms operating under guidance of the invisible hand in order to convey this information.[11] Galbraith found, however, very little support for the view that consumer behavior is managed through a wide variety of mechanisms of which advertising is only the most obvious.[12] Consumer sovereignty is always assumed and consumption "is a process by which the individual imposes his will on the producer" (Galbraith 1970: 473).[13]

This is not, of course, the general view of most non-economists. Most of the public, other social scientists, and those who work in marketing and advertising recognize that firms play a considerable role in shaping as well as serving consumer demand. We know, in other words, that Standard Oil and Wal-Mart, along with most other firms, pay considerable attention to how they can move goods through the final link of the supply chain. Interestingly enough, neither Standard nor Wal-Mart made heavy use of advertising, which is the firm activity that has attracted most critical attention from those who have disagreed with the conventional wisdom of economists, so in a sense they might be said to fit the pattern of the economic texts in which passive firms supply fully formed consumer wants.[14] However, it is not quite so simple as that because both Standard Oil and Wal-Mart took considerable care to develop and shape the markets for their goods.

For Standard Oil, the final link from $C' \to M'$ involved the movement of refined products, initially kerosene, to consumers. Kerosene was the primary, but by no means the only, product of the refineries of the first three crucial decades of Standard's existence, and, as surprising as it may seem today, the greatest part of the output of American refiners was exported during the early years of the industry. In Europe, to which a great portion of kerosene was originally shipped, manufactured ("artificial") illuminants had been in use for half a century before the development of the American oil industry. But, costs had been high, and the use of lamplight remained a privilege of the well off. As relatively inexpensive kerosene became available, use expanded quickly, and marketing was handled by import houses.[15] Though there were complaints lodged about the safety of the illuminant, and particularly against Standard as it became the major source, demand seems to have been assured without major marketing efforts.

By the 1880s, a far greater percentage of US-produced petroleum was being consumed domestically, in large measure as kerosene which served as illuminant for the less well off in the cities (where gas light was available for those who could afford its higher cost) and for all who could afford it in rural areas. Williamson and Daum note that kerosene was assured rapid adoption because households that had lamps in which to burn coal-oil could easily substitute kerosene and kerosene rapidly became the cheaper product. And, for many rural households, kerosene was the first source of lighting other than candles. Williamson and Daum cite Hamlin Garland's story of how much kerosene lanterns meant to farm families during the winter months on the northern plains:

> Living on a newly "homesteaded" farm in northern Iowa late in 1868, Garland recalls that candles and a square candle-lantern were the family's only source of artificial light during an unusually severe winter. During the threshing season in the fall of 1869 a wonderful transformation took place when the men came into the dining room for their evening meal and found the table lighted with a kerosene lamp. A year later a new kerosene lantern brought welcome illumination as the members of the family performed long hours of chores and cared for the animals in the darkness of early morning and late evening.
> (Williamson and Daum 1959: 339)

Demand also grew for lubricants and other products to service the rapidly increasing number of machines found on both farms and new and expanding factories. The task that faced Standard Oil was, therefore, more one of managing distribution to its advantage rather than establishing a growing market for its output. This it did by increasing control over sales made directly to retail distributors.

Chernow provides a vivid description of the process whereby Rockefeller began, in the 1870s, to "assemble a marketing organization to eliminate the middlemen, independent agents who had earned three to five cents per gallon of gasoline" (Chernow 1998: 252). His goals were several in creating this organization. In the first instance, he wanted distributors to handle only Standard products. He also wanted more emphasis on expanding the market than on the margin on sales. Chernow writes that

> Standard's refinery flow was now too huge to depend upon ... [a] fragmented, obsolete distribution system.... To have high-volume, low-cost production, the Standard needed huge guaranteed sales. This forced Rockefeller to integrate vertically the entire industry, controlling everything from the wellhead to the consumer.
> (Chernow 1998: 252)

In the early 1880s, Standard developed a system of storage tanks to which it delivered, either by railroad tank cars or pipelines, the kerosene that was then taken by wagon to grocery and hardware stores. Further, Standard provided canisters for storage of the kerosene in the stores and sold, at what Chernow says was almost cost, heaters, stoves, lamps, and lanterns to those who would be consumers.

In the process of developing this network, Rockefeller put wholesalers and local distributors who refused to abide by Standard's terms out of business, thereby earning the enmity of "tens of thousands of small businessmen located in every congressional district" (Chernow 1998: 252). It was this enmity, says Chernow, that eventually led to the end of the Trust. Whether or not this is true, it is clear what Rockefeller was doing. If his systematic control of the industry was to work, if it was to be managed as a large and integrated machine, then the refined products had to flow out and the M' be retrieved. If the efforts in Europe were less dramatic, in good measure because the domestic market became so much more important, and if the marketing of products other than kerosene occupied less attention, they were not of a different kind. All was to be moved forward in a systematic and profitable manner. The throughput and its speed was the key.

So, too, for Sam Walton. Remember that the first Wal-Mart was created because the powers that were in the Ben Franklin chain were concerned with margins rather than total sales. Walton had begun to think about how to increase sales through discounting with his first store in Newport, Arkansas, and it was there that he first ran into trouble with Butler Brothers, the wholesale supplier with whom he had a purchasing agreement. At this early stage in his retailing career, he advertised regularly and, according to Vance and Scott, paid particular attention to sales promotions and did well. However, he was also aggressive in studying the growth of suburban discount stores and became convinced that generalized discounting, with an emphasis on low cost of supplies and volume of sales, was the route to retail success. He tried to persuade what had become, by 1962, the Butler Brothers division of City Products Corporation of the wisdom of his plan, but it was apparently horrified by the idea of reducing the standard margin of 20 to 25 percent to Walton's proposed 12.5%. After another failed attempt to affiliate with a supply house on these terms, Walton moved out on his own with a plan to provide variety and everyday low prices (Vance and Scott 1994: Chapter 3).

As he built his empire on that basis, Walton relied primarily upon word-of-mouth advertising and upon providing goods that moved quickly off the shelves. If Rockefeller had a ready market among the farm families that, before kerosene, had little or no artificial light, Walton had a ready market among the small-town dwellers who either had to drive a distance to choose from a variety of goods, order from stodgy catalogs, or make do with the very limited range of products sold in small-town stores where there were slow turnover and relatively high prices. A ready market did not, however, cause Walton to rest upon his laurels. He needed to move goods quickly, did not want to pay for advertising, but did realize that he could, by careful tracking of customer purchases, achieve his goal. His use of computer technology to track sales has already been described, and examples abound. Wal-Mart even knows what people buy as hurricanes approach its area. Most retailers would know without difficulty that plywood, flashlights, and bottled water are going to be in demand, but only Wal-Mart analysts, using "trillions of bytes' worth of shopper history," would know that strawberry Pop-Tarts and beer lead the list of items the sales of which increase before a predicted storm landfall (Hays: November 14, 2004). This story reinforces what has already been said: Sam Walton gave consumers what they wanted, but he also fed the consumption boom of late-twentieth-century America, some would say, perhaps unfairly, with both low-cost and low-quality goods.[16]

Both Rockefeller and Walton stepped into markets where neither had to worry about creating demand for totally new products, but neither Standard Oil nor Wal-Mart took the final link in their supply chains for granted.[17] They ensured that the goods would move out and be converted quickly to M′. However, that is not the end of the story. Successful management of the $M{\to}C{\to}C'{\to}M'$ chain involved, for both Rockefeller and Walton, more than careful control of the constituent parts.

Holistic management/holistic problems

Holistic control of the interconnected segments is the key to understanding the effectiveness of supply chain management. Such management involves the use of power, whether the power of persuasion or of command (Blanchard 2007: 9).[18] The success of Rockefeller and of Walton was in the integration of their management of the different segments and it is this integration that has been stressed by modern advocates of supply chain management.

The idea and practice of supply chain management is not new but explicit recognition and wide publicity for the concept is only a quarter century old. Although the management consultant Keith Oliver is credited with being the first to use the term in print, the modern idea of supply chains began in full force with Michael Porter's book on *Competitive Advantage* (Blanchard 2007: 9). Porter's articulation of integrated management came at a time when there was great concern that American management of manufacture and distribution was less effective than Japanese practice. It was also important that those who studied and taught about management could draw upon the technical work of Jay Forrester, an engineer at MIT. What Forrester provided that resonated with modern management specialists was the idea that "inventories in a company's pipeline (i.e. supply chain) tend to fluctuate the further they are from the ultimate end user" and that this fluctuation could be shown through computer simulation. More importantly, Forrester and those who expanded on his ideas were able to show, often in convincingly technical format, that these fluctuations could be contained to the advantage of the firm. Containing the "bullwhip effect" that Forrester noted is what supply chain management is about.[19]

As important as Forrester and Porter have been in creating new ways of thinking about management practice, there seems little doubt that Rockefeller and his colleagues had an implicit understanding of the bullwhip effect and knew how important it was that they control it. To prevent an overabundance of crude oil from a new oil field in Bradford, Pennsylvania, Rockefeller needed to tame the crude oil producers. Had Rockefeller been able, instead, to increase quickly the movement of more C (crude oil) into C' (kerosene) and then into M' (sales revenue) he might have done that. But, in the late 1870s, he could not. What he could do, and did do, was to refuse to buy oil for temporary storage at the same time that he lowered the price he would pay for oil to be transported through his pipeline, and he stalled on payments. The producers were forced, though not without loud protests, to curtail output. That is to say that the effect of a new supply of crude oil was prevented from working its way fully through the Standard supply chain, and, by virtue of the power of his pipeline in moving oil out of the producing regions, he prevented potential rivals from taking advantage of cheap oil. His supply chain remained well managed, M' continued to exceed M, and the process moved speedily. But there were residual effects felt by the producers of crude oil who found themselves not pumping oil that could have produced for them equally speedy revenues.

It is not difficult to see that a similar effect occurs in the Wal-Mart chain. If sales of a particular item slow, this information is instantly fed backward through the Retail-Link to suppliers, and shipments to Wal-Mart slow down. But this does not mean, as we have already seen, that something like the bullwhip effect is totally prevented. Rather, it is the manufacturer of the shirts who is left holding the cloth and whose income is affected.[20]

Both of these examples of the ways in which supply chain management was used by Rockefeller and Walton reveal that when the concept is moved from the realm of management and into the realm of economic discourse what emerges is that containment of the bullwhip effect presents problems for the larger society in which such management occurs. The more effective Rockefeller and Walton became in controlling the bullwhip effect, the greater the problems were for the people and their communities who lost the cushioning effects that previously loose management of the supply chains had allowed. There would still have been consequences, some happy and some unhappy, of disturbances in any one part of an integrated and self-regulating market system, but those effects were more likely to be randomly distributed in the absence of centralized power.

Several things seem obvious to this point. Both Rockefeller and Walton understood that power over the whole of the supply chain was crucial if they were to build business empires that would survive. And management through use of persuasive and coercive power is central to building successful supply chains. Once these chains are built and successfully executed, their control has widespread – and not always beneficial – economic effects on suppliers and users of the goods that are part of the controlled supply chain. What is difficult, however, is to translate these reasonably obvious conclusions into the language that most economists have used in describing the activities and consequences of large firms. Both the concepts of power and of interstitial management were effectively deleted by American economists from the analytical spectrum as they developed the twentieth-century explanations of big business, though, as we shall see, not from the popular accounts of big business that informed a large part of the American public.

It is worth considering how these omissions occurred. In some part the path taken was deliberate and explicitly mapped as, for example, in an early article entitled "Trusts From an Economic Standpoint." There W. M. Coleman strongly urged economists to leave concerns about any power other than classic monopoly power over pricing to political economists. A gullible public, said Coleman, might succumb to the "picture of a great nation in thrall to a combination of capitalists," but their technical analysis of the effects of the invisible hand of competition could protect economists from being swayed by this public if they would let it do so (Coleman 1899: 19). In the years that followed, economists did just that with the result that, as John Kenneth Galbraith described it in his presidential address to the American Economic Association, "the commonplace feature[s]" of the mainstream of modern economic analysis are "the assumptions by which power, and therewith political content, is removed from the subject" (Galbraith 1973: 2). The key assumption, of course, is, as Galbraith put it:

The business firm is subordinate to the instruction of the market and, thereby, to the individual or household. The state is subordinate to the instruction of the citizen.... If the business firm is subordinate to the market – if that is its master – then it does not have power to deploy in the economy save as this is in the service of the market and the consumer.

And, Galbraith continues,

> The decisive weakness ... is not the error in the assumptions by which ... [economic analysis] elides power.... Rather in eliding power – in making economics a nonpolitical subject – neoclassical theory ... destroys its relation with the real world.
>
> (Galbraith 1973: 2)

One aspect of the real world that Galbraith emphasized in his presidential address to the American Economic Association and in *The New Industrial State* was the extent to which the American economy is a planned economy, one in which the planning is done by large corporations.[21] Galbraith was not alone in making this observation. As we have already seen, Coase made a similar, if less sweeping, observation in 1939. And, even earlier, in 1899, in an exchange between Frank S. Monnett, Attorney General of Ohio, and Representative L. F. Livingston of Georgia, the following words were recorded:

> Q: (by Representative LIVINGSTON): Is it your opinion that the evolution that is now going on, if unchecked, will lead to a control of the industries of this country, and after that to the control of the government by a few hundred or a few thousand men?
> A: [Monnett] Well that is the merest conjecture....
> Q: (Livingston) Would not the result which I suggested be realized if other industries were controlled in the way a few men control the Standard Oil Company and the oil production of the country?
> A: (Monnett) Yes sir; that would be the result. The socialists are advocating that this be speedily gone on with and continued to its ultimate conclusion.... It is their theory that the government ought to own all of these industries; that the only way to demonstrate the possibility of that is to allow a few people, a few brainy men like Mr. Rockefeller and others, to demonstrate that they can be run by a few.
> Q: (Livingston): That is the point I was referring to, Mr. Monnett.
> A: Well, if we could always have a man like Mr. Rockefeller to run them he might be able to run them better than they would be run under governmental ownership.
>
> (United States Industrial Commission 1901: 175)

While this exchange may have been based on a lot of conjecture, the much more recent observation by Robert E. Hall in the *Brookings Papers on Economic Activity* was offered as a sober assessment of a not dissimilar reality:

Wal-Mart's systems make possible a completely Stalinesque organi-zation involving an astonishing 1.4 million employees. It is wonder-fully ironic that the dreams of the Soviet central planners have come true – thanks to modern information technology – in a worldwide empire run from a small town in Arkansas rather than from Moscow.

(Baily, Hall: 2002: 187)

Irony aside, it does appear that supply chain management, whether couched in the language of business strategists who talk of value chains or as a process of managing the interstices in $M \rightarrow C \rightarrow C' \rightarrow M'$, provides a relevant approach to understanding the rise of Standard Oil and Wal-Mart. These mega firms, and many others like them, are organizations that coor-dinate a wide range of activities; they are not simply production or distrib-ution units as is implied by focus on $C \rightarrow C'$ alone. This recognition, one that both emerges from and is consistent with the analyses of Veblen, Chandler, and modern management specialists, may provide more than understanding. It may also serve as the basis for more relevant public pol-icies, and that is the concern of the next and last chapter.

7 Toward relevance

Economic and business history, the history of economic thought, and popular literature have, in Chapters One through Six, given us a look into the past. In this chapter, focus shifts to ask a different question from a different perspective: Does seeing the firm as $M\rightarrow C\rightarrow C'\rightarrow M'$ provide a narrative that will give us a better template for addressing current social and economic issues than the more customary $C\rightarrow C'$ emphasis? The answer must necessarily be speculative, for it deals with the present, where the trees are always clearer than the forest, and with the future, which is contingent and unknowable. Further, it should be noted that the earlier chapters of this book have offered evidence drawn primarily from two supply chains during two relatively short periods of time: Standard Oil from the late 1860s until the early twentieth century and Wal-Mart from its founding in the 1960s to the first decade of the twenty-first century. The proposition that this is a sufficient sample over sufficient time on which to base predictions about a new and more appropriate meta-narrative for explaining and dealing with big business must, therefore, be offered with some caution.

Nevertheless, convergence of views suggests that a narrative based on supply chains as the source of both commercial power and potential threat to broadly defined human welfare might be a useful foundation for effective public policy. The theory that Veblen proposed, translated into the descriptive language used earlier by Karl Marx, which is the same theory that is implicit in Chandler's stories of the rise of big business, has been shown to be coincident with successful modern management theory. That such a diverse group of scholars and writers, working from very different perspectives, converged on a like understanding bodes well for the accuracy and usefulness of the supply chain as a way of thinking about the American economy.[1] However, before exploring public policy as seen through the lens shared by this group, a brief review of the relationship of stories told about the rise of big business and the evolution of public policy is in order.

The meta-narrative about the rise of big business in the US has been a story of both service and threat to public well-being, but with many variations in tone and detail. To adequately sort the stories told about the rise of big business one would need a matrix of overlapping explanations that would include technological change, institutional innovation, greed, laxity or favoritism on the part of governments, and opportunism often combined with genius. Moreover, the matrix would need to be multidimensional and without firmly fixed cell boundaries, for explanations have shifted through time in overlapping and sometimes contradictory manner. Given the difficulty of attaching such a matrix to the pages of a book, the following words are offered instead.

The pure technological explanation is one that ties size of firm to the size of the mill, which is, in turn, dictated by the best available technology in a world where ongoing technological change often increases the best mill size. This is the explanation that draws on parallels between large firms and the railroads, where high fixed costs, size of initial investment required, and increasing returns to scale over a wide range of activity produce cut-throat competition and ultimate combination. The consensus about such industries at the end of the nineteenth century, consensus that continued through the twentieth in most quarters, was that the appropriate public policy was regulation or public ownership. In the US, out of this reasoning came railroad, airline, and public utility regulation, all of which have been weakened in recent years as the boundary between railroad-type firms and different types of business enterprises has become blurred.[2]

The explanation that has bled over into the arena of regulated industries combines elements of the pure technological explanation with the view that concentration is simply a consequence of the fact that, wherever they can, businessmen will conspire to gain monopolistic advantage. This composite view emerged as the US struggled with the growth of ever larger firms that seemed to be characterized by weaker technological imperatives to large size than was the case with railroads. Neither regulation nor the always in the US less-favored solution of public ownership seemed appropriate, but neither was inaction acceptable. This was made absolutely clear at the Chicago Conference on Trusts. John Bates Clark's leap of reason in his lectures at Cooper Union in 1904 provided a solution: technological change did indeed demand larger firms, but technologically justified concentration might combine with that which was illegitimately allowed by unfair tariff and other public policies that tilted the playing field. Unfair business practices could also contribute to illegitimate growth in size and sacrifice of the public good. Out of this reasoning came the Federal Trade Commission and other regulation of the Progressive Era and eventually the antitrust consensus of the late 1930s and forward. This consensus merged with and, over time, came to be dominated by the Chicago School view that the invisible hand of competition would drive firms, even very large and powerful firms, to forgo significant oligopolistic or monopolistic pricing and restraint of output. In tune with a move toward deregulation in industries once thought to be natural monopolies or nearly so, the antitrust stance has been weakened in recent decades as faith in the powers of the invisible hand has increased, at least among those charged with effecting public policy. With the notable exception of the breakup of AT&T and the highly publicized, but in the end ineffectual, assault on Microsoft's dominance, antitrust policy has tended to be limited to relatively minor issues, with an exclusive focus, not surprisingly, on prices of products.[3]

As against the technological and technological-plus-collusion explanations of the growth of large firms, the accounts in Chapter 5 stressed administrative innovation in combination with technological change. This is the explanation Alfred Chandler offered in his lifetime of work, and, as was argued above, it is in many ways similar to the more skeletal explanation that had been offered by Thorstein Veblen during the initial phases of consolidation. Further, it is an explanation that bears marked resemblance to the views now being taught in business schools throughout the US. What the Chandlerian explanation lacks, however, is any clear remedy for possible large-firm abuse of power. The technological explanation leads to regulation or public ownership as the routes to ensure general welfare. The composite technological-plus-collusion view leads to pro-competition policies. Chandler's explanation of big business, on the other hand, offers no clear route to insure that the public interest is protected.[4]

However, such a neutral stance is, once again, not sufficient in the face of the persistent view that big business exists by and for exploitation of some considerable portion of mankind. This was the view of the muckrakers of the late nineteenth and early twentieth centuries; it underlay the suspicions of Frank Fetter when he led the charge of economists to beat back the associationist challenge to the Sherman Antitrust Act; it persists in the work of scholars such as Perrow, Sklar, Fligstein, Roy, and others who see the darker side of the technological imperatives that, given the power structure in the US, have led to great firm size; and, most importantly, it persists in the public view that continues to be expressed as one of "the people" against "big business." As criticism mounts of the economy of the early twenty-first century, a time that is now routinely called a second gilded age, with its skewed income distribution, conspicuous consumption by the ultra-rich, and economic insecurity for many, the American meta-narrative in which big business is seen as a threat to most people has reappeared.

In the film *Wal-Mart: The High Cost of Low Price*, an employee of a small-town hardware store that was driven out by Wal-Mart says, "They busted up Standard Oil, and they busted up Ma Bell, but in this case, nobody seems to be paying attention" (quoted by Gates 2005). For good reason, Chandler's explanation of the rise of big business has been accepted by most economic and business historians, but the suspicion that something is wrong with an explanation that ignores perverse results persists in history textbooks, in the work of economic sociologists, in the classrooms where American literature is taught, and in films about corporations and about Wal-Mart. There is also suspicion and mistrust in towns and cities where Wal-Mart construction is proposed and then opposed by citizen groups, and in the public arena in discussions of trade policies, employment and labor management practices, immigration, outsourcing of jobs, provision of medical care and other basic services, and much more.

A template to drill by

The question, then, is, if we adopt the explanation offered in Chapter 5 of the rise and persistence of big business, what can we say about the effects upon workers, consumers, citizens? What remedies for real ills can be offered? How do we go about answering these questions? In Chapter One, I expressed the hope that a template for pragmatic approaches to problems of the current economy might emerge from use of a monetary theory or supply chain approach to the analysis of firm size and in saying this chose the word template deliberately. Template is a word of many usages, but the one that I intend here is that of a "flat plate or strip perforated with holes used as a guide in marking out holes for riveting or drilling" (OED). A template is not a set of specific solutions to specific problems. Rather, it is a guide to where we need to drill for solutions.

It is relatively easy to use the model of big business formation presented in Chapter 5 to say where we do *not* need to drill. Prices of products and quantity of output, the usual suspects of conventional analysis, are not and have not been problems. Stanley Lebergott calculated that

> [o]ver the Trust's entire life, Standard Oil's net earnings averaged 1.4 cents per gallon of illuminating oil. Now a competitive rate of return in such a risky, technologically fast-moving industry might have been about 10 percent. Had the Trust earned a competitive 10 percent instead of its actual monopoly rates, its earnings would have been only 46 percent of what they actually were. Hence consumers paid .0066 cents a gallon in monopoly profits. During these years the average family bought about 30 gallons of illuminating oil a year. Standard Oil's monopoly profits from each consuming family thus came to 21 cents a year. (American workers at that time earned an

average of $450 to $500 a year.) Under mass consumption, it turned out, massive profits went hand in hand with low prices and low unit profits.

(Lebergott 1984: 333–4)

In the twenty-first century, Petra Rivoli estimates that we buy our Chinese-made T-shirts for perhaps twenty-five cents less than we would without the "Wal-Mart squeeze," but, she asks, "at what cost?" (Rivoli 2005: 150). It seems little wonder that the Antitrust Division of the Justice Department, with its almost exclusive focus on price, is an irrelevant agency for most Americans.

The template that emerges from supply chain theory *does* suggest that we should drill at the interstices of the chain. It also suggests that we should drill where, through containment of the bullwhip effect, the consequences of oscillations are minimized for the firm but transferred to those linked to but not actually part of the supply chain. This is simply another way of saying drill at the interstices. Those linked to but not inside the supply chain would include workers whose hours of work and total pay are flexible, as is the case with many who work for Wal-Mart and for firms that have copied their management practices. It would include suppliers of goods, whether foreign or domestic. It would include towns whose economic base has been changed by arrival of a Wal-Mart but whose claim on that store is tenuous in the face of Wal-Mart's willingness to pick up and move to more profitable locations. Focus on the problems of these groups is not new, but what the supply chain analysis does that more traditional approaches do not is to force recognition that it is control of the interstices that has been crucial to the building of large firms and to their survival. Wal-Mart's strength comes not from simple monopsonistic power in a labor market but, rather, from the ability to control sources of supply by choosing from an array of willing participants. Wal-Mart's managers can turn the supply spigot on and off as they choose. Much the same could be said of Standard Oil. For Standard the issue was not simply one of the prices it would pay producers of crude but its willingness to let the suppliers of the Oil Regions participate in the supply chain. Put more generally, management is use of power, and the power that successful supply chain managers have is power over much more than quantity and price.

It is obvious that even those who are securely part of the supply chain may not receive the incomes or perquisites to which they may feel, and perhaps should be, entitled. Wal-Mart does have power in determining the salaries and benefits of full-time employees and they may or may not be well paid. The point here, however, is that they are part of the supply chain and so receive some degree of protection from far-distant fluctuations. If there is a significant decline in consumer spending, then the core of the supply chain will be affected. What those who are members of that core are, however, protected from are the fluctuations that are an inherent part of a large and complex supply chain even during periods of overall growth, fluctuations that are magnified by that complexity. For those in the core, Walton and his colleagues tamed the bullwhip effects of these fluctuations, so that it is only, and especially, those who are outside but still connected to the supply chain who suffer the boom and bust cycle that was, back in Rockefeller's early days, the bane of all.

The disorder in the market that Rockefeller so disliked can be thought of as Forrester's bullwhip in action. Rockefeller tamed that bullwhip in the interests of Standard Oil, its stockholders, its employees, the railroads who served it, those who sold to it, and even the consumers who bought kerosene at low prices. Those not served were denied a secure place in the supply chain: the oil producers whose products might not be purchased in the amounts they produced, the rail lines who were excluded, the distributors who did not cooperate, and the many others who were simply squeezed out of the petroleum business by Standard's organizational efficiency. People and places not part of this supply chain did not count in its management. Much the same can be said of Wal-Mart and Walton and it is those who are affected but not protected by this modern supply chain who should be considered for protection by the larger society.

The recognition of the importance of control of the supply chain which is given emphasis by imagining Forrester's bullwhip in Walton's hands takes us to an obvious problem in the existing template for social and political action. *We do not have agencies that are specifically designed to serve public interest that have power over the supply chains that have come to organize our economic activity.* This is true for several reasons.

The first reason is geography and jurisdictional boundaries. Almost by definition supply chains that matter extend across such boundaries and American federalism, a structure of government that allows states to be innovative and to respond to local issues, also limits response to national issues that are not also being dealt with by active federal policy. Naomi Lamoreaux notes that when the courts in the years leading up to adoption of the "rule of reason" in its 1911 breakup of Standard Oil struggled and issued what seem today to be inconsistent and confusing rulings, they were not only dealing with changing economic organization. They were also

striving to respond to ... public demands for action in a way that would be consistent in jurisprudential terms. The main problem they faced was structural: how the federal government could fulfill its responsibility to regulate interstate corporations when it did not have the power to charter them.

(Lamoreaux 1985: 180)

Harry Scheiber makes the related point that, throughout US history, there is no evidence that *laissez faire* ideology has gotten in the way of industrial policy, whether regulatory or promotional, nor is there evidence of "ideological adherence to individualism or egalitarian orthodoxy ... at the expense of other objectives such as planning" (Scheiber 1987: 418). Rather, "Active state intervention" has been "effective, equitable and consistent with a fair and just distribution of income and resources only so long as the overriding national policies [have] encourage[d] them to be" (Scheiber 1987: 444).

State versus federal ability to control was clearly an issue in the building of Standard Oil. When Rockefeller was first involved in the oil industry in Cleveland, he was operating in a country where corporations could not own property outside of the state in which they were incorporated. As described earlier, the creation of the Trust was a way of getting around this state control, and the Sherman Antitrust Act was the response of a nation that attempted to regain control of that which the States could no longer manage on their own.

State versus federal control is also problematic today as is abundantly clear in two instances of concern about Wal-Mart. Consider first the case of health insurance. Wal-Mart is by no means the only large firm that does not provide easily affordable health insurance to the bulk of its employees. Indeed, one reason why the story of Wal-Mart has resonated so widely among Americans, even those who neither shop nor seek work there, is that health insurance has become a major worry and debating point in the US. Employment-related coverage for both catastrophic and routine medical costs became a feature of the American economy during labor shortages in the 1940s and expanded in the years after World War II. A combination of international competition, rising health costs, and changes in the labor markets for most firms have changed this pattern so that employment-related health insurance, even for full-time workers, has become less common than it once was. For part-time workers, the coverage is even skimpier.

States faced with increasing numbers of uninsured citizens have struggled to find ways to provide medical services for the uninsured, and focus has turned to large employers whose workers are not covered or not covered adequately. And, the largest of these is, not surprisingly, Wal-Mart. In a fine example of the kind of state-level innovation that federalism allows, the legislature in Maryland passed a law that required corporations with 10,000 or more workers to spend 8 percent of their pay-rolls on health insurance or pay the difference into a state fund. This law would have affected only Wal-Mart. However, the United States Court of Appeals for the Fourth Circuit found the legislation to be inconsistent with federal law, in this case with the Employee Retirement Income Security Act (ERISA), which provided for uniform national plans to be provided by companies if they chose to provide such benefits (Barbaro: January 18, 2007).

Even Wal-Mart's critics admit that the threat of the Maryland law in combination with fierce criticism in the press and other public venues has led the company to offer somewhat more generous health benefits. Even though it currently covers fewer than half its 1.4 million US employees, press coverage is better and the story is clearly an evolving one (Barbaro and Abelson: November 13, 2007). What is important here, however, is not that Wal-Mart may respond to bad publicity and public pressure but that state policies are limited in effect on a national company, and, in this case, an international one. Not only does distributed political authority limit the ability of the public to deal with national and international supply chains, but in some cases it may lead to undesirable competition among local political authorities.

An entirely understandable reaction of state and local governments to the shifts in employment and industrial location called globalization has been to develop enticement programs to persuade job-providing firms to locate in their areas. Wal-Mart has been, as we have already seen, the beneficiary of such programs, as have a variety of other firms, retail and industrial. It is dif-ficult to determine the magnitude of the subsidies provided, as they are typ-ically granted at the local level making it difficult to compile aggregate statistics and, in some cases, are provided to developers of sites rather than directly to Wal-Mart. Nevertheless, we do know that Wal-Mart has been the beneficiary of a variety of subsidies. Because such enticement programs operate at the local level while Wal-Mart operates nationally and interna-tionally in making its decisions about location of both retail stores and distri-bution centers, it is obvious that Wal-Mart has the upper hand. Given the boost that a Wal-Mart center can give to a town or county, local govern-ments will quite reasonably compete with each other for Wal-Mart's favor and all to the advantage of Wal-Mart as it gains greater concessions.

The problem of local competition for jobs and tax-producing firms is by no means limited to subsidies to Wal-Mart. It is a much broader issue, one about which Scheiber wrote pessimistically:

When the national government is willing to establish floors and accept broad responsibility for minimum services and regulatory standards, the competition among states is placed on a basis that is not damaging to social policy objectives other than the objective of industrial growth itself. Today, however, the states confront the harsh reality of a national administration hostile to uniform national standards except where they reduce or eliminate regulatory powers, hostile to state autonomy when states prefer conservationist over developmental standards, and hostile to federal tax-deductions policy which would encourage the states to play their traditional role as "laboratories of democracy."

(Scheiber 1987: 443)

The problems caused by an imbalance of power go well beyond the difficulties that states have in dealing with Wal-Mart and other large and powerful supply chains. The real question in the twenty-first century, when supply chains reach round the world, is whether or not nation states can be laboratories of democracy and effective policy formation when well-managed supply chains have become global. As troubling as local subsidies to Wal-Mart may be, and as difficult as the issues of health coverage may seem, even more troubling to large numbers of people has been the lack of internationally effective oversight of the activities of firms that have become, in effect, independent of any nation state.

States in the US and some nation states have attempted to deal with specific issues raised by Wal-Mart's power, but this has proven difficult and not simply because power remains diffused among governmental units even as it has been centralized by the management practices of Wal-Mart and like companies. There has also been increased reluctance, developed in close accord with a returned faith in the invisible hand, to intervene in the workings of private firms. As Harry Scheiber noted, the years of Wal-Mart's rise have been years during which national administrations in the US have been hostile to increased regulation or national standards. It has also been an era in which governments that have played strong roles in their national economies have seen their power reduced by the forces of international competitiveness. By being so firmly in control of the bullwhip, those managers in Bentonville, Arkansas, have been able to transfer the effects of oscillation in the supply chain from their firm and onto increasingly vulnerable workers even in nations with strong worker protection and welfare programs. And, in the absence of any organization with effective power to impose international labor, environmental, and product quality standards, the power of Wal-Mart seems beyond reach. It may be true, as Rivoli wrote: "A bit more stability, a bit more community, a bit more of a dike against the bashing waves from China are worth more than small savings for each of us on the cost of a T-shirt" (Rivoli 2005: 150). But, how do we get there?

It seems reasonably obvious that agencies will have to be created and empowered that have the geographic reach of the supply chains whose effects they need to control. Such a process is arguably under way, if haltingly. Beginning in 1992 when NAFTA (the North American Free Trade Agreement) was signed into law, labor and environmental goals were made part of an economic agreement designed primarily to ensure relatively unhindered flow of goods, people, and ideas across political boundaries. The intent is to protect against harmful effects that are likely to result from management of these unhindered flows. However, this process of incorporating multiple goals into international agreements has been slowed because discussions of public policy have remained chained to a nineteenth-century notion of trade among nations that is managed primarily through tariff barriers or lack thereof. This allegiance to the past has persisted even in the face of trade that is managed through supply chains in which managerial decisions and negotiating power among participants are of far greater importance than are government-imposed tariffs. In spite of this, the stated goal and ideal has been "free" trade, meaning free of government taxation at national boundaries, and such freedom has been touted as the overriding and inviolable goal of NAFTA and similar agreements.

Critics of NAFTA have argued that it is less a free trade agreement and more a protection of firms that want to invest in regions outside their nations of origin and there is considerable truth to this charge. Given the importance of cross-boundary management of manufacture and distribution, it would be surprising if this were not the case. From the reality that freedom of management, rather than the freeing of goods from traditional tariff barriers, has been both goal and consequence of the "free trade" agreements of recent years, both problems and possibilities follow, as does complexity.

To clarify this point it helps to recognize that NAFTA, CAFTA (Central American Free Trade Agreement), and the nascent Middle East Free Trade Area, which was initiated with the US–Oman Free Trade Agreement, contain provisions that prevent governments of the nations involved from restricting investment on grounds of national origin of firms. Where such restrictions are applied, firms can appeal to a tribunal, and they have done so. As illustration of what this means, consider the case in which a Canadian company complained that a US ban on a fuel additive for which the company supplied a component chemical amounted to discriminatory action of the kind prohibited by NAFTA. This complaint was rejected by the appeals tribunal, but the way in which the claim was made and the type of issues involved make it an important case, for it goes right to the heart of the barriers to trade that are most important today and to questions of national sovereignty (Knox 2006: 429–33).

The simple case is this: If a company from Canada or Mexico is prevented from establishing a plant in the US by restrictions on the sale of its output, as in the case above, this can be deemed discriminatory, but it can also be seen as appropriate action taken to guard citizen health and well-being. It is up to the appeals tribunals and to the courts as to which further appeals may be made. If restrictions are judged to be a matter of standards, and if standards for products sold are higher in one country than in another, then the issue becomes one of negotiating common standards. That is the key issue, and one directly related to the need to use the supply chain template to identify those points of intersection between the supply chain itself and those who are on the outside but are nevertheless affected by it. If seen, on the other hand, as qualitative restrictions on free trade, then a wide variety of protections, whether of the environment, of labor, or of existing industry, seem inappropriate for they are indeed likely to prevent the reductions in prices that are assumed by most to be the primary goal of freeing of trade across national boundaries.

The crux of the matter is that protections that may be a good way of buffering those individuals and communities that do not enjoy the protection afforded by being part of the supply chain may also be seen as restrictions on trade. If the overriding goal is to produce and distribute more goods at lower prices, freedom of trade will trump. If regulation of supply chains by agencies charged with the public interest is given equal standing as a worthy goal, then restrictions can be seen as serviceable. Simply by recasting the issue a different perspective is gained. Seeing international trade agreements as agreements about how supply chains should be managed, and what bullwhip effects are allowable when visited upon those not offered supply chain protection, the agenda for negotiation is altered significantly.

As noted, critics of inclusion of an array of public concerns such as labor standards and environmental protection in trade agreement paint them as restrictions on free trade. From the supply chain perspective, inclusion of such issues simply involves a broadening of trade management agreements, a broadening for the purpose of affording to those who are subject to the oscillations of the supply chain the protection already offered for those in the safer confines of the supply chain itself. But viewing national restrictions and standards as legitimate does not solve the whole issue by any means. The case of NAFTA is once again instructive.

Fierce debate about NAFTA made it politically necessary, if approval was to be gained in the US, to create the "side agreements" on labor and the environment. Although the dispute resolution process created as part of these agreements may indeed be "the premier attempt to date to provide a modality in international trade law for reconciling trade values with social and environmental values," the hard fact is that this process has had little effect (Garvey 1995: 439). The reason is simple: "The Side Agreements on labor and the environment do not contain labor or environmental norms; they constitute legal processes" (Garvey 1995: 440). These legal processes may indeed be a "revolutionary linkage," which will "guarantee that pressure on a variety of issues of health, labor and environment" will be part of negotiations "to a degree never before experienced by the makers of trade policy" (Garvey 1995: 453). However, the fact remains that the effectiveness of such pressure has not been sufficient to offset the substantial power of Wal-Mart and other controllers of international supply chains, and precisely because the norms are those of nations where protection has tended to lag behind private managerial innovation.

To be even more explicit, consider that income security and distribution, both within the US and abroad, are crucial issues for those who protest the practices of Wal-Mart as well as for those worried in a more general way about the twenty-first century economies. As already noted, it has become commonplace in the US to talk of a second "gilded age", and news stories about children working in sweatshops to produce clothing for affluent American and British consumers contribute to the unhappiness of affluent and poor alike in a world awash with goods.

In the US, it has been well documented that real incomes of the majority have not kept pace with the rate of economic growth, but what is arguably much more important is that work for many has become less certain both in hours and in long-term continuity. As many commentators have noted, the era of lifetime (or near lifetime) employment with a guaranteed number of hours and benefits has become increasingly difficult to find for many Americans. In its place we have Wal-Mart-type employment with flexible hours (determined by the employer) and few or no benefits for a majority. We have already seen why this pattern of employment makes good and economically rational sense from the standpoint of Wal-Mart. By tracking sales volume, managers are able to determine precise times at which employees will be needed in what numbers and this allows the cost minimization that is the foundation of everyday low prices. In the US the norm, that which NAFTA's legal processes can protect should anyone wish to appeal violations, is such that workers have no rights to full-time work or to a minimum income or to benefits so that Wal-Mart is entirely on the good side of the law in pursuing its highly efficient policies.

The difficulty for those who wish to argue for a different set of norms to be enforced as part of international agreements, ones that would be based upon a greater degree of concern with overall income equality and worker welfare, is that the stories on which current policies are based make this a difficult reach. The story that continues to guide the thinking of most economists and many policy makers is one that dates from the remake by John Bates Clark and other neoclassicists of the old Smithian story about the invisible hand and economic growth. This is a story that says that what people earn, except in the presence of unfair market practices, equals the value of what they contribute. If unfair business collusion is prohibited – and we do have laws that prevent such collusion – the employers will pay the worth of each worker. To compel them to pay more would be unfair to them and would only result in unnecessarily high costs and slower growth that would be detrimental to all. That story is brilliantly logical but unfortunately irrelevant to a lot of twenty-first-century public concerns.

Again, consider income inequality. In the neoclassical story it follows that the answer to income inequality is to make people more productive while at the same time prohibiting unfair practice by firms. If these steps are taken, inequality will eventually be erased. More education is the suggested remedy. But, in a world where Wal-Mart's decisions about location have major consequences for the ability of local areas to support education, the recommendation of providing more and better education to young people seems almost as irrelevant as does insistence that T-shirts will be cheaper still in a better world. If we were to adopt the perspective of supply chain managers, it would be reasonably clear that only by controlling oscillations affecting all factors determining individual productivity would we be able to ensure an equal playing field and greater equality and fairness of economic outcomes for all. This is an ambitious goal.

Exhortations for education fall flat in a context where the health of children is undermined by inadequate medical care and other support needed to ensure an ability to learn. Not only in the US, in rural areas and urban ghettos, but most especially in sweatshops in India and elsewhere and in many, many other parts of the world, there are needs to incorporate the welfare of people into consideration in the privately planned economic systems that, in reality, determine the flow of products, of jobs, and of funds. This can be rephrased in the traditional language of economists. We can say that greater attention needs to be given to making sure that the privately owned and managed supply chain internalizes the full costs of production. This can mean that the health costs associated with use of toxic-to-humans components and their biota should be included in the prices of products produced and sold. It can, however, also and perhaps more realistically mean greater attention paid to the way in which accounting is done.

John Maurice Clark, the son of John Bates Clark, and his collaborator on the second edition of *The Control of Trusts*, published in 1923 an important, but not largely forgotten, book called *Studies in the Economics of Overhead Costs*. In the first chapter, "The Gradual Discovery of Overhead Costs," Clark tells the story of how a move from handicraft to machine production led to a slowly dawning realization that idle machines involved costs that needed to be taken into account both by economic theorists and by accountants. The railroads rammed this point home, but Clark moved further to make two additional points that deserve great consideration by those who would use the supply chain template to think and manage for broader social and economic welfare in the twenty-first century.

The first has to do with cost accounting, a practice that was in early stages of development when Clark wrote:

> business has developed the technique of cost accounting, including methods of allocating costs which cannot be directly traced to given units of product. This may be confined to seeing that all products are charged with a share of all operating expenses, or it may also include a share of interest on investments. This obviously offers great possibilities in the way of developing a standard of sound or conservative practice in fixing prices.... It also offers great opportunities for the development of arbitrary and fictitious notions of cost, through the necessity of apportioning items somehow, even if there is no satisfactorily scientific basis on which to do so.
>
> (Clark 1923: 14)

The second point was that labor itself can and perhaps should be thought of as an overhead cost. Clark wrote:

> Once the holding of unused productive capacity is conceived as "idle overhead," it was inevitable that the idea should be extended to human powers as well as to the powers of physical plant and machinery.... Wherever a laborer has invested time and money in specialized training, the result is, in a certain sense, fixed capital which is useful in one occupation and in no other, and which must earn whatever return it can, because the investment cannot be withdrawn and moved into some other line of business. In such a case it seems fairly clear that labor involves an overhead cost.
>
> In a more general sense, however, there is a minimum of maintenance of the laborer's health and working capacity which must be borne by someone, whether the laborer works or not: that is, if it is

not borne, if the maintenance is not forthcoming, the community
suffers a loss through the deterioration of its working power which is
at least equivalent to the cost of maintaining the laborer. Thus the
burden is there in any case: it cannot be avoided.

(Clark 1923: 15–16)

Viewed in this light, we can restate the problem and possibilities. Supply
chain management practices have been a powerful innovation based on
recognition that control of the entire $M{\rightarrow}C{\rightarrow}C'{\rightarrow}M'$ process is of critical
importance to the profitability of a firm, and particularly so where low
transport costs and highly effective international communication makes
close management possible. However, the norms and laws that govern
employment, environmental, and health practices have remained fragmented, not simply because of jurisdictional complexity but also because
individuals are seen as independent of any larger and causal sequence.
Investment in education is seen as an individual choice as is place of resi-
dence, work taken, health decisions and much, much more. Efforts to minimize the impact of economic change on individuals, as by guaranteed
incomes or employment or other forms of worker security, have been criticized as counterproductive measures that would increase costs and prices
and slow or distort increases in output. If, however, we see these decisions
as subject to bullwhip oscillations, it is clearer that individuals may be
severely limited in the choices that they make, and in ways that distort and
limit the impacts of increased economic capacity.

Saying this is not anything new. Economists have long talked of externalities, which is to say of effects outside of the firm, and sociologists and
others have written much about the influence of community. It has also
become traditional to try to calculate a ratio of costs and benefits of major
endeavors, both public and private. What may be new and useful about the
approach suggested here is to use the stories of Rockefeller and Walton in
order to see supply chain management as a practice that could be
amenable to a broader application, a practice that could be implemented
through broadened use of the now widely acceptable practice of cost
accounting.

John Maurice Clark was aware of the dangers inherent in cost accounting, the dangers of fictitious and arbitrary notions of cost, but he also had
high hopes for the use of "true statistical method" as a way to make cost
accounting a valuable tool. What Clark wanted was to gather data not
unlike that which Albert Fink put together for the railroads. What John D.
Rockefeller did, perhaps intuitively, and what Sam Walton did with more
precision because of the tools available to him, was to use statistical
methods to manage economic empires. Surely, public officials and public

servants could do likewise. The use of a supply chain template in conjunction with broadened cost accounting could be used to monitor the costs of the supply chains that provide so many of the goods that we purchase. Norms and laws and international trade agreements could be based upon this data. What are needed are not so much new techniques; we have those. What is needed is public will to put these tools to work.

Three-quarters of a century after Clark wrote, his discussion of labor as an overhead cost seems somewhat naïve, but not because we do not have the social statistics that would allow better measurement of the costs of idle capacity. Rather, it appears naïve because we have convinced ourselves, at least in the US, that the crucial economic story is about efficiency in the transformation of C into C′. Perhaps, however, Clark's proposition is worth revisiting. With a different story, a story of supply chains and interstitial management as the key to big business, a new approach may yet emerge.

Stories and policies: a final word

The evolution of public policies designed to cope with water suppliers in London, railroads and manufacturing trusts in the US, and the oligopolistic firms that followed, suggests that articulation of the issues that trouble us as a people is of critical importance both in inducing and directing change. Policies evolve from the understanding that stories provide. It might be nice to think that there is a purely scientific progression toward truth about human interactions – social, economic, and political – that could guide the development of "correct" public policy. The stories told in this book suggest otherwise. Stories evolve and do so as inherited ideas are modified by changing circumstances and appreciation of new opportunities for a better world. The stories we create and use serve to identify both problems and potential solutions. Supply chain analysis, and the need to beware of and control the bullwhip effects on society of supply chain management require a new story that can serve the twenty-first century.

In Chapter 1 the point was made that public policy is path-dependent, meaning that policies are the outcomes of QWERTY-like choices made at various times, and often for what seem, at the time, as the best of reasons. They are also an amalgam of expert and public opinion. Because policies that will be put in place in the coming years are emerging now, it is not possible to know what they will be. At best, the effort to understand how narratives of big business have evolved and how they have informed public policy can give only limited powers of prophecy. However, if economists are to have a major influence upon the evolution of the new stories it would probably be wise to pay heed to current public concerns and to the considerable wisdom of their colleagues who have struggled to understand more precisely what Rockefeller and Walton actually did to earn their places in history.

The story told in this book, one that may be helpful in creation of new and useful stories, is one in which the reality of greatly increased output and lowered real prices in the era of Standard Oil's prime led quite sensibly to the view that some very large and powerful firms deserved to survive. Wal-Mart has reaffirmed this sensible conclusion. The survival test that John Bates Clark touted to the Chicago Conference made sense, but the reasoning that was associated with it was flawed. By focusing on economies in production, Clark began a long-lived tradition of ignoring the efficiencies in management associated with size, which is to say the gains to the managing firm of tight control over supply chains. Most often it was this control that prompted the unhappiness of rival producers, of suppliers, and of groups other than consumers.

To date, economists have not fully used the analytical tools that can be had from thinking of the firm as a manager of $M \rightarrow C \rightarrow C' > M'$ rather than simply as producer of goods. John D. Rockefeller and Sam Walton earned their places in American history because they did understand the importance of controlling the entire process. They succeeded in very different lines of endeavor but what they had in common was an understanding of the importance of such control. Business strategists have now caught up with Rockefeller and Walton with their current focus on supply or value chains but their concern is with the welfare of firms. Such welfare may, however, not be consistent with public welfare as the farmers, the laborers, the anti-Wal-Mart activists, and as those now rallying against free trade and uncontrolled immigration have said and said loudly. If economists are to play a role in shaping a new meta-narrative for the twenty-first century, they will almost certainly need to think in terms of $M \rightarrow C \rightarrow C' \rightarrow M'$. New stories will emerge. Perhaps by recognizing how the stories of our past have been constructed we, economists and non-economists alike, can do a better job of creating them.

Notes

1 Introduction

1 Though not to Deirdre McCloskey who has long and bravely argued that economists should recognize that they too tell stories (McCloskey 1998).
2 For an excellent discussion of the meaning of these terms as they apply to the
  history of economic thought, see the discussion on "Whiggish history" available
  in the electronic archives of the History of Economics Society
  (http://ehnet.lists/search). Economic historians have given less explicit attention
  to the possible perils of "Whiggishness," though the discussions of path dependence, about which more will be said shortly in the text, relate to the issue.
  However, in the discipline of History, the idea that history is sometimes, or
  perhaps often, written more for applauding or deriding the present than for
  understanding the past is of long standing. See Butterfield (1965) for a classic
  example of a critique of "Whiggishness."
3 The original institutionalists were those economists who, in the early part of the
  twentieth century, adopted the newly emerging goals and methods of social science
  in order to describe production and distribution systems as evolving through time,
  as integrated with other social systems, and as amenable to deliberate efforts to
  improve them. This approach contrasted with the neoclassical approach, which also
  took shape during roughly the same period and which was built upon the notion of
  a natural order of economic behavior and outcomes. Deduction from a relatively
  small set of fixed principles assumed to be part of this natural order was the prin-
  cipal tool of neoclassicism. There were and are many variations on these themes,
  but discussion of these lies well beyond the scope of this work.
4 This is a good place to acknowledge my intellectual debt to Alfred D. Chandler
  and the business historians who through their written work have taught me so
  much. Though I was never fortunate enough to study directly with Chandler or
  his associates and students, I found in their work a treatment of business enterprise as economic institution that fit well with my own direct training in institutionalism in the tradition of Thorstein Veblen, John R. Commons, Wesley C.
  Mitchell, Karl Polanyi, and their students. This is a tradition that is sometimes
  seen as anti-business but should not be, for business enterprises, whether small
  and local or large and global, are as surely humanly instituted and inherited parts
  of our culture as are religious or kinship practices. Some anthropologists, some
  sociologists, and the Chandler-influenced business and economic historians
  know this; unfortunately, many economists have preferred to treat business

organization and practice as straightforward manifestations of universal and invariant human nature.

5 The arrangement of letters was technologically desirable in the case of early typewriters because the relative frequency of letter use determined the tendency of the bars that connected the keyboard to the print mechanism to get stuck together, especially when accomplished typists struck the keys rapidly. Paul David's article "Clio and the economics of QWERTY" (1985) is the classic statement of the case for the reality of QWERTY. Since that time, others, and particularly Liebowitz and Margolis (1995), have questioned whether or not technologies that are less than optimally efficient will be used over any period of time. Vernon Ruttan (1997) makes a good case that, over time, changing factor prices may cause firms to adopt better technology even though existing technologies create some incentives to stay with the tried and true. However, the real argument over QWERTY has become a larger one about whether or not "network externalities" associated with path dependence represent market failures. For my purposes it will suffice to say that the QWERTY keyboard can be explained in terms of a technology of the past; it may still be the most efficient for typists or it may not be, but it is what we have. So, too, with public policies. Path dependence need not imply anything about desirability unless, as economists and some economic historians are wont to do, you adopt the extreme Whiggish position that all lasting change is for the better.

6 The phrase "flat world" is, of course, that of Thomas Friedman (2005) who argues for the advantages that globalization brings.

2 The agreed upon stories

1 For this section I have relied most heavily upon Harold F. Williamson and Arnold Daum's 1959 work, *The American Petroleum Industry*. There are a number of other good sources, but for a technical discussion of the new industry, Williamson and Daum's work remains a reliable and comprehensive source.

2 Chernow's book, *Titan*, is a recent and very thorough treatment of all aspects of Rockefeller's life. A full account of his early years can be found there in Chapters 1–6. See also Allen Nevins (1940 and 1953) and Ralph and Muriel Hidy (1955) are also excellent sources.

3 For more on Drake and his well, see Chernow (1998: 73–6).

4 It is interesting to note that refining remained throughout this period a "batch" process. This was not, as Williamson and Daum explain, because of a lack of interest in continuous distillation. Rather, in the case of Standard Oil, where Henry Rogers, who was an early developer of a modern-style fractionating tower, was employed from 1874,

> "pressure for sharper, narrower fractions was insufficient to stimulate the modest mechanical modifications of his tower necessary to bring it into commercial use. Surpluses of both crude-oil and refining capacity, emphasis on throughput and kerosene fractions, and limited production of by-products in a general refinery were among the influences contributing to this neglect. Not until the introduction of J. W. Van Dyke's stone-packed tower in the first decade of the twentieth century by some of Standard's refineries did any American refiner turn to multi-stage distillation"
>
> (Williamson and Daum 1959: 270–1)

5 Of Rockefeller's concern with tight operation, Ron Chernow notes that he paid great attention to detail by, for example, reducing the drops of solder used to seal kerosene cans, and fractionally reducing the length of staves and the width of iron hoops on barrels. He was also notoriously thrifty in his own personal expenditures. Chernow adds that he was "never a foolish penny-pincher" and that he also pressed for Standard to branch into petroleum by-products so as to take best advantage of the crude oil that flowed through his refineries (181).

6 A cartel is an organization of producers of like products undertaken for the purpose of controlling output and prices.

7 The development of tank cars, of storage facilities, and of "gathering" pipelines in the oil fields themselves all contributed to improved transportation and lower costs. On these topics, see Williamson and Daum 1959: 178–94.

8 As with the story of John D. Rockefeller, there are a number of accounts of Sam Walton's rise to fame and riches. Walton's own account of his career, written with John Huey (1992), is particularly interesting, and I have also relied heavily upon Slater (2003) and Vance and Scott (1994) for this account. Among other major works on Walton and Wal-Mart are these: Charles Fishman, (2006); Don Soderquist, (2005); and Anthony Bianco (2006). Two important collections of scholarly essays are those edited by Stanley D. Brunn, (2006) and Nelson Lichtenstein (2006). Other sources, particularly news stories and movies, will be referred to in Chapter 3.

9 Ben Franklin stores were variety stores, much like the Woolworth's of a few decades ago, that operated primarily in small towns.

10 Slater says that it was only after Walton's death and when David Glass became CEO that "far-reaching decisions on technology were made," but Walton himself says that "If I really hadn't wanted the technology, I wouldn't have sprung the money loose to pay for it" (Slater 2003: 85; Walton 1992: 91). By his own account and that of others, including Slater himself, Walton sought out advice on the use of new technology and went seeking those who understood it better than he did. The probable explanation for the somewhat different views is that, in Walton's words, "I always questioned everything. It was important to me to make them think that maybe the technology wasn't as good as they thought it was, or that maybe it really wasn't the end-all they promised it would be. It seems to me they try just a little harder and check into things a little bit closer if they think they might have a chance to prove me wrong" (Walton 1992: 91).

11 The concept of "supply chains" will be discussed in much greater detail in Chapter 6.

12 Levinson's book on containers and containerships provides a fascinating account of a revolution in shipping brought about by technological change and logistic innovation that parallels the kind of revolution that Rockefeller and Walton oversaw in their industries.

13 Just-in-time trucking involves onboard computers; "back-hauling," meaning having trucks that would otherwise return from stores pick up goods from suppliers to return to distribution centers; and "cross-docking," which involves movement of supplies straight across a dock into a waiting truck for delivery to stores. All of this, says Soderquist, seems minor but, in fact, "resulted in millions and millions of dollar savings and countless hours of savings in the movement of merchandise" (Soderquist 2005: 161).

14 Monopsonistic power is that exercised by a sole buyer; it parallels monopoly power where there is only one seller of a product.

15 See, for example, Miu in the *Washington Post*, September 7, 2007 and November 16, 2007.

16 There is an extensive literature on the role of individual entrepreneurs in economic and business history that in some ways parallels debate over the "great men theories" in history. In Economics and related history, the debate has had an additional edge because great fortunes and income disparity between entrepreneurs and their workers have been justified by the individual contributions of owners/capitalists who lead firms during expansion. I do not propose to add to the theoretical disputes on this topic but will let the reader relate the stories of Rockefeller and Walton to the issue if they so wish.

3 Popular accounts and wider contexts

1 Ida Tarbell (1904) and Henry Demarest Lloyd (1894) were the major muckraking reporters. The novels of William Dean Howells, Willa Cather, Upton Sinclair, Frank Norris, and the short stories of Hamlin Garland are particularly important as economic narratives and will be used and cited in the pages that follow. The photographs of Jacob Riis in *How the Other Half Lives* provided vivid illustration of life in New York tenements. Stephen Crane's *Maggie: A Girl of the Street* and Rebecca Harding Davis's *Life in the Iron Mills* were early works in literary naturalism, a style that focused on the hard, and often tragic, lives of factory workers and urban dwellers.

2 Differences between muckraking in the age of Standard Oil and of Wal-Mart tell the story of how technology has changed investigative reporting and political organization. Google™ provides, as of September 2007, 21,400,000 links to material about Wal-Mart. Much has been written, said, and acted, a lot of it in the muckraking tradition. While many of the stories to be found by using Google are factual accounts of new stores, new plans, fluctuations in sales and the like, many others take the form of twenty-first century electronic muckraking. Wal-Mart Watch, an organization for the purpose of its name, is one of the central sites for blogging about the company, its excesses, and its responses to their criticisms. There are also a number of books on Wal-Mart, ranging in virulence, acceptance, admiration, and anger from Anthony Bianco's *The Bully of Bentonville* to Vance and Scott's straightforward business history, *A History of Sam Walton's Retail Phenomenon*. Much of this work will be cited in the pages that follow.

3 The total number of people living on farms was 21.9 million in 1880, the first year for which this number was reported by the US Census, and 29.9 million in 1900. This represented a decline from 43.8 to 41.9 percent of the total population. The farm population is a measure of "rural civilian population living on farms, regardless of occupation" and not a direct measure of engagement in agriculture (*Historical Statistics of the United States*, Chapter K and Series K 1–3).

4 Comparison with other countries gives an appreciation of the rapidity of the rate of growth. In 1870, the aggregate production per capita of the UK, the leading industrial power of the time, was 133 percent of the US level; by 1890, the ratio had fallen to 120 percent and by 1913 to 95 percent. And, even in the case of Germany, another newcomer to the industrial scene, the same pattern

prevailed with German per capita aggregate product falling from 78 percent of the US level in 1870 to 75 percent in 1890 and 72 percent in 1913 (Gallman 2000: 20).

5 "The Unholy Alliance" is the title of a chapter in Tarbell's work (1904), a book based on articles published in the "muckraking" *McClure's Magazine*. The "Oil Regions" was the term widely used to describe the area of Pennsylvania, Ohio, and Indiana, where crude oil was first produced in quantity and for sale in the US. This was, until the twentieth century, by far the most important oil-producing region in the US and the world.

6 Robert Fogel (1964) and Albert Fishlow (1965) both made brave attempts to estimate the contributions of the railroads to economic growth. For a good review and critique of these efforts and an explanation of the difficulties involved, see McClelland (1968).

7 Many, including Lebergott (1984: 23), cite George Rogers Taylor's estimates of a pre-Civil War comparison of 15¢ for a ton-mile of freight hauled by wagon as compared to 2¢ by rail. McClelland (1968) questions the general validity of this comparison because it is based on a small sample of rates, but he does not question the general proposition that shipping by rail was cheaper in most cases. It seems entirely reasonable to agree and to note as well that wagon transport for heavy goods was at best an iffy proposition in various parts of the country, especially during winter and rainy times.

8 For more details on the railroads themselves, the addition of miles of track, and the often entertaining and dramatic struggle to build a system of roads, see Taylor and Neu (1956); Chandler (1965); Lebergott (1984).

9 Morris (2005, p. 169) mentions the importance of the balloon style of construction, and interesting material is available at www.uh.edu/engines/epi779.htm and at www.pbs.org on the "Death of The Dream" program.

10 For a good summary of what is known about the economic well-being of farmers during this era, see Atack, Bateman, and Parker (2000) and Mayhew (1972).

11 I make a point of this because Thorstein Veblen, whose work will be used extensively in my later analysis, contrasted the role of the engineers with that of businessmen in management of the economy. In his view, the engineers were concerned with making the interconnected industrial system operate smoothly and efficiently, while the businessmen/owners frequently found their advantage in disrupting orderly working in order to gain pecuniary advantage.

12 The phrase is almost obligatory as it has been used so often to describe the farmers' views of their plight. It was originally uttered by Mary Elizabeth Clyens Lease, a populist activist from Kansas and has been widely quoted.

13 The literature on the Progressive Movement is large. For a reasonable summary and description of the current state of scholarship on this complex era of reform, see Brinkley (1997).

14 The American economy grew not only in extent and absolute size during the antebellum decades; per capita income also grew, and then sometime in the middle of the nineteenth century began to grow even more rapidly. Though the Civil War slowed growth, rapid increases resumed after the end of the War so that by the end of the nineteenth century, and certainly by 1914, each American worker, on average, was producing considerably more than had been the case in 1800 or in 1850. Of course, these aggregate measures do not answer the question about what happened to workers and farmers. In fact, the evidence of rapidly growing output may only serve to reinforce the view that Rockefeller

and his fellow tycoons made off with a hugely excessive amount of income that could have been allocated instead to alleviate poverty among the many who did not get their fair share. Once again, however, the evidence does not lend strong support to this pessimistic view. Through painstaking reconstruction and evaluation of data, economic historian Stanley Lebergott estimated that between 1870 and 1910, the earnings of workers advanced at roughly the same rate as did net product per person employed and did so with fair rapidity (Lebergott 1984: Fig. 29–1, 378).

One difficulty, of course, is that these are aggregated numbers and do not tell us how workers in eastern cities fared in comparison to those further removed from the influx of migrants, or how rapidly the wages of relatively unskilled workers compared to those with more skills. One thing that we do know is that the last four decades of the century saw some increased regional inequality, with a growing and substantial discrepancy in income and wealth between the North and South (Williamson and Lindert 1980: 5). There is also evidence of an increasingly skewed distribution by income level as opposed to skewedness by source of income. Put in simpler terms, there is evidence that the rich throughout the nation did get richer faster than the poor got better off, though there is no evidence from regions other than the more impoverished areas of the South of declining income for major groups of the population such as workers or farmers.

15 Moreton tells the story told by Wal-Mart officials themselves about how, with encouragement from Sam Walton, Senior Vice President Ron Loveless told a group of investors that Wal-Mart used the number of dead chickens found on the side of the road in Arkansas as a guide to market demand. The claim was that in good times the chickens that fell off trucks carrying them out of Northwest Arkansas were left dead by the roadside while when times were bad, people picked them up for food. Moreton, who got this story in an interview with Loveless, reports his claim that "the audience sat there nodding and frowning and writing it all down" (Moreton 2006: 59–60). However accurate Loveless's memory may or may not have been in the retelling of this story, the point is well made that those who created Wal-Mart were fully aware of and manipulative in their use of their hillbilly image.

16 It has been well documented that American households did begin to purchase more durable goods in the years just before World War I and during the 1920s, with the shift to such purchases measured as a percentage of household income continuing in the post-WWII period (Olney 1991). The earlier shift to more durables was revolutionary, for it involved not only a new pattern of equipping homes and a change in attitude toward indebtedness, the use of consumer credit, and the pattern of household saving. But, the *continued* growth of expenditures after WWII was also revolutionary, even though it has received less attention. There is some discussion of the types of goods and the rate of diffusion (see Offer 2006 on this), and some texts do discuss the relatively low rate of saving in the US, which is sometimes noted as being the flip side of high rates of consumption, but otherwise surprisingly little is said. This is even more surprising given the conclusion of Moses Abramowitz and Paul David about the relative importance of new consumer goods in the twentieth century:

It seems to us that these important twentieth-century developments in consumer goods, which are unmatched, in our view, by equally important nineteenth-century advances, create a strong presumption that a measure of per capita output growth [and consumption] that took into account the true values of new and improved goods and services would show a more pronounced rise in the pace of growth between the centuries than the standard figures now show.

(Abramowitz and David 2000: 33)

17 The only explicit comparison of Rockefeller and Walton that I have located in the literature is that provided by Bianco in *The Bully of Bentonville*: "Like Rockefeller, Walton built a company that defined its era and changed the way business was done in America as much through sheer bullying force as through the inspirational power of its example" (Bianco 2006: 46). Bianco notes similarities between the two men, their rural upbringing, frugality, and tee-totaling characters but then goes on to allege that whereas Rockefeller was truly pious and committed as a Baptist, Walton "was not a true believer." The evidence for this may or may not be convincing and, more importantly, it may or may not be relevant, but it gives a sense of the ill will toward Walton that is hard for Bianco (and presumably others) to maintain for the long-dead Rockefeller. This ill will continues through a discussion of Walton's failure to equal Rockefeller in charitable giving and in his comparative shortcomings as father and family man. What is, however, of much greater importance for this analysis is what Bianco says about the business approaches of the two men:

Rockefeller and Walton took opposite approaches to their shared goal of market domination. An industrial virtuoso, Rockefeller spun out organizational structures and commercial arrangements of staggering complexity. Standard Oil's creator was an ingenious administrator who did as much as anyone to pioneer the form of the modern corporation even as he concocted countless devious schemes to advance his self-interest at the expense of free and open competition. By contrast, there was nothing nefarious about Walton, who did business with all the subtlety of a fullback hitting a hole off tackle. Relishing the sort of head-on competition that Rockefeller went to great conniving lengths to avoid, Walton created a business model that was no less brilliant in its contrarian simplicity.

(Bianco 2006: 49)

As in much of the other literature of condemnation, Walton's accomplishments are seen as simply ugly.

18 This may seem strange to those young enough to think that Internet and catalog shopping are perfectly acceptable and perhaps to be preferred. In the 1950s and 60s, the kind of catalogs that now fill mailboxes were rare, the old-style catalogs were seen as stuffy and the Internet did not exist. What was wanted was the experience of window-shopping, which had by then become transformed into a much more interactive process of trying things on and trying things out.

19 Kenneth E. Stone, an extension economist with Iowa State University (Stone 1988 and 1997), in a widely cited study, established that in Iowa, small towns in which a Wal-Mart was located gained in total sales revenues but at the expense of sales in neighboring small towns. However, in the small towns in which the Wal-Marts located, retailers who competed directly with them were likely to lose sales, but others who offered services or goods not offered by

Wal-Mart tended to benefit. The effects were much the same but more diffused in larger cities. None of this is surprising and, as Vance and Scott and others point out, the same effects would be found if studies were done of the impact of shopping malls on downtown retailers or, in an earlier period, of supermarkets on small grocery stores or drugstore chains on local pharmacies.

20 It is the case, however, that in the last months of 2007, Wal-Mart is receiving favorable publicity for a new health care plan. The possibility that Wal-Mart will redeem itself in the public eye will be discussed further in Chapter 7.

4 Economists, trusts, and big business

1 It is necessary to say something here about the word "trusts." The Standard Oil Trust, formed in 1882, set off what seemed to the public to be a rush to turn all major industries into the same kind of monster that Standard Oil of Ohio had become. Not only had Standard grown in size, but it had also taken a new legal form, that of a trust. Trusts in a legal sense were an old device that allowed the transfer to "trustees" of the rights of management of assets without transfer of the income derived from those assets. What Rockefeller and his associates did was to use this old device to get around prohibitions on ownership by one corporation of the assets of another, especially across state lines. Voting rights that accompanied shares of corporations were placed in the hands of Standard owners who then had management rights, though not the income from, firms that had once been competitors. In spite of the public perception, the number of trusts actually formed during the decades at the end of the nineteenth and the beginning of the twentieth centuries was relatively small. As Chandler notes,

> Despite widespread use of the term trust (as distinguished from a trade association or holding company) I have been able to identify definitely only eight that were formed to operate in the national market. Two – the cattle and cordage trusts – were short-lived. The other six – petroleum, cottonseed oil, linseed oil, sugar, whiskey, and lead processing – came to dominate their industries for a decade.
>
> (Chandler 1977, p. 320)

Even though the actual number of genuine trusts was small, the public did not draw a sharp distinction between those combinations organized as trusts and those that grew by internal expansion or by other means of horizontal or vertical integration. They were all "trusts" in the language of the 1880s, 90s and even beyond, and I will also use the word in that way, which is to say that all companies, whatever their legal form, that grew large will be called trusts.

2 A recent work by Michael Perelman entitled *Railroading Economics: The Creation of the Free Market Mythology* (2006) covers some of the same ground that I cover here, though his intent, which is to show how "conventional economics ... mostly exists as a justification for an unjust and inefficient means of organizing society" (199), is different than mine. My goal is to understand how the grounds for judging justice and efficiency have changed through time, by interrogating the multiple stories told by economists, conventional and otherwise, as well as others.

3 Hans Thorelli makes the point that even as some economists came to advocate state regulation of railroads, others – perhaps the majority and including the widely read textbook authors Amasa Walker and Arthur L. Perry – continued

to maintain that "nuisances" in the form of monopoly "could simply not exist without artificial buttresses of governmental privilege and power." Seeing what Mitchell did in his skylark allusion, Thorelli concluded that "It is eloquent evidence of the massive belief of most American political economists in the eternal validity of the old doctrines that they continued to propagate a substantially unmodified version of laissez-faire theory long after its premises had been overthrown by the appearance of big business and huge fixed investments" (Thorelli 1955: 110).

4 I have relied heavily for this presentation of Adams' thought on the account given by Thomas McCraw (1984). McCraw emphasizes that even though Adams was trained as a lawyer, he reasoned as an economist, and he lived and wrote before the academic credentials required to acquire the official title "economist" had been firmly established in the academy. I treat him as part of the group of economists who created the first stories of big business in America because he so clearly drew upon the thought of political economy as it then existed.

5 The reader who is an economist will (or should) object that what was involved in the railroads was not diminishing returns to variable inputs but, rather, increasing returns where all inputs are variable. However, for Adams, not all inputs were variable, as railroads were of technological necessity of a large scale. I will discuss the sometimes subtle distinction between diminishing returns to a variable input and economies of scale at some length in the next chapter.

6 Among the economists who wrote about and spoke on the issue were Arthur T. Hadley, President of Yale; Benjamin Andrews, President of Brown; and Henry Carter Adams, of the University of Michigan and Cornell.

7 Hans Thorelli (1955), whose careful survey of the literature of the time provides the best and most detailed discussions of the reactions of economists to the trusts and to the Sherman Act, gives other reasons as well for the lack of enthusiasm, but he also provides ample evidence for the conclusion that economists who wrote or spoke on the topic saw falling costs and prices as a major reason not to panic. George Stigler (1982) offered a Whiggish view that ignores the empirical basis for the opposition to the Act, arguing instead that economics did not have sufficiently satisfactory theories of monopoly behavior to lead them to support what was, in any event, a somewhat muddled piece of legislation. Still others, among them DiLorenzo and High (1988), find the source of silence to be based on early foresight that the Sherman Act did more harm than good. I will say more about these interpretations later in this chapter.

8 Some modern treatments of the Sherman Act assume that the Act was a simple response to rising prices. For example, in a 1997 article in the *Wall Street Journal*, Roger Lowenstein wrote that both political parties were "keenly aware of the populist agitation" that followed from the failure of the prices of consumer goods to fall as grain prices did. This is simply untrue. The reality is that the wholesale price index fell from 135 in 1870 to 100 in 1880 to 82 in 1890 and the agricultural terms of trade improved (North 1966: 137–48). Prices of products of several industries where trusts or other combinations had been formed fell even more rapidly. The Sherman Antitrust Act cannot be explained by concern with rising prices of goods produced by the trusts.

9 The Civic Federation had as its goal the preservation of industrial peace. It was to call another conference in 1907, once again to discuss progress in resolving

issues of industrial organization and strife. The 1907 Conference, as judged by the printed proceedings, was a much more sedate affair, though many of the issues raised in the 1899 conference were once again debated (The National Civic Federation 1907).

10 Glenn Porter, drawing on Arthur S. Dewing's work (1914), gives the following list of some, but only some, of the "giants that might have been but which failed to achieve long-run success": American Bicycle, National Starch, U.S. Leather, American Glue, National Salt, National Cordage, Standard Rope & Twine, United Button Company, American Wringer, American Grass Twine, National Novelty, Consolidated Cotton Oil, American Woodworking Machinery, U.S. Dyewood and Extract, American Soda Foutain, National Wallpaper, and Mt. Vernon-Woodberry Cotton Duck (Porter 2006: 87).

11 See Dorfman (1971: 17) for a discussion of the important role that the work by the Clarks played in the drafting of these Acts.

12 This is a paraphrase of J. B. Clark's own statement of his goals in suggesting new legislation.

13 Morris (2005) is quite harsh in his discussion of this omission and of the emphasis on Frederick W. Taylor's widely regarded efforts to make batch pro-duction more efficient. He suggests that business historians and analysts were forty years late in recognizing the causes of efficiency (Morris 2005: 316). His complaint is legitimate, but not entirely well-founded as will be explained in Chapter 5.

14 See Chandler (1977: 348–52) for a discussion of the continued concentration of the petroleum and tobacco industries.

15 For different but overlapping views on the arguments and compromises that led to these Acts, see Letwin (1965); McCraw (1984).

16 The descriptor "neoclassical" was created by Thorstein Veblen to describe the work of Alfred Marshall and his followers. The term served to emphasize the continuity between the giants – Smith, Ricardo, Malthus, Marx – who had created the master narrative of the early years of the Industrial Revolution and those who transformed that vision to better suit the maturing industrial economies of the late nineteenth and early twentieth centuries. It is a phrase that continues to be widely used, though with fraying meaning, today.

17 See Kitch (1983) for descriptions of these Chicago years by Bork, Friedman, and others.

5 Alternative stories

1 I add the phrase legitimately because, as the alert reader will note, accounts of predacious behavior by firms often includes use of power to borrow money more cheaply or of restriction of output in order to sell at higher prices. These are the behaviors that public policy, such as the FTC, was designed to prevent in the interests of maintaining an appropriate degree of competitiveness.

2 For more on this see Smithin (2004).

3 For readers who know Marx only as a prophet of centrally directed economies of the twentieth century, it is worth quoting Wesley Mitchell, who in his mag-isterial survey of the history of economic thought said this:

> as far as theoretical political economy is concerned, the influence of Marx was, for a time at least, almost altogether indefinite. It was productive of

further controversies, of many efforts simply to refute the socialistic conclusions at which Marx arrived, but of very few efforts to use that extraor-
dinarily skillful combination of study of recent records of the industrial
development which England was going through with an analysis of economic processes similar in character and intellectual temper to Ricardo's
analysis. It seems to have been one of the cases where the feelings of a set
of scholars regarding conclusions arrived at blinded them to the possible
contribution of the underlying work.

(Mitchell 1969: 117)

4 Joseph Dorfman (1969) gives some idea of the place that Henry Carter Adams
has in the history of American economic thought by noting that the first publication of the American Economic Association was Adams' essay "The Rela-
tion of the State to Industrial Action." In his introduction to the reprint of this
and "Economics and Jurisprudence," Adams' 1896 presidential address to the
American Economic Association, Dorfman gives an account of Adams' career
and the relevance of his work to changing economic thought.

5 It was for this reason that he stressed the relationship of Marshall and Clark to
the classical economists. Theirs was a neoclassical view, but a sharper break
was needed to reflect the dramatically changed circumstances of businessmen
in a thoroughly industrial economy.

6 Economic sociologists Perrow, Roy, and Fligstein have emphasized the break
with past organization represented by the corporate form of business organization as it was given shape by powerful interests in the Rockefeller era. John
R. Commons in *The Legal Foundations of Capitalism* (1924) presented a
similar argument and traced the court decisions that transformed business
organizations into legal persons whose future stream of earnings became a
form of property with constitutional protection. While Veblen stressed the continuity of commercial and legal practice that made interstitial adjustments so
important, he, too, recognized the radical changes in business organization and
law of his era. For more on this see his Chapter VIII in *The Theory of Business
Enterprise* (1975).

7 For those who know Veblen primarily through his reputation as a satirist, it
may be necessary to point out that although he often wrote with sarcastic wit,
he also meant his points seriously, and that is certainly the case here.

8 In *The Theory of Business Enterprise*, Veblen also considered the effects of
industrialization and business reorganization on the organization of finance,
and in so doing developed a theory of business cycles that in some ways
anticipated the later work of John Maynard Keynes, but a discussion of that
theory lies beyond the scope of this work. On this, see Dillard (1980).

9 Veblen had been an undergraduate student of John Bates Clark at Carleton
College and his work was frequently cited, often quite favorably, by John
Maurice Clark.

10 In 1959, Chandler published an article entitled "The Beginnings of Big Business" that provided a concise statement of the thesis of *The Visible Hand*, and
in 1962, *Strategy and Structure* was published. However, *The Visible Hand*
marked the definitive break with the "robber barons or industrial statesman"
approach to business history. Richard R. John (1997) and Glenn Porter (2006)
in his "Bibliographic Essay" provide good accounts of the impact that Chandler's work had on the writing of business history.

It must be noted that John quite specifically argues that Chandler's explanation of the rise of big business was unlike Veblen's because: "According to Veblen, business leaders intent on maximizing profits routinely stifled technological advances pioneered by engineers. Chandler, in contrast, highlighted the interdependence of science, technology, and business" (John 1997: 165). It is true that Veblen posited an opposition of engineers to businessmen but not in any major way for the reasons that John suggests. Rather, and as is explained above, Veblen, too, saw business enterprise as it was in the early part of the twentieth century as a consequence of an "interdependence of science, technology and business." He was less sanguine about the outcome than was the apparently more optimistic Chandler but for a wide variety of reasons having to do with pecuniary rather than engineering dominance over a range of firm decisions. His perspective was, as is noted elsewhere in this work, not unlike that of Herbert Hoover, as odd as that may seem.

11 See Chandler (1977: 6–14) for the full list of propositions.

12 It is very important for the reader, and especially the reader who is a trained economist, to keep in mind that when Clark said that the large firms that had the right to survive would not be monopolists, he was not using Mason's spectrum of market power that ran from competitive through monopolistically competitive and oligopolistic to monopolistic. That is, he was not saying that such firms would be oligopolistic or monopolistically competitive. They could be sole providers of products with no good substitutes, but if they provided the products at a lower cost than could be provided by other producers, they would have that "right to survive."

13 Bain phrases the distinction as one between "real" economies, "reflecting a reduction in the physical quantities of productive factors needed to produce a unit of output" and "strictly pecuniary" economies that reflect "only a reduction in the prices at which the firm acquires productive factors, no real cost savings being involved" (Bain 1968: 492). Clark needed to assert the existence of real economies for large-scale manufacturing industries.

14 See Edwards and Starr (1987) for a more elegant phrasing and answer to the question. They make the point that scale economies can result from labor specialization if there is indivisibility in the use of labor, though this is not always made clear, especially in introductory texts.

15 On this point, see Tynan (2007).

16 The "law of diminishing returns" was articulated by David Ricardo and others in the debates over tariff protection for British farmers in the early part of the nineteenth century. This law describes the rate of change of output when variable inputs are added to fixed inputs (labor being variable and land fixed in Ricardo's development of the law). Economies of scale or size, when the concept is correctly used, refer only to cases where all inputs are variable. For more on earlier confusion of the two principles, see Bullock (1902: 484 and following). Unfortunately, the two concepts are still sometimes confused when there is discussion of increasing, decreasing, and constant returns.

17 Bela Gold describes Marshall's dilemma and his essential honesty this way:

> It is not at all surprising that Alfred Marshall was sympathetic to ... observationally-rooted perceptions. As a systematic economic theorist, however, he was confronted by some basic problems.... How ... was he to explain why larger plants often yield larger returns than smaller plants within the static framework of fixed factor prices and a given state of technology? ...

> It seems quite clear ... that, despite his tremendous efforts to develop a completely integrated system of static economic theory, Marshall's extensive knowledge of the factors associated with widespread increases in the size of plants and firms prevented his acceptance of an unrealistically restricted concept of the nature of scale increases.
>
> (Gold 1981: 7)

18 See Stigler (1941: 76–83) for his dismissal of Marshall's list of advantages related to size, which include discounts for quantity purchases of inputs, reduced selling costs, and lowered credit costs. Stigler dismisses these on the grounds that they would not be relevant in a competitive economy.

19 There were a good many economists who stuck resolutely to the observational path and found cause to doubt that size of production unit alone accounted for most of the increase in size of firm being observed in those years. One fine example of this is J. M. Clark in "Overhead Costs in Modern Industry" (1923).

20 Bain provides useful definitions: a plant is "a factory, mill, or other assemblage of connected productive facilities located on a single site," and a firm is "an independent administrative and control unit which manages a plant or plants and distributes their outputs (Bain 1968: 492).

21 See also Silbertson (1972).

22 See, for example, Haldi and Whitcome (1967).

23 Gold does offer examples in which the "six-tenths rule" of engineering is said to hold and to contribute to genuine economies of scale in production. The six-tenths rule has

> two roots: first in the fact that volume increases more rapidly than the enclosing surface of rectangular, cylindrical, and spherical shapes; and second, in the simple-minded assumption that the output of productive facilities is generally correlated with their volume, while their investment costs tend to be correlated with the size of their enclosing surfaces. Such a relationship may hold, of course, in respect to some kinds of facilities, especially in respect to the construction of hollow shells, such as tanks, furnaces, boilers, pipes, and some simple buildings.
>
> (Gold 1981: 12)

24 For more on this see Gold (1981: 11 and Liebhafsky (1968: 288–304). See also Edith Penrose (1955) who has written extensively about the tendency of firms that are organized as corporations to grow, with results that may or may not be advantageous to society.

25 Some readers may object to the certainty of this conclusion by pointing out that workers can be made to work faster. This is the point of the famous scene from Charlie Chaplin's film *Modern Times*, in which the tramp (Chaplin) is shown desperately trying to keep pace with the machine. It is also well known that unskilled labor that is paid by the hour may be required to work faster so as to produce more. The reality, Alchian seems to be saying, is that even if the pace of the machine may seem brutal to a worker, it is a pace that is determined by the choice of machine. You cannot take a machine and run it to advantage at higher speeds. In the case of hand work, the story is different and a tyrannical boss may get more hems sewed by compelling workers to move faster, but this is not the kind of case that is important for understanding arguments about economies of speed and scale in modern manufacture.

26 On this, see Lamoreaux (1985). She argues that excess capacity was the major factor in the increased number of mergers that took place between 1895 and 1904, and that it was also important in explaining some of the internal growth that Chandler attributes to genuine economies of scale/speed.

27 There was a great flurry of interest in a related aspect of this question a few years ago when it appeared that the vertically and horizontally integrated firms that dominated the US economy in the middle of the twentieth century were being replaced by a greater number of specialist firms, each linked into a loosely integrated unit. Wal-Mart might be considered from a legal standpoint to be such a loosely integrated unit for it does not own the assets of its suppliers in the manner that the giant corporations that are sometimes described as "Fordist" did. However, as the story of Wal-Mart told in Chapters Two and Three, and to which we will return in Chapter 6, makes clear, the control is still sufficiently tight so that it makes sense to think of Wal-Mart as a giant administrative umbrella, one that covers a well-managed supply chain. More will be said about this below.

28 See Williamson 1985, 1996 and Williamson and Winter 1991. Richard R. John, in an article (1997) entitled "Elaborations, Revisions, Dissents" on *The Visible Hand*, objects strenuously to Oliver Williamson's translation of Chandler's ideas into a transaction cost framework. He does so because "Chandler .. . always distinguished between the modest cost savings obtainable through reduction of transaction and information costs and the much larger cost savings obtainable through administration coordination." John also quotes William Lazonick who wrote that "By imposing a transaction cost interpretation of Chandler's historical material Williamson failed to comprehend the nature of the dynamic interaction between organization and technology that is central to [Chandler's] approach" (1997: 152). I agree with both John and Lazonick but want to show that if you seriously truncate Chandler's argument, you *can* squeeze it into Coase's formulation and thus save the day for J. B. Clark's foundational assertion that a combination of "the size of the mill" and potential competition would force firms to act in the larger interests of society as a whole.

For a somewhat different view of the relationship between the work of Chandler and of Williamson, see Lamoreaux and Raff 1995.

29 It should be noted that John R. Commons proposed in 1934 in *Institutional Economics* that the fundamental unit of economic analysis should be the transaction. However, as Yngve Ramstad has pointed out, the meaning of the word varies with context. Although Williamson credits Commons as a precursor, Commons was looking for a way to incorporate into economic analysis many of the aspects of economic power to be considered in the next chapter, elements that are excluded from Coasian-Williamsonian analysis.

6 Supply chains and $M \rightarrow C \rightarrow C' \rightarrow M'$

1 Glenn Porter writes that "Most Americans had come ... [by the time of WWI] to believe that big business was inevitable, that the new world of complex organizations, bureaucracy, and giant enterprise had permanently transformed their civilization" (Porter 2006: 101). And – in an article entitled "What Happened to the Antitrust Movement?" – Richard Hofstadter describes it as a "faded passion" (Hofstadter 1965: 188) and talks of the uneasy acceptance by most Americans of

the big and powerful businesses of the post-World War II era. What Porter and Hofstadter say is true, and while it is true that big business in general is no longer so often blamed for a variety of ills, particular big businesses do still come under attack. I will say more about this later in this chapter.

2 Formalization of the strategy of coordinated interaction between suppliers, producers, and consumers of a product was undertaken at a surprisingly late date. Modern advocates of such supply management trace this formalization to the 1980s and 1990s. This was indeed late in the day, for Charles Morris is undoubtedly correct in attributing Standard Oil's advantage to just such coordination. Morris writes that Standard "may have been the only big business [of its era] to control its entire value chain from production and processing ... through distribution...." (Morris 2005: 150). Morris faults business analysts for failing to understand this. A more generous (at least to business theorists) way of putting it is to say that part of John D. Rockefeller's genius lay in anticipating what Michael Porter (1985) was to tell the community of business strategists some one hundred years later in his seminal work.

3 Vance and Scott (1994: Chapter 3) provide details about the public offering. In his article "Discounting Northern Capital: Financing the World's Largest Retailer from the Periphery," William Graves (2006), a geographer, stresses the inadequacy of Southern financial markets as a problem for Walton. However, Walton's own account of his borrowing and of his negotiations suggests that regional difficulties were not great. Although the South as a whole may have suffered from some degree of "capital starvation" in the first part of the twentieth century, it is difficult to think that was a big problem in a region in which the financial centers of Atlanta and Dallas, along with Charlotte and Raleigh, are located. Moving from the generalized regional picture that seems to animate Graves' analysis to the details of Walton's story, it seems more reasonable to conclude that creditors, both in the Northeast and in the old Confederacy, were more likely deterred by their failure to appreciate the growth potential of Wal-Mart than from lack of capital in lending all that Walton might have liked when he wanted it. And, it seems reasonably obvious that in the end Walton got all the funding that he wanted.

4 To delve into the confusions that exist between national income accounting, where saving is defined as that portion of annual income flows to households that is not spent on output of the same year and the act of household saving by purchase of interest-bearing assets, and, in addition, to relate either of these to the ability of banks to extend lines of credit or other loans in anticipation of repayment, would require many pages. Suffice it to say that the apparently simple concept of "saving" is defined in many different ways in economic theory and in economic measurement. Beyond that, the connection between saving, however defined, and the ability of banks (or other financial organizations) to lend money is not a simple matter. There is an enormous and complicated literature devoted to this and related topics.

5 As economists will know, there is an extensive literature in economics about the nature of risk, uncertainty, and profits. For present purposes, however, the exchanges between S. M. McVane, Alfred Marshall, and Francis A. Walker in the pages of the *Quarterly Journal of Economics* of the late 1880s may be cited as sources that display both the contentiousness and the basic issues that have continued to characterize debates over the role of profits and income inequality in a capitalist economy.

6 Although attention has been given to networks of finance in early Ameica, there has been relatively little attention paid to their importance in the modern economy, at least by economists and business historians. This is probably due to acceptance of the notion that efficient financial markets developed by the end of the nineteenth century, thus allowing such markets to be analyzed without attention to personalities and personal ties. More attention to networks would provide a point of intersection between the work of economic sociologists such as William D. Roy and that of business historians.

7 See Cobb 1984 and 1993. He writes:

> Some enterprising boosters fashioned schemes whereby employees contributed to their own factory's "building fund" by allowing deductions from their pay checks. Such a method financed a factory in Dickson, Tennessee, where workers sacrificed 6 percent of paychecks that often totaled less than $10 per week. Albany, Georgia, leaders raised $10,000 to subsidize a new hosiery plant when executives promised to hire high school graduates who were to be paid only after successful completion of a six-month training period.
>
> (Cobb 1984: 37)

8 That it was batch rather than flow is an important point because the real economies of scale in production discussed in Chapter 5 were largely a consequence of flow processes, as Morris and others have emphasized. Chernow writes of "economies of scale" in the industry in the early 1870s, but these were organizational and had to do with flow through the supply chain, which is to say, with speed of throughput rather than with production of refined products from crude.

9 Actually, this may have been the case as well for manufacturing firms such as Toyota, Boeing, and Dell that dealt with suppliers over which they had considerable power. The early enthusiasm for just-in-time production probably led enthusiasts to underestimate the extent to which cost saving was actually cost shifting. Without doubt, however, the practice saved costs for powerful firms and was a good and clever move on their part.

10 On this, see Bonacich and Wilson (2006: 235).

11 This view has been put forth in formal terms by Nichols (1985).

12 Galbraith, like Veblen before him, had concluded that "The need to manage consumer behavior ... arises from the circumstances of modern industrial life – sophisticated technology, large commitments of capital, long-time horizons in product development and production and, in consequence, large inflexible and vulnerable organization" (Galbraith 1970, p. 472 and see also Galbraith 1967). On this same point, see Veblen (1997: Chapter 11).

13 Galbraith's analysis of the views of economists on consumer sovereignty was published in 1970, but, if anything, the stricture against considering the effects of advertising, marketing, or other social processes in determining and changing consumer behavior has grown stronger even as both consumption and advertising expenditures have multiplied. In Paul Samuelson's 1948 introductory textbook, the book that became the model for economic instruction for decades thereafter, almost two pages (out of some 600 pages of text) are devoted to "The Backward Art of Spending Money." (The phrase is Wesley Mitchell's.) Samuelson acknowledges the effects of advertising and changing social norms on consumption, but in the more recently dominant text, that of

Gregory Mankiw, neither advertising nor marketing appears in the index. This is what Mankiw says about consumer choice: "The most obvious determinant of your demand is your tastes. If you like ice cream, you buy more of it. Economists normally do not try to explain people's tastes because tastes are based on historical and psychological forces that are beyond the realm of economics" (2004: 69).

14 In late 2007, as consumer confidence in the US has been shaken by rising rates of mortgage default and higher energy prices, Wal-Mart has been advertising heavily on television in an effort to shore up holiday spending. This is a departure from its earlier reliance on word-of-mouth advertising.

15 That costs could fall by half, as they did between 1874 and 1884, and still be competitive is remarkable given that Williamson and Daum report that it took a month to load and unload cargoes that ran from 7,000 to 14,000 fifty-gallon barrels and that the sea voyage from New York to Bremen took forty-five days over and thirty-five back (1959: 497). This clearly speaks to the shortage of alternative illuminants as well as to the cheapness of kerosene.

16 Most of the critical focus on the quality of Wal-Mart goods seems to be on clothing, for the range of other goods that it carries is quite similar to that to be found in other big box stores and supermarkets. It is probably impossible to determine how much of the "low quality" reputation stems from successful branding efforts by its rivals, how much from its association with rural and regional taste often assumed to be of lower quality than that of the cities and the more sophisticated coasts, and how much is indeed a consequence of pressure on suppliers to cut costs of production that actually lead to lower-quality goods.

17 Business and economic historians have described the growth of many other firms where demand had to be nurtured. Singer Sewing Machine Company, Xerox, to an extent the early automobile firms, and manufacturers of a variety of electrical products are all examples of firms whose products caught on quickly but required a network of instructors in the use of the new products. Brand advertising is another form of market management, but that was not particularly relevant for either Rockefeller or Walton, though Rockefeller did seek to establish an automatic link in the mind of consumers between quality of product and Standard Oil. However, his greater concern was simply with controlling distribution points. Wal-Mart has, as we have already seen, outpaced its rivals in low prices and until recently has relied upon that reputation rather than direct advertising against those rivals.

18 The key word in Blanchard's how-to-do-it book on supply chains is management, not power, and for the practitioner there is an important distinction. Power implies force, management cooperation. Seen from our perspective of understanding how such chains work, there is no distinction, and Blanchard's book can be read as a how-to guide to use of available power to coordinate all elements of chains.

19 Somewhat confusingly known as "the bullwhip effect," which may suggest to some that Forrester proposed use of a bullwhip on those further along the supply chain, the idea is also a relatively simple one that might be called more easily to mind for many as similar to the effect achieved in the "crack the whip" game of childhood. Forrester's term "the bullwhip effect" will be used here.

20 Economists will recognize that these examples, though couched in the language of supply chains, represent nothing new, for the advantages of vertical

integration to the integrating firm have long been recognized. What is different, however, is that the supply chain emphasis is on the power of the integrating or managing organization, and a rapidly acquired excess of M' over M is both the goal and the outcome. Where vertical integration is used as explanation, the emphasis is on a drive for efficiency (in $C \rightarrow C'$), and even though speedy acquisition of M' over M may be the goal, the ultimate outcome is that efficiency.

21 This is by no means a new or novel proposition. Robert T. Averitt in *The Dual Economy* said the same way back in 1968, and the recognition underlay the impetus toward development of the conjoint governmental planning that Tugwell and Berle hoped the New Deal would adopt. Indeed, one could argue, and with considerable evidence, that Herbert Hoover proposed such planning while he was Secretary of Commerce in the Harding administration. On this, see Barber (1985).

Toward relevance

1 Though it takes us away from the main line of reasoning, it could also be argued that the story told by one of the best of the muckraking novelists, Frank Norris, was based on his understanding of a supply chain that stretched across the US and into both Asia and Europe. *The Octopus*, which was cited in Chapter 3, told the story of the clash between railroads and farmers in California but it was only the beginning of a larger saga that Norris planned to create. The second novel in what was to have been a trilogy was called *The Pit: A Story of Chicago*. It told of how the trading of claims to the wheat grown far to the west of that new city gave rise to fortunes and disasters. Crucial to the financial and personal disasters with which the novel ends was the effect of fluctuations in the supply of wheat on the ability of even the cleverest of traders to anticipate the price of that in which they were trading. To use Forrester's language, those traders were subject to bullwhip fluctuations; using Veblen's language, we can say that some prospered and others perished as they sought to control the interstices. Norris clearly shared this vision when he wrote about wheat in California and Chicago. Here is how Norris described it:

> "The wheat [Jadwin, a destroyed trader said] cornered itself. I simply stood between two sets of circumstances. The wheat cornered me, not I the wheat."
>
> And all those millions and millions of bushels of Wheat are gone now. The Wheat that had killed Cressler, that had ingulfed Jadwin's fortune and all but unseated reason itself ... had passed on, resistless, along its ordered and predetermined courses ....
>
> (Norris 2006: 240)

Norris, who sadly died before he could complete it, had planned a third novel in which bread made from the wheat that moved through Chicago was consumed "in a village in Western Europe." "The Wolf," as Norris planned to call the third novel would "probably have for its pivotal episode the relieving of a famine in an Old World community" (Norris 2006: 4). In a preview of this relief of hunger abroad, Norris had ended *The Octopus* with wheat being shipped from San Francisco to Calcutta. Though he did not use the language of either the management specialists or the economists, what Norris did accomplish, and what he might have completed, was a supply chain saga of a particular kind, but one that supports the view that many people have seen essentially the same thing in the modern American economy. As goods were and are moved there are great benefits and enormous opportunities in managing the interstices, opportunities for fortunes and for failures.

2   By 1984, when Thomas McCraw published his survey of the "prophets" who had led in the creation and modification of firm regulation in the US, belief in the efficacy and desirability of regulation was waning rapidly. When Ronald Reagan was elected as President in 1980, his conclusion that "government was the problem" was widely shared, and especially so by economists who increasingly accepted the Chicago School argument that the invisible hand of competition was almost always and almost everywhere a sufficient and superior form of regulation. In what McCraw called "the economist's hour," as compared to the time of the muckrakers and the lawyers who had earlier held center stage, a wave of deregulation was begun and has not yet ended. As I write, there is a news story about the plan of the head of the Federal Communications Commission "to relax decades-old media ownership rules" (Labaton: October 18, 2007). This follows a quarter century of deregulation in airlines, trucking, railroads, and financial markets among others. McCraw commented on the irony of this deregulation in context of a simultaneous move in the 1980s toward "additional social and environmental regulation" (McCraw 1984: 304). However, even that trend has been reversed in the first years of the twenty-first century.

3   There was a little flurry of interest in antitrust law when the Supreme Court struck down, in its June 2007 session, the long-standing prohibition of resale price maintenance agreements. However, the interest was almost entirely in the fact it indicates that the Court seems willing to overturn precedents and not in any economic effects of this ruling. That is appropriate for there are not likely to be many.

4   Although Chandler has been criticized for this failure, his goal was that of a social scientist trying to describe causes of existing phenomena. He did not try to say what should be done nor did he, except by implication and a generally non-critical stance toward big business, nod approval of the present order.

Bibliography

Abramovitz, M. and David, P. A. (2000) "American Macroeconomic Growth in the Era of Knowledge-Based Progress: The Long-Run Perspective," in S. Engerman and R. E. Gallman (eds) *The Cambridge Economic History of the United States*, New York and Cambridge: Cambridge University Press.

Adams, H. C. (1899) "A Statement of the Trust Problem," in Civic Federation of Chicago *Chicago Conference on Trusts* (1900), Chicago: The Lakeside Press; reprinted (1973) New York: Arno Press.

Adams, H. C. (1904) "Trusts," *Papers and Proceedings of the American Economic Association* 5: 91–107.

Alchian, A. (1959) "Costs and Outputs," in M. Abramowitz *The Allocation of Economic Resources*, Stanford, California: Stanford University Press.

Andrews, E. B. (1889) "Trusts According to Official Investigations," *Quarterly Journal of Economics* 3(2): 117–52.

Atack, J., Bateman, F. and Parker, W. N. (2000) "The Farm, the Farmer, and the Market," in Engerman, S. and Gallman, R. E. (eds) *The Cambridge Economic History of the United States*, New York and Cambridge: Cambridge University Press.

Atkinson, A. B. and Piketty, T. (eds) (2007) *Top Incomes over the Twentieth Century: A Contrast between European and English-Speaking Countries*, Oxford: Oxford University Press.

Averitt, R. H. (1968) *The Dual Economy*, New York: W. W. Norton.

Babbage, C. (1963) *On the Economy of Machinery and Manufactures*, New York: Augustus M. Kelley.

Baily, M. N. and Hall R. E. (2002) "Intangible Assets: Computers and Organizational Capital: Comments and Discussion," *Brookings Papers on Economic Activity* 2002(1): 182–98.

Bain, J. S. (1956) "Advantages of the Large Firm: Production, Distribution, and Sales Promotion," *Journal of Marketing* 20(4): 336–46.

Bain, J. S. (1968) "Economies of Scale," in Sills, S. L. (ed.) *International Encyclopedia of the Social Sciences*, New York: The Macmillan Company & The Free Press, 4: 491–5.

Balisciano, M. L. (1998) "Hope for America: American notions of Economic Planning between Pluralism and Neoclassicism, 1930–1950," in Morgan, M. S. and Rutherford, M. *From Interwar Pluralism to Postwar Neoclassicism*, Durham and London: Duke University Press.

Barbaro, M. (2005) "Wal-Mart to pay $11 Million," *The Washington Post*, March 19, online edition.

Barbaro, M. (2007a) "Appeals Court Rules for Wal-Mart in Maryland Health Care Case," *The New York Times*, January 18, online edition.

Barbaro, M. (2007b) "Leader of Wal-Mart's Effort At More Stylish Clothes Quits," *The New York Times*, July 21, online edition.

Barbaro, M, and Abelson, R. (2007) "A Health Plan for Wal-Mart: Less Stinginess," *The New York Times*, November 13, online edition.

Barbaro, M. and Dash, E. (2007) "At Wal-Mart, A Back Door into Banking," *The New York Times*, June 21, online edition.

Barber, W. J. (1985) *From New Era to New Deal: Herbert Hoover, the Economists and American Economic Policy*, New York: Cambridge University Press.

Barber, W. J. (1996) *Designs Within Disorder: Franklin D. Roosevelt, The Economists, and The Shaping of American Economic Policy, 1933–1945*, New York: Cambridge University Press.

Basker, E. (2005) "Job Creation or Destruction? Labor Market Effects of Wal-Mart Expansion," *Review of Economics and Statistics* 87: 174–83.

Berry, T. S. (1943) *Western Prices Before 1861*, Cambridge: Harvard University Press.

Bianco, A. (2006) *The Bully of Bentonville: How the High Cost of Wal-Mart's Everyday Low Prices is Hurting America*, New York: Doubleday.

Blanchard, D. (2007) *Supply Chain Management Best Practices*, Hoboken, New Jersey: John Wiley & Sons, Inc.

Bonacich, E. and Hardie, K. (2006) "Wal-Mart and the Logistics Revolution," in N. Lichtenstein *Wal-Mart: The Face of Twenty-First Century Capitalism*, New York and London: The New Press: 169–87.

Bonacich, E. W. and Wilson, J. B. (2006) "Global Production and Distribution: Wal-Mart's Global Logistics Empire," in S. D. Brunn *Wal-Mart-World*, New York and London: Routledge.

Brinkley, A. (1997) *The Unfinished Nation*, New York: Alfred A. Knopf.

Brue, S. L. and Grant, R. R. (2007) *The Evolution of Economic Thought*, Mason, Ohio: Thomson Southwestern.

Brunn, S. D. (ed.) (2006) *Wal-Mart World*, New York and London: Routledge.

Buck, S. J. (1913) *The Granger Movement*, Cambridge: Harvard University Press.

Bullock, C. (1901) "Trust Literature: A Survey and a Criticism," *Quarterly Journal of Economics* 15: 167–217.

Bullock, C. (1902) "The Variation of Productive Forces," *Quarterly Journal of Economics* 16(4): 473–513.

Butterfield, H. (1965) *The Whig Interpretation of History*, New York: Norton. (First published in 1931.)

Calvert, R. A. (1977) "A. J. Rose and the Granger Concept of Reform," *Agricultural History* 51(1): 181–96.

Cather, W. (1933) *O Pioneers!*, Boston: Houghton Mifflin.

Cather, W. (1999) *My Antonia*, New York: Penguin Books.

Chamberlin, E. H. (1933) *The Theory of Monopolistic Competition*, Cambridge: Harvard University Press.

Chandler, Jr., A. D. (1959) "The Beginnings of 'Big Business' in American Industry," *Business History Review* 33 (Spring): 1–31.

Chandler, Jr., A. D. (1965) "The Railroads: Pioneers in Modern Corporate Management, *Business History Review* 30 (Spring): 16–40.

Chandler, Jr., A. D. (1977) *The Visible Hand: The Managerial Revolution in American Business*, Cambridge, MA: The Belknap Press of Harvard University Press.

Chandler, Jr., A. D. (1988) "Administrative Coordination, Allocation and Monitoring: Concepts and Comparisons," in McCraw, T. K. *The Essential Alfred Chandler*, Boston: Harvard Business School Press.

Chandler, Jr., A. D. (1990) *Scale and Scope: The Dynamics of Industrial Capitalism*, Cambridge, MA: Belknap Press of Harvard University Press.

Chandler, Jr., A. D. (1992) "Organizational Capabilities and the Economic History of the Industrial Enterprise," *Journal of Economic Perspectives*, 6 (Summer): 79–100.

Chernow, R. (1998) *Titan: The Life of John D. Rockefeller, Sr.*, New York: Random House.

Civic Federation of Chicago (1900) *Chicago Conference on Trusts*, Chicago: The Lakeside Press; reprinted (1973) New York: Arno Press.

Clark, J. B. (1900) "The Necessity of Restraining Monopolies While Retaining Trusts," Chicago Conference on Trusts, Chicago: The Lakeside Press; reprinted (1973) New York: Arno Press.

Clark, J. B. (1901) *The Control of Trusts*, New York: Macmillan.

Clark, J. B. (1904) *The Problem of Monopoly*, New York: The Columbia University Press.

Clark, J. B. and Clark, J. M. (1971) *The Control of Trusts*, New York: Augustus M. Kelley Publishers. (First published 1912.)

Clark, J. M. (1923) "Overhead Costs in Modern Industry," *Journal of Political Economy* 31(5): 606–36.

Coase, R. H. (1937) "The Nature of the Firm," *Economica* 4(16): 386–405.

Cobb, J. C. (1984) *Industrialization and Southern Society 1877–1984*, Lexington, Kentucky: The University of Kentucky Press.

Cobb, J. C. (1993) *The Selling of the South: the Southern Crusade for Industrial Development 1936–1990*, Urbana, Ill: The University of Illinois Press.

Coleman, W. M. (1899) "Trusts from an Economic Standpoint," *Journal of Political Economy* 8: 19–33.

Commons, J. R. (1924) *Legal Foundations of Capitalism*, New York: Macmillan.

Commons, J. R. (1934) *Institutional Economics*, New York: Macmillan.

Crane, S. (2006) *Maggie: A Girl of the Streets*, Peterborough, Ont.: Broadview Press. (First published 1893.)

David, P. A. (1985) "Clio and the Economics of QWERTY," *American Economic Review* 75(2): 332–7.

Davis, R. H. (1972) *Life in the Iron Mills*, New York: Feminist Press. (First published 1861.)

Dewey, D. (1990) *The Antitrust Experiment in America*, New York: Columbia University Press.

Dewing, A. S. (1914) *Corporate Promotions and Reorganization*, Cambridge: Harvard University Press.

Dick, E. N. (1937) *The Sod-House Frontier, 1854–1890*, New York: D. Appleton-Century Co. Inc.

Dillard, D. (1980) "A Monetary Theory of Production: Keynes and the Institutionalists," *Journal of Economic Issues* 14(2): 255–73.

Dillard, D. (1987) "The Evolutionary Economics of a Monetary Economy," *Journal of Economic Issues* 21(2): 575–85.

DiLorenzo, T. J. and High, J. C. (1988) "Antitrust and Competition, Historically Considered," *Economic Inquiry* 26: 423–35.

Dorfman, J. (ed.) (1969) *Two Essays by Henry Carter Adams with an Introductory Essay and Notes*, New York: Augustus M. Kelley.

Dorfman, J. (1971) "Introductory Essay," in Clark, J. B. and Clark, J. M. *The Control of Trusts*, New York: Augustus M. Kelley.

Doyle, W. (1993) "A Reappraisal of the Role of Finance in the Corporate Revolution of the Late Nineteenth Century," *Business and Economic History* 22(1): 223–33.

Drucker, J. (2007) "Inside Wal-Mart's Bid to Slash State Taxes," *The Wall Street Journal*, October 23: 1.

Dunbar, C. F. (1886) "The Reaction in Political Economy," *Quarterly Journal of Economics* 1(1): 1–27.

Dunlavy, C. A. (1989) "Technological Change," *Science* 245(4921): 991.

Edwards, B. K. and Starr, R. M. (1987) "A Note on Indivisibilities, Specialization, and Economies of Scale," *American Economic Review* 77(1): 192–4.

Ehrenreich, B. (2001) *Nickel and Dimed: On (Not) Getting By in America*, New York: Metropolitan Books.

Ehrenreich, B. (2005) *Bait and Switch: The (Futile) Pursuit of the American Dream*, New York: Metropolitan Books.

Feder, B. J. (2004) "Wal-Mart's Expansion Aided by Many Taxpayer Subsidies," *The New York Times*, May 4, online edition.

Fetter, F. A. (1932) "The Economists' Committee on Anti-Trust Law Policy," *American Economic Review* 22: 465–9.

Fishlow, A. (1965) *American Railroads and the Transformation of the Antebellum Economy*, Cambridge, MA: Harvard University Press.

Fishman, C. (2006) *The Wal-Mart Effect*, New York: The Penguin Press.

Fligstein, N. (1990) *The Transformation of Corporate Control*, Cambridge, MA: Harvard University Press.

Fogel, R. W. (1964) *Railroads and American Economic Growth: Essays in Econometric History*, Baltimore, MD: Johns Hopkins Press.

Forrester, J. W. (1975) *Collected Papers of Jay W. Forrester*, Cambridge, MA: Wright-Allen Press, Inc.

172   *Bibliography*

Friedman, T. (2005) *The World is Flat*, New York: Farrar, Straus and Giroux.

Galbraith, J. K. (1958) *The Affluent Society*, Cambridge, MA: The Riverside Press.

Galbraith, J. K. (1967) *The New Industrial State*, Boston: Houghton Mifflin.

Galbraith, J. K. (1970) "Economics as a System of Belief," *American Economic Review* 60(2): 469–78.

Galbraith, J. K. (1973) "Power and the Useful Economist," *American Economic Review* 63(1): 1–11.

Gallman, R. E. (2000) "Economic Growth and Structural Change in the Long Nineteenth Century," in Engerman, S. and Gallman, R. E. (eds) *The Cambridge Economic History of the United States*, New York and Cambridge: Cambridge University Press.

Garland, H. (1891) "Up the Coolly," in Garland, H. (ed.) *Main-Traveled Roads*, New York: Harper & Brothers.

Garvey, J. I. (1995) "Trade Law and Quality of Life–Dispute Resolution under the NAFTA Side Accords on Labor and the Environment," *American Journal of International Law* 89(2): 439–53.

Gates, A. (2005) "A Look Inside the Outsize Company That is the Biggest Retailer on the Planet," *The New York Times*, November 4, online edition.

Geisst, C. R. (2000) *Monopolies in America*, New York: Oxford University Press.

Gold, B. (1964) "Economic Effects of Technological Innovations," *Management Science* 11(1): 105–34.

Gold, B. (1981) "Changing Perspectives on Size, Scale, and Returns: An Interpretive Survey," *Journal of Economic Literature* 19(1): 5–33.

Gold, B. (1986) "Technological Change and Vertical Integration," *Managerial and Decision Economics* 7(3): 169–76.

Goodwin, C. (1998) "The Patrons of Economics in a Time of Transformation," in Morgan, M. S. and Rutherford, M. *From Interwar Pluralism to Postwar Neoclassicism*, Durham and London: Duke University Press.

Goodwyn, L. (1978) *The Populist Moment: A Short History of the Agrarian Revolt in America*, Oxford: Oxford University Press.

Graves, W. (2006) "Discounting Northern Capital: Financing the World's Largest Retailer from the Periphery," in Brunn, S. D. *Wal-Mart World*, New York and London: Routledge.

Greenhouse, S. and Barbaro, M. (2006) "An Ugly Side of Free Trade: Sweatshops in Jordan," *The New York Times*, May 3, online edition.

Greenwald, R. (2005) *Wal-Mart: the High Cost of Low Prices*, a DVD available from www.bravenewfilms.org and www.robertgreenwald.org.

Hadley, A. T. (1885) *Railroad Transportation: Its History and Its Laws*, New York and London: G. P. Putnam's Sons.

Haldi, J. and Whitcomb, D. (1967) "Economies of Scale in Industrial Plants," *Journal of Political Economy* 75(4): 373–85.

Hawley, E. W. (1966) *The New Deal and the Problem of Monopoly; A Study in Economic Ambivalence*, Princeton, NJ: Princeton University Press.

Hays, C. L. (2004) "What Wal-Mart Knows About Customers' Habits," *The New York Times*, November 14, online edition.

Hicks, J. D. (1961) *The Populist Revolt*, Lincoln, NE: University of Nebraska Press.

Hidy, R. (1955) *History of Standard Oil Company*, New York: Harper.

Hofstadter, R. (1965) "What Happened to the Antitrust Movement?" in Hofstadter, R. (ed.) *The Paranoid Style in American Politics and Other Essays*, New York: Alfred A. Knopf.

Howells, W. D. (2002) *The Rise of Silas Lapham*, New York: Penguin Putnam Inc. (First published 1885.)

Hugill, P. J. (2006) "The Geostrategy of Global Business: Wal-Mart and its Historical Forbears," in Brunn, S. D. *Wal-Mart World*, New York: Routledge.

Jenks, J. W. (1899) "Elements of the Trust Problem," in Civic Federation of Chicago (1900) *Chicago Conference on Trusts*, Chicago: The Lakeside Press; reprinted (1973) New York: Arno Press.

John, R. R. (1997) "Elaborations, Revisions, Dissents: Alfred D. Chandler, Jr.'s, 'The Visible Hand' after Twenty Years," *Business History Review* 71(2): 151–200.

Johnson, B. C. (2002) "Retail: The Wal-Mart Effect," *McKinsey Quarterly* (1): 40.

Kitch, E. W. (1983) "The Fire of Truth: A Remembrance of Law and Economics at Chicago, 1932–1970," *Journal of Law and Economics* 26(1): 163–234.

Knoedler, J. and Mayhew, A. (1999) "Thorstein Veblen and the Engineers: A Reinterpretation," *History of Political Economy* 31(2): 255–72.

Knox, J. H. (2006) "The 2005 Activity of the NAFTA Tribunals," *American Journal of International Law* 100(2): 429–42.

Krugman, P. (2005) "Big Box Balderdash," *The New York Times*, December 12, online edition.

Labaton, S. (2007) "Plan Would Ease Limits on Media Owners," *The New York Times*, October 18, online edition.

Lamoreaux, N. (1985) *The Great Merger Movement in American Business, 1895–1904*, New York: Cambridge University Press.

Lamoreaux, N. R. and Raff, D. M. G. (eds) (1995) *Coordination and Information: Historical Perspectives on the Organization of Enterprise*, Chicago: The University of Chicago Press.

Lamoreaux, N. R. and Raff, D. M. G. (1995) "Introduction: History and Theory in Search of One Another," in Lamoreaux, N. R. and Raff, D. M. G. *Coordination and Information: Historical Perspectives on the Organization of Enterprise*, Chicago: The University of Chicago Press.

Layton, E. (1969) "Science, Business, and the Engineers," in Perucci R. and Gerstl, J. E. (eds) *The Engineers and the Social System*, New York: John Wiley & Sons.

Lebergott, S. (1964) *Manpower in Economic Growth: The American Record Since 1800*, New York: McGraw-Hill Book Company.

Lebergott, S. (1984) *The Americans: An Economic Record*, New York: W. W. Norton & Company.

Letwin, W. (1965) *Law and Economic Policy in America: The Evolution of the Sherman Antitrust Act*, New York: Random House.

Levinson, M. (2006) *The Box: How the Shipping Container Made the World Smaller and the World Economy Bigger*, Princeton: Princeton University Press.

Lichtenstein, N. (2006) "A Template for Twenty-First-Century Capitalism," in Lichtenstein, N. (ed.) *Wal-Mart: The Face of Twenty-First-Century Capitalism*, New York: The New Press.

Lichtenstein, N. (ed.) (2006) *Wal-Mart: The Face of Twenty-First Century Capitalism*, New York: The New Press.

Liebhafsky, H. H. (1968) *The Nature of Price Theory*, Homewood, Ill: Dorsey Press.

Liebowitz, S. J. and Margolis, S. E. (1995) "Path Dependence, Lock-in, and History," *Journal of Law, Economics, & Organization* 11: 1: 205–26.

Lloyd, H. D. (1894) *Wealth Against Commonwealth*, New York: Harper & Brothers.

Lloyd, H. D. (1910) *Lords of Industry*, New York: G. P. Putnam's Sons.

Lowenstein, R. (1997) "Trust in Markets: Antitrust Forces Drop the Ideology, Focus on Economics," *The Wall Street Journal*, February 27, p. A1.

Lowenstein, R. (2007) "The Inequality Conundrum," *The New York Times*, June 10, online edition.

McClelland, P. D. (1968) "Railroads, American Growth, and the New Economic History: A Critique," *Journal of Economic History* 28(1): 102–23.

McCloskey, D. N. (1998) *The Rhetoric of Economics*, Madison, WI: The University of Wisconsin Press.

McCraw, T. K. (1984) *Prophets of Regulation*, Cambridge, MA: The Belknap Press of Harvard University Press.

McCraw, T. K. (ed.) (1988) *The Essential Alfred Chandler*, Boston: Harvard Business School Press.

McMath, Jr., R. C. (1993) *American Populism: A Social History 1877–1898*, New York: Hill and Wang.

Macvane, S. M. (1887) "Analysis of Cost of Production," *Quarterly Journal of Economics* 1(4): 481–7.

Macvane, S. M. (1887) "The Theory of Business Profits," *Quarterly Journal of Economics* 2(1): 1–36.

Mankiw, N. G. (2004) *Essentials of Economics*, Mason, Ohio: Thomson Southwestern.

Marshall, A. (1887) "The Theory of Business Profits," *Quarterly Journal of Economics* 1(4): 477–81.

Marshall, A. (1890) *Principles of Economics*, London: Macmillan and Co. Ltd.

Marshall, A. (1919) *Industry and Trade*, London: Macmillan & Co. Ltd.

Marx, K. (1906) *Capital*, New York: The Modern Library. (Vol. 1 first published in 1867.)

Mayhew, A. (1972) "A Reappraisal of the Causes of Farm Protest," *Journal of Economic History* 32(2): 464–75.

Mayhew, A. (1998) "How American Economists Came to Love the Sherman Antitrust Act," in Morgan, M. S. and Rutherford, M. *From Interwar Pluralism to Postwar Neoclassicism*, Durham and London: Duke University Press.

Medema, S. G. (1998) "Wandering the Road from Pluralism to Posner: The Transformation of Law and Economics in the Twentieth Century," in Morgan, M. S. and Rutherford, M. *From Interwar Pluralism to Postwar Neoclassicism*, Durham and London: Duke University Press.

Mill, J. S. (1878) *Principles of Political Economy*, London: Longmans, Green, Reader and Dyer.

Mitchell, W. C. (1969) *Types of Economic Theory: From Mercantilism to Institutionalism*, New York: Augustus M. Kelley.

Moreton, B. E. (2006) "The Agrarian Origins of Wal-Mart Culture," in Lichtenstein, N. *Wal-Mart: The Face of Twenty-First Century Capitalism*, New York: The Free Press.

Morris, C. R. (2005) *The Tycoons: How Andrew Carnegie, John D. Rockefeller, Jay Gould, and J. P. Morgan Invented the American Supereconomy*, New York: Henry Holt and Co.

Mui, Y. Q. (2007) "Green Valley in Wal-Mart's Back Yard," *The Washington Post*, September 7, online edition.

Mui, Y. Q. (2007) "At Wal-Mart, 'Green' Has Various Shades," *The Washington Post*, November 16, online edition.

Mui, Y. Q. (2007) "Wal-Mart Extends Its Influence to Washington," *The Washington Post*, November 24, online edition.

National Civic Federation (1907) *Proceedings of the National Conference on Trusts and Combinations*, New York: National Civic Federation.

Nevins, A. (1940) *John D. Rockefeller, the Heroic Age of American Enterprise*, New York: C. Scribner's Sons.

Nevins, A. (1953) *Study in Power: John D. Rockefeller, Industrialist and Philanthropist*, New York: Scribner.

Nichols, L. M. (1985) "Advertising and Economic Welfare," *American Economic Review* 75(1): 213–18.

Norris, F. (1986) *The Octopus*, New York: Penguin Books. (First published in 1901.)

Norris, F. (2006) *The Pit: A Story of Chicago*, Middlesex, UK: The Echo Library. (First published in 1903.)

North, D. (1966) *Growth and Welfare in the American Past*, Englewood Cliffs, NJ: Prentice-Hall, Inc.

Offer, A. (2006) *The Challenge of Affluence: Self-Control and Well-Being in the United States and Britain Since 1950*, New York: Oxford University Press.

Olney, M. (1991) *Buy Now, Pay Later: Advertising, Credit, and Consumer Durables in the 1920s*, Chapel Hill: University of North Carolina Press.

Ortega, B. (1998) *In Sam We Trust: The Untold Story of Sam Walton and How Wal-Mart is Devouring America*, New York: Random House.

Panzar, J. C. and Willig, R. D. (1981) "Economies of Scope," *American Economic Review* 71(2): 268–72.

Penrose, E. (1955) "Limits to the Growth and Size of Firms," *American Economic Review* 45(2): 531–43.

Perelman, M. (2006) *Railroading Economics: The Creation of the Free Market Mythology*, New York: Monthly Review Press.

Perrow, C. (2002) *Organizing America: Wealth, Power, and the Origins of Corporate Capitalism*, Princeton, NJ: Princeton University Press.

Petrovic, M. H. and Hamilton, G. C. (2006) "Making Global Markets: Wal-Mart and Its Suppliers," in Lichtenstein, N. (ed.) *Wal-Mart: The Face of Twenty-First Century Capitalism*, New York: The New Press.

Piketty, T. and Saez, E. (2003) "Income Inequality in the United States, 1913–1998," *Quarterly Journal of Economics* 118(1): 1–39. Updated version published in Atkinson, A. B. and Piketty, T. (eds) (2007) *Top Incomes over the Twentieth Century: A Contrast between European and English-Speaking Countries*, Oxford: Oxford University Press.

Pindyck, R. S. (1979) "The Cartelization of World Commodity Markets," *American Economic Review* 69(2): 154–8.

Porter, G. (2006) *The Rise of Big Business 1860–1920*, Arlington Heights, Ill: Harlan Davidson, Inc.

Porter, M. E. (1985) *Competitive Advantage: Creating and Sustaining Superior Performance*, New York: The Free Press.

Public Broadcasting Service (2004) *Is Wal-Mart Good for America?* A Frontline TV Film available at http://www.pbs.org/wgbh/pages/frontline/).

Ramstad, Y. (1996) "Is a Transaction a Transaction?" *Journal of Economic Issues* 30(2): 413–25.

Ray, G. F. (1981) "Review of Gold, B. *et al.*, Evaluating Technological Innovations: Methods, Expectations," *Journal of Economic Literature* 19(1): 140–1.

Ricardo, D. (1911) *The Principles of Political Economy and Taxation*, London: J. M. Dent.

Riis, J. (1996) *How the Other Half Lives: Studies Among the Tenements of New York*, Boston: Bedford Books of St. Martin's Press. (First published 1890.)

Rivoli, P. (2005) *The Travels of a T-Shirt in the Global Economy*, Hoboken, NJ: John Wiley & Sons, Inc.

Robinson, J. (1933) *The Economics of Imperfect Competition*, London: Macmillan and Co., Ltd.

Roy, W. G. (1997) *Socializing Capital: The Rise of the Large Industrial Corporation in America*, Princeton, NJ: Princeton University Press.

Ruttan, V. W. (1997) "Induced Innovation, Evolutionary Theory and Path Dependence: Sources of Technical Change," *Economic Journal* 107(444): 1520–9.

Samuelson, P. A. (1948) *Economics: An Introductory Analysis*, New York: McGraw-Hill Book Company, Inc.

Samuelson, R. J. (2006) "Capitalism's Next Stage," *The Washington Post*, October 26, online edition.

Scheiber, H. N. (1987) "State Law and 'Industrial Policy' in American Development, 1790–1987," *California Law Review* 75(1): 415–44.

Schumpeter, J. A. (1994) *Capitalism, Socialism & Democracy*, London and New York: Routledge.

Shannon, F. A. (1945) *The Farmer's Last Frontier: Agriculture, 1860–1897*, New York: Farrar and Rinehart, Inc.

Silbertson, A. (1972) "Economies of Scale in Theory and Practice," *Economic Journal* 82(325): 369–91.

Silvestre, J. (1987) "Economies and Diseconomies of Scale," in Eatwell, J. Milgate, M. and Newman, P. (eds) *The New Palgrave: A Dictionary of Economics*, New York: Stockton Press.

Sinclair, U. (1906) *The Jungle*, Boston: Bedford/St. Martins.

Slater, R. (2003) *The Wal-Mart Decade*, New York: Penguin Books Ltd.

Smith, A. (1937) *The Wealth of Nations*, New York: Random House. (First published in 1776.)

Smith, C. S. (2007) "British Grocer Set to Tackle U.S. Market," *The New York Times*, June 6, online edition.

Smithin, J. (2004) "Keynes, Chicago and Friedman: A Review Essay," *Journal of Economic Studies* 31(1): 76–88.

Soderquist, D. (2005) *The Wal-Mart Way: The Inside Story of the Success of the World's Largest Company*, Nashville, TN: Thomas Nelson Inc.

Stabile, D. (1986) "Herbert Hoover, the FAES, and the AFofL," *Technology and Culture* 27(4): 819–27.

Stigler, G. J. (1941) *Production and Distribution Theories*, New York: The Macmillan Company.

Stigler, G. J. (1982) "The Economists and the Problem of Monopoly," *American Economic Review* 72: 1–11.

Stone, K. E. (1988) "The Effect of Wal-Mart on Businesses in Host Towns and Surrounding Towns in Iowa," unpublished paper, Ames, Iowa, Iowa State University, available online at http://www.econ.iastate.edu/faculty/stone/.

Stone, K. E. (1997) *Impact of the Wal-Mart Phenomenon on Rural Communities. Increasing Understanding of Public Problems and Policies*, Chicago, IL: Farm Foundation.

Tarbell, I. (1904) *The History of Standard Oil*, New York: McClure, Phillips and Co.

Taylor, G. R. (1951) *The Transportation Revolution 1815–1860*, New York: Rinehart & Co. Inc.

Taylor, G. R. and Neu, I. (1956) *The American Railroad Network, 1861–1890*, Cambridge, MA: Harvard University Press.

Teece, D. J. (1993) "The Dynamics of Industrial Capitalism: Perspectives on Alfred Chandler's Scale and Scope," *Journal of Economic Literature* 31(1): 199–225.

Thorelli, H. (1955) *The Federal Antitrust Policy: Origination of an American Tradition*, Baltimore: The Johns Hopkins Press.

Tynan, N. (2007) "Mill and Senior on London's Water Supply: Agency, Increasing Returns, and Natural Monopoly," *Journal of the History of Economic Thought* 29(1): 49–65.

Uchitelle, L. (2007) "The Richest of the Rich, Proud of a New Gilded Age," *The New York Times*, July 15, online edition.

U.S. Bureau of the Census (1975) *Historical Statistics of the United States: Colonial Times to 1970, Bicentennial Edition, Part 1*, Washington, DC: U.S. Bureau of the Census.

U.S. Industrial Commission (1901) *Pure Oil Trust vs. Standard Oil Company, being the report of an investigation by the United States Industrial Commission*, Oil City, PA: Derrick Publishing Company.

Vance, S. S. and Scott, R. V. (1994) *Wal-Mart: A History of Sam Walton's Retail Phenomenon*, New York: Twayne Publishers.

Vassilakis, S. (1987) "Increasing Returns to Scale," in Eatwell, J., Milgate, M. and Newman, P. (eds) *The New Palgrave: A Dictionary of Economics*, New York: Stockton Press.

Veblen, T. B. (1975) *The Theory of Business Enterprise*, Clifton, NJ: Augustus M. Kelley. (First published in 1904.)

Veblen, T. B. (1997) *Absentee Ownership*, New Brunswick, NJ and London: Transaction Publishers. (First published in 1923.)

Walker, F. A. (1888) "On the Source of Business Profits: A Reply to Mr. Macvane," *Quarterly Journal of Economics* 2(3): 263–96.

Walton, S. with Huey, J. (1992) *Sam Walton: Made in America*, New York: Doubleday.

Wiebe, R. H. (1967) *The Search for Order, 1877–1920*, New York: Hill and Wang.

Williamson, H. F. and Daum, A. R. (1959) *The American Petroleum Industry*, Vol. 1, Evanston, IL: Northwestern University Press.

Williamson, J. G. and Lindert, P. H. (1980) *American Inequality: A Macroeconomic History*, New York: Academic Press.

Williamson, O. E. (1985) *The Economic Institutions of Capitalism: Firms, Markets, Relational Contracting*, New York: Free Press.

Williamson, O. E. (1996) *The Mechanisms of Governance*, New York: Oxford University Press.

Williamson, O. E. and Winter, S. G. (eds) (1991) *The Nature of the Firm*, New York: Oxford University Press.

Wooten, D. G. (1899) "Principles and Sources of the Trust Evil as Texas Sees Them," Chicago Conference on Trusts, Chicago, IL: The Lakeside Press, R. D. Donnelly & Sons.

Zook, M. and Graham, M. (2006) "Mapping the Reach of a Retail Colossus," in Brunn, S. D. *Wal-Mart World*, New York and London: Routledge.

Index